# A NOTE FROM STEPHEN CURRY

There are two things everyone needs to make strides in this world: a place to call home, and a sense of community. Missing just one can upend a person's life. This is a story about a mom who suddenly finds she has neither. Staring down a hopeless situation, she pursues an unlikely path to restore community for herself and her daughters —and accidentally starts a nationwide movement. Her journey shows us that no matter where you are in life, you can create something world-changing. All it takes is a spark. And maybe some Girl Scout cookies. I'm excited to read this one with you.

THE GIRL SCOUT

TROOP THAT

BEGAN IN A SHELTER

AND INSPIRED

THE WORLD

# TROOP 6000

# Nikita Stewart

BALLANTINE BOOKS
NEW YORK

Published in the United States by Ballantine Books, an imprint
of Random House, a division of Penguin Random House LLC, New York.

BALLANTINE and the HOUSE colophon are registered trademarks
of Penguin Random House LLC.

Photo credits: pages 56, 71, 78, 84, 201, 204 (top, third, and fourth),
215, 227, 243 courtesy of Giselle Burgess; pages 118, 192 courtesy of
David Browne; page 204 (second from top) courtesy of Corinthia Fludd;
pages 228, 259 courtesy of the author.

Library of Congress Cataloging-in-Publication Data
Names: Stewart, Nikita, author.
Title: Troop 6000: the Girl Scout troop that began
in a shelter and inspired the world
/ Nikita Stewart.
Description: First edition. | New York: Ballantine Books, 2020.
Identifiers: LCCN 2019038599 (print) | LCCN 2019038600 (ebook) |
ISBN 9781984820754 (hardcover) | ISBN 9781984820778 (ebook)
Subjects: LCSH: Girl Scouts of Greater New York. Troop 6000. |
Girl Scouts—New York (State)—New York. | Homeless girls—New York
(State)—New York. | Homelessness—New York (State)—New York.
Classification: LCC HS3361.N49 S74 2020 (print) |
LCC HS3361.N49 (ebook) |
DDC 369.46309747/1—dc23
LC record available at https://lccn.loc.gov/2019038599
LC ebook record available at https://lccn.loc.gov/2019038600

Proprietary ISBN 978-0-525-61703-7

Printed in the United States of America on acid-free paper

randomhousebooks.com

2   4   6   8   9   7   5   3   1

*Design by Jen Valero*

*To JoAnn, who saved up enough money to buy me a Brother word processor and a Pentax camera to support me in my dream of becoming a journalist*

# CONTENTS

# ≡ TROOP ≡
# 6000

# "QUEENS PEOPLE OF THE WEEK"

HAILEY SMOOTHED DOWN her wavy hair and tried not to be nervous. She was thirteen and it was a big deal, being on television. If you lived in New York and had cable, the city's twenty-four-hour news channel, NY1, was the first thing you saw when you turned on the TV. Hailey took another deep breath and thought about what she might say to the interviewer. The butterflies in her stomach danced the way they did every year on the first day of school.

It was a Wednesday in July 2016, and the humidity was so high that her hair, which she'd combed into a half-up, half-down style, had turned into a sort of billowing Afro in the back. It was puffier than she had planned. Hailey told herself that was okay because no one could see the back, right? She sat perched on the edge of the brown leather sofa in the lobby of Pam's Place, a homeless shelter for single women in Long Island City, Queens, tugging at her khaki Girl Scouts vest to straighten it. Then the reporter, a friendly brown-haired woman whose calm voice helped put Hailey at ease, started asking her questions. The camera zoomed in and out on Hailey's face. Although her thirteen-year-old body had grown into an adult one seemingly overnight—a fact that she hated because now men and boys stared at her and sometimes made rude remarks—her baby face was unchanged, and when she smiled, as she did now, it lit up, looking almost cherubic.

Months earlier, in November, her troop, the Girl Scouts of Sunnyside & Woodside, had served a Thanksgiving lunch to the women who lived at Pam's Place. Now Hailey, her sisters Karina and Christina, and the rest of their troop—who were always doing community service, volunteering to clean up a park or to bring cheer to children with chronic illnesses—had returned to Pam's Place as part of Operation Cookie, a service project that allowed customers to buy the coveted cookies and donate to people whose spirits needed lifting, like veterans, military personnel, senior citizens, and people experiencing homelessness. The Scouts then delivered the cookies. A couple of reporters, including the one who was sitting across from her now, showed up to cover the event. The troop had picked Hailey to represent them on camera that day. Her mother, Giselle, was a leader of the troop and worked as a community development specialist for the Girl Scouts of Greater New York, so even though Hailey had been a Girl Scout for only two and a half years, she knew a lot about Girl Scouting and the history of the organization. And although she was a little shy, which may not have made her an obvious choice as a public representative, she was thoughtful and affable.

"People do so much for us and the least we can do is do something for them," Hailey told the reporter. She blinked, paused, and then smiled as she tried to think of what else to say. "The women in the shelter have experienced many hardships and are really struggling. To see us come in and do all these things for them really makes their day."

After the interview, NY1 collected footage of Hailey standing with her sisters in their Girl Scout vests. Within the Scouts, girls were organized based on grades in school. Hailey's khaki vest indicated that she was an older Scout; she was going into the eighth grade and was a Cadette. Karina, who was approaching her eleventh birthday, would be a fifth grader, so she wore the green vest of a Junior Girl Scout. Christina's vest was brown; at seven years old she would start second grade in the fall, which made her a Brownie. All three of them tried not to look at the camera as they handed out Thin Mints and Samoas and Do-si-dos, but they couldn't help it. It was *television*, after all, and they were going to be on it.

Two days later, on Friday, the sisters and their younger siblings, Gillesy and Judas, who were two and three, gathered in their grandmother's living room to watch the segment. "Giving back is a way of life for thirteen-year-old Hailey Vicente," the reporter narrated as Hailey's face appeared on the flat-screen TV that hung on the wall of the cramped apartment where her mother, Giselle, had grown up. The apartment never got a lot of natural light but the dimness made it cozy and familiar, and on that day, with everyone piled into the living room, squeezing onto the worn faux leather couch, it felt especially homey. They were all there—Hailey's mother, sisters, and brother, along with Evelyn and Manny, Giselle's mother and stepfather, and Mateo and Miranda, Giselle's half brother and half sister—and all were proud of Hailey for speaking so eloquently about helping people who did not have homes of their own. The segment was called "Queens People of the Week," and for the one minute and forty-five seconds that it played, Hailey and her mother and siblings forgot about their secret. Few people outside the family knew about it, certainly not the girls' classmates, not even the Scouts who had helped them give out cookies at Pam's Place.

And if the nice reporter from NY1 had for some inexplicable reason asked Hailey about it, Hailey would have lied to her.

The secret was that Hailey and her family were homeless, too.

IIIIIIIIIIIIIIIIIIIII

The eviction had happened just days before the television interview.

Even though the description in court records read "forcible

entry/detainer," nobody had beaten down any doors or strong-armed their way in. Giselle had known this moment was coming for at least two months, and she'd opened her apartment door without protest to allow her landlord and the marshal entry. The day before, she'd explained to her five children what was about to take place.

"Mommy has some bad news," she said, talking more to the youngest three, Christina, Gillesy, and Judas, than to Hailey and Karina. "Unfortunately, we can't stay here anymore. The owner needs us to leave. I tried to find a new house, but it's hard and I don't have enough money or anyone to help us find a home."

Hailey could see that toddler Gillesy and preschooler Judas had no idea what was happening, and that seven-year-old Christina was confused, too.

Giselle was trying hard not to cry. Her voice quavered but she willed herself to keep talking as if this wasn't a terrible thing. She said they were going to a homeless shelter, just for a short time, until they could figure out their next move. "It will be scary because it's something different and new, but we won't be there long, and I promise we will make it fun."

Giselle smiled, like she often did to hide her emotions.

*Fun?* Hailey thought. What about losing their home could possibly be fun?

As the firstborn, Hailey was her mother's right hand; her name was tattooed alongside an angel on Giselle's arm. While she challenged her mother inwardly, she could see that Giselle was not only upset but scared. She kept her head down and started packing.

When the landlord and the marshal arrived the next morning, Giselle had already packed her clothes and was stuffing throw pillows and photo albums into thin black garbage bags. She wasn't crying—thank goodness for that, because if she had started crying her children would have, too—but Hailey could tell that she was just barely keeping it together. It was Hailey and Karina's job to finish clearing out the kitchen. The day before, Giselle had bought moving boxes at a nearby Home Depot, and now Hailey worked to fill them as quickly and purposefully as she could, even though her chest was so tight she was having trouble breathing and her heart was pounding so hard she thought it might explode. Karina, never big on doing chores but always eager to obey, was working especially slowly, methodically transferring red plastic bowls from the kitchen's cabinets to the boxes. Hailey noticed that she kept staring off blankly into space. Christina, Judas, and Gillesy were unusually quiet, dutifully gathering extraneous belongings that did not have a designated box.

They all paused when the landlord showed up with the marshal, who had the kind of skin that didn't tan but instead burned; he was red-faced after days spent hovering over families as they dragged mattresses and sofas onto the street in the summer sun.

"You have to vacate the premises," he told Giselle.

Giselle was moving as fast as she could. She had rented a nearby storage unit for $160 a month. She figured she would need it for only a month or two, maybe three, until she had saved enough money for a deposit and then found an apartment. Under the extreme duress of eviction, Giselle had already been looking for an apartment. She thought that maybe if she could take her time now, she might be able to find one that she could afford.

"Can I please have a few more hours to get my things out? I have people coming to help me move."

"You gotta get your bags and leave now," the marshal said, but then he shrugged and gestured to the landlord to see if there was any leeway. "It's up to him."

The landlord nodded okay.

A little while later some men from the storage company arrived to take the furniture and boxes to the warehouse. The marshal left once they pulled up, but the landlord stayed, walking around the apartment, monitoring the family as they packed up the pieces of their lives.

Hailey wished everything weren't so complicated. She longed for a day when she and her family could stay put once and for all. She was sick of moving from place to place in recent years. She loved her mom and knew that Giselle was doing her best. Her mother even had a job she loved and was succeeding at the Girl Scouts. How could they be losing their home when their mom worked so hard? None of it made sense to her.

||||||||||||||||||||||||||

All of the moving around had started five years earlier, in 2011, although the roots of what caused the instability went back much further than that. Hailey was eight years old, and she and Karina were attending P.S. 151 in Woodside, Queens. She looked up from the playground one October day to see Giselle across the street in the driveway of their home loading a U-Haul in preparation for a move to Florida—a move that didn't include Hailey or her sisters. Hailey's mom had already sat down with her, Karina, and Christina and explained to them that she would be gone for a little while so that she could make a better life for the family. They'd be under the joint care of the girls' grandparents, Evelyn and Manny, and Karina and Christina's father, Chris; Hailey's father was not a steady presence in her life. Her mom had tried to reassure them that the separation was just for now, until she'd started her new job at the dental office in West Palm Beach, and she and her boyfriend, Wally, had established themselves.

"Mommy! Mommy!" Hailey screamed as she tore across the playground. When she reached the chain-link fence that enclosed the blacktop play area, she wrapped her fingers between the metal diamonds and shook it. Tears fell on her white button-down shirt. "Don't leave!"

Giselle quickly made her way to the fence as Wally finished loading the truck. Though they'd been a couple for just five months, Giselle had dated him back in middle school and had never got over a feeling that they shared something special. He had no children, and the only thing he'd ever taken care of was a pit bull named Blue, who was in the U-Haul. Giselle caressed her daughter's fingers through the links and tried to reassure her. "I love you. Please behave. I'll be back. I promise I'll be back."

Later that day Giselle called her daughters from the road.

"Mommy, we miss you," Hailey and Karina screeched in unison.

"Me too," Christina hollered in the background.

And then Giselle said something that helped to ease the girls' anxiety. "Whatever you do, before you go to bed, look up at the moon and Mommy will watch the same one, like I'm right there with you. I'll always be there."

It had helped a little—but not enough.

True to her word, Giselle returned to Queens with Wally three months later to take the girls to Florida, where they'd start the second half of the school year. Giselle described all the great things about their soon-to-be new home: It was warm in Florida even when it was cold in Queens; they had a back porch of their own, and just yards away from it was a lake. Ducks waddled on the lawn, and they had three whole bedrooms and two bathrooms for the five of them. Hailey couldn't wait to see it all.

What she saw instead when they walked in was a ransacked apartment. The TV was gone. Giselle's laptop, which was filled with pictures of the girls that she had never downloaded, was gone. Wally had thrown Blue's rawhide dog bone into the glass door before they'd left—it turned out that he had a violent temper—and he'd covered it with heavy plastic sheeting, the kind meant for weatherization, as a quick fix. The broken door had given burglars an easy entrance.

Giselle burst out sobbing.

The girls froze, and then Hailey and Karina began to apologize, as though they were to blame, and Christina, a month away from her third birthday, began to wail.

"It's not your fault, okay," Giselle told them through her tears.

*Whose fault is it?* Hailey wondered.

Wally was a complicated man. After his parents abandoned him, which left a gaping emotional wound, he was raised by his grandmother. Like Giselle, Wally pined for romance. He also desperately hoped to win the lottery so he could stop living paycheck to paycheck. When his dreams clashed with the reality of his life, he sometimes turned to violence, taking his frustrations out on Giselle. Christina once saw Wally choke her mother in a terrifying rampage as Blue barked and protected her until the police arrived and arrested Wally. She had been too young to remember it later, and for the most part, the kids did not witness the physical abuse Giselle endured.

Wally was attentive to Giselle's daughters, though, and he could be a lot of fun. He was an expert fortress builder, he plied the girls with McFlurry slushies and sundaes from McDonald's, and he took them to Chuck E. Cheese. He called them "my daughters" and loved them the best way he knew how.

Hailey didn't know exactly what to make of it all—a nice Wally who also hit her mother, a happy home that could so quickly become a frightening place to live. By the time the family left Florida for good in early 2013 and moved back to Queens, Giselle and Wally had brought a baby boy, Judas, into the world.

# 2

# BACK TO THE FUTURE

RETURNING TO QUEENS meant splitting up: Giselle and Wally did not have the money to afford a place roomy enough to keep everyone together, so Hailey, Karina, and Christina moved back in with Chris, the younger girls' father, who had a room in his mother's house. Wally moved in with relatives, and Giselle stayed with Judas, the newest arrival, in her grandparents' apartment in Woodside, where she'd stayed ten years earlier when she was pregnant with Hailey. At the time, she'd been newly married to Hailey's father, but they couldn't afford a place together either. Now she was there again, sleeping on a futon and pregnant with her fifth child, having to fold up the heavy bed each morning.

Being scattered around like that was a horrible state of affairs. Before they left Florida, Giselle had been diagnosed with epilepsy and prescribed two heavy-duty medicines that were supposed to keep her from convulsing. The episodes she'd had as a child now made sense. At the time, people around her thought she had been daydreaming. Her face would become blank for a few seconds, as if she couldn't hear or see or feel anything—

almost as if her brain had clicked off. The doctors in Florida explained that these episodes were called absence seizures, and that the far more physically debilitating episodes she was currently enduring were called grand mal seizures. One of the seizure triggers was stress, they told her. Try to avoid stress.

But there was one ray of light: Giselle had managed to land work at a dental office in Manhattan. Despite all the challenges of raising four children and carrying another one inside her, and the occasional epilepsy flare-up, she soldiered on, taking the subway to Manhattan in the mornings and back to Queens in the evenings. She was dead set on working hard and earning enough to reunite her family—including Wally, who seemed unable to contribute much in the way of income and even less emotionally—under one roof.

Keeping her family together felt like a do-or-die situation. Her own father, a graffiti artist named GWIZ, had split up with Evelyn, her mother, and moved out of the apartment when she was thirteen and her younger brother, Greg Jr., was nine. The breakup shook Giselle, and her relationship with her mother grew toxic. There'd been a few times when Evelyn, who had not been able to control her hot temper when she was younger, had assaulted her.

Her romantic life had been volatile, too. Giselle knew that she'd made plenty of choices that turned out to be wrong, and sometimes the weight of those choices, and the judgments that other people had about them, lay heavy on her heart. When she returned to Queens, she was twenty-eight, had four children by three different men, and was pregnant with one more. Her children were *good* decisions, she never doubted that. And she'd loved each of them right from the start; she would never have considered not having them once she knew they were on the way. She loved the thrill of watching each of them grow a little every day, learning more, understanding the world. They were the bright lights of her life.

She had thought that each of their fathers, in turn, was the right choice, someone she would love and who would love her back. Now she was beginning to understand that her optimism, her tendency to see the best in others, and her longing—her *desperation*—to be loved had clouded her ability to see clearly. The fathers of her children were simply men with their own troubles and their own histories of poor judgment, just like her. They may have cared for her or even loved her, but they were never going to be the answer to her problems.

Still, even though she knew Wally wasn't perfect, she was also willing to do whatever it took to keep them together. Back in middle school when they'd dated, he had been her first—her first love, her first time, the first guy who prompted her to sneak out of the house and to keep secrets from her parents. He'd come into her life just as her father was leaving it, and she'd never forgotten him and how he'd helped her through that painful period. And when he wasn't losing his temper, he was a wonderful father to all of her children.

||||||||||||||||||||||||

Relatives, friends, and nosy neighbors who lived in the same complex of low-income buildings where Giselle's grandmother and grandfather, Papi and Lucy, lived, knew about Giselle's move to West Palm Beach and her unceremonious return to Woodside. Although the community was too sprawling to create any general feeling of easy neighborliness, some families made lifelong bonds. That had been the case with Giselle and Luana Orengo; Luana's older sister and Giselle's mother had been play cousins, so they were, too.

Luana was Woodside through and through and a modern-day Renaissance woman: On the street she straddled a hot-pink motorcycle—her biker name was "Allure"—while at home she'd care so lovingly for her pernil as it was roasting in the oven that by the time it was done, the pork would fall from the bone by the simple application of gravity.

Renewing a relationship with Luana was definitely not on Giselle's to-do list, even though it seemed every time she turned around, her play cousin was there. Luana had a daughter, Aleijah, who was about the same age as Hailey, and the two girls had become inseparable. They were the third generation of their families to attend P.S. 152, and they took the play-cousin tradition to another level: Aleijah introduced Hailey as her *real* cousin when Hailey returned to the school she had attended in kindergarten. That was just the affirmation Hailey needed to help her fit back in. This was Hailey's third school transfer, and each one was getting harder. She had started at P.S. 152, transferred to P.S. 151, moved to Florida, where she had attended Benoist Farms Elementary School, and now she was back at P.S. 152. Although she'd never had a problem adjusting academically, the emotional dislocation was taking a toll.

Aleijah exuded confidence. She had deep dimples, a wide smile that spread across her entire face, a good reputation at school, and an exotic extracurricular title that fascinated Hailey: Girl Scout.

Field trips. Cookies. Sleepovers. Friends. Aleijah was always giving Hailey the reasons she should join.

But whenever Luana tried to talk to Giselle about Girl Scouting, Giselle either avoided her or nodded politely with absolutely no plans to buy anything she was selling, including those cookies, no matter how addictive they were.

Woodside was right next to Sunnyside; the neighborhoods were often lumped together in census records and on websites and blogs that guided New Yorkers looking for inexpensive "ethnic" food. But Queens natives knew the difference. Sunnyside had a reputation as bright as its name, hopeful and solid, filled with longtime residents rooted in working-class sensibilities with paychecks to match. Woodside also had its share of the middle class but had achieved a notoriety so negative that certain blocks were considered off-limits for safety's sake. The neighborhood was on a gang watch list, with squads like the Woodside 8 Trey Crips. When Giselle was a teenager, she bonded with gang members who initiated girls by making them endure beatings to prove that they could fight them off.

The Girl Scouts had been a visible presence in both communities when Giselle was growing up. In her circle, though, the Girl Scouts were seen as an elusive, uncool, white-people thing. *Badges? Cookies? Who needs it?* But that reputation was misleading and unfair; in fact, black girls were included in the third official troop ever formed, in 1913 in New Bedford, Massachusetts. Though the Scouts were largely segregated, like the rest of the country, by the 1950s, several decades after their founding, they were recognized as so inclusive that the Reverend Martin Luther King, Jr., called the organization "a force for desegregation." In 1975, the national Girl Scouts named Gloria Dean Randle Scott as its first black board president. Under Scott's leadership, the organization's symbol—the iconic trefoil, with its three leaves representing each Girl Scout's promise to serve God, help people, and live by Girl Scout Law—was developed. Barbara Murphy-Warrington, a black lawyer who was the former deputy attorney general of New Jersey, was the chief executive officer of the Girl Scouts of Greater New York beginning in 2011.

The Girl Scouts had all but disappeared from Sunnyside and Woodside, so when Meridith Maskara, a fair-skinned Maine transplant who was looking for a troop for her daughter, asked "Where's the Girl Scout troop?" at St. Sebastian Church in Woodside, she was met with blank stares. "We haven't had Girl Scouts in decades," she was told.

*No troop? No problem,* thought Meridith, who earned the Girl Scout Gold Award, the Scouts' highest honor, as a teenager. She set about creating one from scratch. She decided that the troop would draw from both Sunnyside, where she lived, and Woodside, where she knew only a few people who attended St. Sebastian. So with limited connections to Sunnyside and even fewer to Woodside, how could she recruit girls to join and try to bring the neighborhoods together? That's where Luana came in. Giselle's childhood friend had tried to start a troop of her own in Woodside. She agreed to become the co-leader, with Meridith, of a joint troop of girls from both Sunnyside and Woodside, and her daughter, Aleijah, became a poster girl for the Scouts' efforts to promote diversity. Between 2009 and 2013, when Giselle returned to Queens, the troop had ballooned from a handful of girls to dozens.

In October 2013, Giselle gave birth to a daughter she and Wally named Gillesy. Just before Christmas break—almost a full year after their return from Florida—Giselle and the entire family cheered Hailey as she performed the cha-cha and fox-trot at a ballroom dancing exhibition at P.S. 152. The flower she wore in her hair gave a little extra flair to her uniform: white shirt, red tie, and blue skirt.

"That was amazing," Giselle gushed. Hailey had spent every day of practice in front of a mirror at home, holding out her arms and dancing as if she had a partner. "You have some moves!"

Luana and her family were at the exhibition, too. *Here we go,* Giselle thought. She knew that Luana had Girl Scout registration forms in her bag—she always carried them, just in case.

But Hailey beat Luana with a soft sale. "Mom, can I join?" She scooped up Judas, who was gnawing on a graham cracker. Hailey was always picking up Judas and baby Gillesy. She was their second mother.

In that moment of familial pride and happiness—surrounded by parents taking photos of their children, even if a few had two left feet all night, aunts and uncles and grandparents laughing and hugging their ballroom dancers—Giselle relented and said yes. Karina could join, too, she added.

But that didn't mean *she* had to participate.

She had made up her mind that she would not be a volunteer, but she was a dutiful enough parent to make sure that her girls would be properly attired for Scout meetings. One day after work at the dental office in Manhattan, she traveled to the store located at the headquarters of the Girl Scouts of the USA on Fifth Avenue. She didn't know what all the different colored vests meant—brown was for Brownies, naturally, but what about khaki and blue? Giselle learned that she needed a green vest for Hailey, who would be a Junior Girl Scout, and a brown one for Karina. She flipped through the vests on the rack and found the appropriate items. She would worry about the other colors if and when the time came.

Hailey and Karina's first meeting with the troops wasn't a meeting at all. They joined dozens of other girls who squealed in delight at sleeping overnight in the gym at St. Sebastian. Dressed in pink and white pajamas, Hailey rolled out her sleeping bag on the floor just like she unfurled it atop the mattress at her stepfather Chris's, but on this night it was right next to Aleijah's. Karina wrapped herself up inside a Spider-Man sleeping bag, feeling happier and more welcome in a group than she had in a long time; at school she was repeating second grade and that was hard on her. The sisters slept soundly on the hardwood, tuckered out from adrenaline and giddiness.

Come the new year, the whole family was able to move into a new home together. Giselle and Wally signed a lease for a house on College Point Boulevard in College Point, which was solidly working middle class, a social status to which the two of them aspired and a rung above the other Queens streets where they'd grown up.

Giselle was thrilled with the family's reaction when they first saw the two-story duplex with three bedrooms. "I love it!" Hailey screamed, running from the car to the front door. "It's the most beautiful house I've ever seen." It sat on a block bursting with Americana. Flags flew in front yards, and residents held a Christmas tree lighting each year in Poppenhusen Triangle, a small park nearby. Karina and Christina were excited to have enough space to sleep in their own beds.

Life had been good since they moved into the College Point house. The home seemed to erase, or at least blur, the poverty and problems of the past, even though the past was just a few short months ago. It was as if the house had coated everyone in a middle-class veneer. And they played their parts: Wally and Hailey made pancakes on weekend mornings. Giselle baked chicken, looking surprisingly domestic in an apron. The house—the family—was acceptable, respectable enough now to welcome people over. In April, Giselle threw Hailey a Girl Scouts birthday party.

The handwritten invitations read "HAILEY & KARINA HOST A GIRL SCOUTS SLEEPOVER! We'll watch a movie and stay up late! What an awesome way to celebrate." The girls used flowers and ribbons to decorate fancy teal-and-brown goody bags with white polka dots.

Giselle loved planning the party. She was good with her hands and artistic, abilities she'd forgotten she possessed after dropping out of high school. And Giselle loved to have fun in a childlike way; she was almost more excited than her children to play tag or hide-and-seek. When she thought something was funny, she guffawed so hard that tears welled. She made sure the sleepover had plenty of activities.

Games like forehead detective went all night long, and the Scouts wore their vests over their pajamas. Christina was welcome even though she was too young to be a Scout. She let them pet Fluffy, a black-and-white rabbit she got for her birthday as a sort of replacement for Wally's dog Blue, who'd been given away in all the chaos of the move from Florida. Little Judas wandered around all the girls in their sleeping bags as they giggled and shouted, "No boys allowed!"

Still, when it came to Girl Scouting, Giselle was not eager to go all in. She had reluctantly taken orders for cookies from her co-workers, complaining about lugging the boxes to the dental office to distribute. She actually seemed cranky about the whole endeavor, posting a meme of a Brownie vest on Instagram with the caption: "So-called 'fun patches.' But fun for whom? Certainly not mom!"

But Meridith, taking notice of Giselle's upbeat personality and can-do attitude, and maybe even hoping to befriend another mother with so many children—Meridith had four children herself, all of them girls, and was pregnant with a fifth—decided to try to engage her. "Hey, why don't you just stay for a little bit?" she asked one Saturday.

Giselle did, and in the following weeks she began hanging around a little longer at drop-off or showing up a little earlier for pickup. She heard stories about the Girl Scouts, about what they represented, and, most strikingly, about a woman named Juliette Gordon Low, who in another era on another continent had founded the organization. Eavesdropping one day as Meridith spoke to the troop, Giselle learned about Low's unhappy marriage and how that proper southern woman had refused to be a victim of her circumstances. She thought it was a pretty deep discussion for elementary school children as she mulled her own troubled, up-and-down relationship with Wally.

In May, Luana cornered Giselle before a meeting and said, "We need a chaperone." She wasn't asking; she was telling Giselle to step up.

The girls were headed to Camp Kaufmann, 425 acres of land owned by the Girl Scouts of Greater New York an hour and a half away from the city.

The land had a history steeped in a circle of ultrarich people who believed it was their duty to spread a portion of their wealth in a way that benefited the greater good. The most important person in its story was Harriet Dyer Price Phipps, who became a troop leader as a young woman in the 1920s. Her mother was friends with Juliette Gordon Low, whom Phipps called "Aunt Daisy." She would have to explain that her mother was not related to Low but that southern culture allowed for "courtesy aunts." Phipps's dedication to the Girl Scouts in New York was legendary: She was wearing the uniform when her fiancé took her into the famed Cartier Mansion of marble and granite on the corner of Fifty-second Street and Fifth Avenue in Manhattan to buy pearls as a wedding gift. She recalled the occasion in a *New York Times* story in which she also corrected the reporter for referring to her as a "den mother."

"Cub Scouts have den mothers. Girls have leaders," she declared.

Phipps cajoled her deep-pocketed family and acquaintances, including the philanthropist John D. Rockefeller, Jr., to donate handsomely so the Girl Scouts could buy the land that originally included a farmhouse and a large chicken coop and transform it into what they called Camp Merrywood. She also had a brainstorm to raised additional funds for the camp: She proposed that the Scouts sell cookies.

The camp was christened in 1959 on an unseasonably cool Tuesday in June. About three hundred people, mostly women, attended the ceremony. Sitting in chairs with their ankles crossed, the women cheered on three Scouts who made a campfire out of a heap of birch logs to mark the occasion. Over the years, the camp expanded to three times its original size and changed its name to honor Henry Kaufmann, a Pittsburgh department store heir who donated millions to create several other camps in the New York region. But remnants of the Phipps era remained. On a stone fireplace inside the mess hall known as Cookie Hall was a plaque that read THE HOUSE THAT COOKIES BUILT.

Though Giselle had gone camping with her family in the Catskills every year until she was seventeen, she had never taken her own children and had no desire to chaperone the Girl Scouts excursion. On the final camping trip of her youth, she'd had a devastating confrontation in the woods with her mother. Furious that Giselle was lying to her about being pregnant, Evelyn had kept after her until she finally yelled, "I'm going to punch you if you're not pregnant!" daring Giselle to lie to her one more time.

"No," Giselle said. Her mother's fist had slammed into her stomach, and Giselle buckled over, hoping no one would hear them, hoping no one would suspect what her mother knew, or that her mother, in that moment, hated her.

Evelyn sobbed, startled by her own rage. She had once dragged Giselle by her hair from her bedroom into the living room after finding a love letter in a backpack, so this wasn't the first, second, or even third time that she had hurt Giselle, but it would be the last.

After finally learning to control her anger, Evelyn had become a better mother to her two youngest children and a doting grandmother to Giselle's children. When Hailey was born, she had gushed, "Oh my God, she's nothing but lashes."

"This is a different kind of love," she repeated again and again, cradling Hailey and wishing she could take back the mistakes she'd made with Giselle.

Evelyn made a real effort to change, to prove that she was sorry for the way she had treated Giselle. She offered to help Giselle with her new granddaughters—first Hailey, and then Karina, and then Christina—by babysitting and cooking.

So all these years later, Giselle had better memories of Evelyn. Mother and daughter had worked to repair their relationship and Giselle had come to count on Evelyn. She wasn't eager to be reminded of that moment in the woods again. But Giselle agreed to chaperone the trip to Camp Kaufmann because she felt she owed it to the troop. Hailey and Karina didn't know it, but the troop had started subsidizing their monthly dues.

Plus Giselle and Wally needed some space. Giselle was struggling with their relationship. They'd been living in College Point for five months now, and Wally had not blown up like he had in Florida, but he seemed to always be on edge. They bickered often, whether about his staying out late or not doing something he'd said he would do. It reminded Giselle of her childhood—her parents were always fighting before their divorce—and she wondered if she was living out some kind of preordained cycle. And Wally's temper wasn't the only thing that was short—he was perpetually short of cash. The rent on the house, the money it took to move from Florida back to New York, and Wally's sporadic work all added up to an unsolvable financial equation.

Giselle's experience at Camp Kaufmann was a rush she wasn't expecting. The freedom, the fresh air, and the breeze ruffling the leaves—as soon as she was out on the land Giselle remembered what she missed about camping, from the pleasure of unfurling her sleeping bag to the gentle aroma of smoke settling into her clothes. She jumped over puddles and pointed out poison ivy to the girls. She showed her daughters and the other Scouts how to roast marshmallows over an open fire, mashing them onto pieces of chocolate and graham crackers, laughing as she burned the roof of her mouth with the hot, gooey concoction. She had never before made the connection between s'mores and the Girl Scouts, who had actually popularized the classic campfire treat. She impressed the girls and the other troop leaders with her athleticism and competitiveness. She scaled the rock-climbing wall, she hit the bull's-eye on the archery range, and she quickly picked up a little trick that set Girl Scouts apart from Boy Scouts—namely, making a fire catch more quickly by using the cotton from tampons, adding a little Vaseline because the petroleum jelly acted as a sort of starter fluid. Her joy, the way she went all in with everything, and her appreciation of the outdoors made her a natural leader, even if an inexperienced one.

Still, Giselle knew she had some things to learn, especially the songs.

"There was a great big moose. He liked to drink a lot of juice. There was a great big moose. He liked to drink a lot of juice. Wee-ooo-wee-ooo-wee-ooo," Luana and Meridith sang out in a call-and-response with the Scouts.

Hailey and Karina had already memorized those and other lyrics; Giselle tried to catch on, mouthing the words she caught, a little embarrassed that she didn't know them all—and a little embarrassed that she liked the songs so much. With all the turmoil in her life growing up, Giselle had skipped through adolescence right into the experiences of adulthood, but there was still a child in there somewhere. On the bus ride home, she dozed with an exhausted smile on her face.

The next weekend, Wally got in a scrape with police and led them on a highway chase in New Jersey. He didn't even bother to call Giselle for help; he reached out to a friend to ask him to sell an old dirt bike to bail him out.

When he came home, he and Giselle finally had the talk they'd both been avoiding. "This isn't working. It's not healthy. I don't want to do this anymore," she said in tears. She told him that they had to break up but he would always be the children's father. She loved him and she hoped that they could be friends— maybe they would even get back together someday—but for now, Giselle had to be on her own. The example they were setting for the children was a bad one. She owed it to them and she owed it to herself to put an end to the turmoil.

Wally left quietly on the day of the breakup, though there would be blowups in the future during his visitations with Gillesy and Judas. Giselle kept hoping that Wally would mature and evolve the way Evelyn had, but she could not wait passively, marking time and holding his hand.

⸻⸻⸻

That summer, there was a Girl Scout outing to Taste of LIC, a celebration of food from restaurants in Long Island City, Queens, as well as a Girl Scout pool party at the St. Sebastian Parish Center, where Hailey, Karina, and Miranda, Giselle's much younger half sister, played Marco Polo with Aleijah and other Scouts. Hailey and Karina loved the Scouts, and Giselle could see how good it was for them. Giselle loved the Scouts, too, her reluctance having been replaced by a happiness to participate in something so obviously positive for her two oldest children, and for herself, too. She was excited that when school began in the fall, Christina would be old enough to be a Daisy Scout.

She was becoming progressively more and more exhausted, though. Between her work at the dental office in Manhattan, the long commute both ways, and single-parenting five children under the age of twelve, including a ten-month-old, she was drained. She was only twenty-nine, and she wondered how long she could keep up with the demands of her life.

In the fall of 2014, Hailey entered sixth grade, Karina started third after repeating second, and Christina was in kindergarten. Judas had just turned two years old and Gillesy would turn one in October. Giselle's mother babysat the little ones during the day. Six weeks after Gillesy's first birthday, Giselle was hospitalized after a seizure. On social media, she posted a photo of herself lying in a hospital bed with unkempt hair and a wistful smile, and a caption saying that she wanted to be home watching movies with her children.

Still, Giselle did her best to help the oldest girls keep up with their schoolwork, and she volunteered with the Girl Scouts as often as she could fit it into her crammed schedule. And when she learned about a trip the troop was planning to take after the holidays, she was almost as excited as if she were going on it herself.

# 3

# SAVANNAH SMILES

ON A COOL February Sunday in 2015, Hailey stood gaping at the house on Oglethorpe Street in Savannah where Juliette Gordon Low, the founder of the Girl Scouts, was born in 1860. A three-story Federal-style mansion with a tan-colored stucco façade, it was a sight to behold for the members of Sunnyside & Woodside troops. Hailey couldn't remember seeing a house that had so many shutters; she was used to high-rises and skyscrapers.

Luana and the other troop leaders of the Girl Scouts of Sunnyside & Woodside had raised money so that the Juniors and Cadettes could travel to Georgia to immerse themselves in Juliette's hometown for four days. The Scouts and their chaperones had taken Amtrak from New York to Savannah, chugging through Virginia and the Carolinas along a route similar to the one that Hailey remembered taking in the car to and from Florida. She was eleven now and had a full year of Girl Scouting and about twenty badges and patches under her belt. She had never before traveled without her family, so she was a little nervous but excited, too.

The troop was still subsidizing dues for Hailey and Karina, and now for Christina as well; Hailey would never have made it to Savannah otherwise. Their home life had taken a bad turn. The College Point duplex that Hailey loved had once and for all become unaffordable. With Wally gone, the rent was just too much for Giselle to handle by herself.

They had downgraded to a ramshackle second-floor apartment on Maple Avenue in Flushing. The poorly painted walls were an unattractive smudged beige. The older girls slept in a bedroom so small that there was just enough space for their bunk beds and two dressers. Giselle's "master" bedroom was no better. She had to move Gillesy's crib back and forth to get into her closet. The bathroom was narrow and had only a shower so Giselle had to bathe Judas and Gillesy while standing up and then hand them to their older siblings to be dried off.

The house had bars on the windows and was the ugliest one on the block. When Hailey first saw it from the outside, she couldn't help blurting out, "This place is a dump." The aging siding was in desperate need of a power washing that would never come. While the neighborhood hadn't yet been swallowed up by gentrification, the construction of a condominium building right next door threw the house into shadow.

Development was changing the city, and Giselle's new block was ripe for the picking—which would mean even fewer apartments available for rental at affordable rates. At the time Giselle moved in, the neighborhood was made up of mostly Asian Americans and new immigrants, followed by a sizable Latino population. It was close to the Queens Botanical Garden and Flushing Meadows Corona Park, the kind of green spaces that developers touted as neighborhood amenities.

But while Giselle was heavyhearted about the move to their new apartment, it also gave her a subtle sense of empowerment and control that she had never felt before. It was the first place she had rented on her own. No help from a man. Her name, and her name only, was on the lease. In spite of all the challenges she faced, she was determined to figure out a way to make this new life work for herself and for her family.

Hailey was thinking about all of it, the move and her mother's new, tenuous independence, as she traipsed around Savannah, where everyone seemed to stroll, not walk—but not like the meandering of tourists she had seen in Times Square. Here, southerners strolled with purpose, if that was possible. Savannah was made up of a series of luxuriously gardened squares, and there was a charm and an ease about the town even as sightseers filled the streets and formed lines outside historic homes. Still, everything around the city seemed so fragile to the girls, including the ground they walked on. There were signs on sets of stairs that read HISTORIC STEPS. USE AT OWN RISK.

The Scouts visited the Savannah College of Art and Design, where they posed like the Oscar de la Renta–draped mannequins; they ate ice cream cones at Leopold's, a shop that was almost a hundred years old; they tiptoed around a cemetery on a ghost tour; they volunteered to keep critically ill children company at the Ronald McDonald House.

And they made it to Juliette's house, which the Girl Scouts organization had purchased in 1953 so it couldn't be torn down. After walking up a grand outdoor staircase, the Cadettes and Juniors from the Sunnyside & Woodside troops entered the mansion. The first thing they saw upon stepping into the foyer was a portrait painted shortly after Juliette's wedding. There she was, the newly named Juliette Gordon Low, awash in pink, appearing gauzy and ethereal. Her blush dress blended in to her porcelain skin as if one and the same. Her rosy lips formed neither a smile nor a frown, perhaps a sign of what she expected of the years to come in her marriage.

The dress was sleeveless—but her discomfort made it resemble a straitjacket.

Juliette, better known as "Daisy" among her friends and family in Savannah, Georgia, had gone against her family's wishes and married the love of her life, William Mackay "Willy" Low. While he was suitable for marriage on paper, having social standing and primed to rake in an inheritance from his father, he had a reputation as a young man who believed his wealth permitted him to be a ne'er-do-well. Willy even acknowledged it to Juliette's father, in a letter asking for money to support their marriage. His own father, he conceded, thought him to be "nothing more than a good-for-nothing boy."

That said, Juliette and Willy had a lot in common. They'd both grown up in families that had accumulated great wealth through enslavement and cotton. William Washington "Willie" Gordon, Juliette's father, had been a Confederate captain. One month before the Civil War ended, the families of Confederate officers were escorted out of Savannah to safety, and Juliette, her older sister, and her mother sought refuge in Chicago, her mother's hometown. The Gordons were able to regroup and retain their wealth because Juliette's mother had her own resources and the sympathy of Union forces, thanks to her family's stature in Illinois and their loyalty: Juliette's great-uncle had led troops of black men during the war.

The Lows eventually moved to England, and Willy ended up making that country his permanent home, returning to Savannah only occasionally.

He and Juliette met during one of those trips, in the early 1880s, and fell in love. He went back across the ocean but soon enough Juliette traveled to England to see him, and by 1885 Willy was penning the "good-for-nothing boy" letter to Juliette's father. In turn, Juliette's father wrote to Willy's father that more money would be needed to support the young couple, both twenty-five years old, and eventually Willy received a promise from his father of $15,000 a year, a substantial amount in the late nineteenth century.

Juliette and Willy married on December 21, 1886, but what should have been an idyllic day was marred by a bizarre accident. As a child Juliette had suffered an ear infection that left her deaf in one ear; now, at her wedding, a grain of rice that guests had thrown like confetti lodged itself in her ear. The procedure to remove the grain left her with worse hearing.

The newlyweds lived briefly in Savannah before moving permanently to England, where Willy introduced Juliette to the country's elite. It was a whirlwind time: There seemed to be no shortage of lords and ladies or elaborate balls and nights at the theater. But the new bride soon saw less and less of her husband on their vast estate with its horses and swaths of orchids. In a nod to their southern roots, the Lows had planted an abundance of lush blooms on the property, almost making it hard to distinguish the sprawling English countryside from the landscape in Savannah. But frequently Juliette's new husband was nowhere to be found.

Their portrait of an idyllic life together was shattered when Juliette found out about an affair Willy had been having with a widow in their social circle. Juliette was humiliated, and by 1895 the couple had separated.

It was a rancorous parting, made all the more ugly by Willy's threat to withhold a settlement from Juliette if she did not agree to a divorce—a threat that should have dissolved when Willy suffered a stroke and later died of a seizure in 1905. But his death only made things worse for Juliette. It turned out that his will was a mess and, in a final insult, it seemed he'd bequeathed much of his orchid-carpeted estate to his mistress. Juliette showed her grit in a tough legal fight and came away with a settlement of properties and holdings worth $500,000, which is equal to about $14 million today.

She was fifty, rich, and in danger of being a permanent lady of leisure when she met Sir Robert Baden-Powell, a British Army officer who had made a name for himself by founding the Boy Scouts and writing *Scouting for Boys,* the organization's bible. The two shared an interest in both sculpting and the outdoors, and Juliette found Robert, who was roughly the same age, charming and attractive.

Robert returned her affection with nothing more than friendship, but what a friendship it was. Beyond being good-looking and accomplished, Baden-Powell had a character that inspired Juliette to want to contribute to the larger world around her, broadening her interests beyond those of her own narrow social circle. She quickly latched on to the Girl Guides, the female counterpart of the Boy Scouts that he had founded, which was led by his sister, Agnes Baden-Powell. The two women became close, and in 1911 Juliette was given her first of many challenges in the combined world of girls and Scouting: establish a troop in a remote glen in the Scottish Highlands, where families were poor and uneducated.

She managed to find seven girls to meet on Saturday afternoons and made a connection with them not only by instilling the beliefs of the Girl Guide organization but by figuring out what the girls needed—like income for their families—and then helping them to develop skills that would be immediately useful to them. Among camping, first aid, mapping, and other things, she taught them how to spin wool—after teaching herself—and even created an export business so they could sell their products in London.

In a letter to her father that August, Juliette sounded like a woman who was finally coming into her own, finding her place in the world, when she wrote: "I like girls and I like this organization and the rules and pastimes, so if you find that I get very deeply interested you must not be surprised!"

She had found her calling, and now she wanted to return to Savannah and share it. On March 12, 1912, Juliette started a Girl Guide troop far from the chill Highlands of Scotland in her own hot southern hometown. Around that time, a small but significant change occurred, almost by accident—Juliette offhandedly and often referred to the girls as Scouts, and everyone around her followed her lead. Soon enough the Girl Guides, a name that endured in the United Kingdom and elsewhere overseas, became the Girl Scouts in the United States. Juliette proposed a merger with the Camp Fire Girls, another leadership, skill-building, and Scouting organization for girls that had sprung up informally in Vermont, and suggested that the combined groups be called the "Girl Scouts." The merger never happened but the name stuck.

Juliette did everything in her power to grow the Girl Scouts, tapping into her personal fund. At one point, she even sold the pearl necklace that Willy had given her as a wedding present when she was expanding the organization and her annual income from her settlement was not coming fast enough. It was just the beginning. Over the years she became a worldwide symbol of female resilience, of what happens when a woman is persistent despite setbacks. An art appreciator and an adept sculptor and painter, Juliette commissioned a Belgian artist to capture her likeness in her Girl Scout uniform. She looked straight ahead sternly, confidently, her self-assured mien so unlike the one in the post-wedding portrait that her husband had commissioned. It was as if she were two different people, not only in terms of age but in terms of fortitude. Juliette was a near-deaf widow who had found her calling in her fifties by helping young girls to find their own callings. She began with eighteen girls in Savannah; when she died of cancer in 1927, fifteen years after her founding of that original troop, there were 168,000 Girl Scouts across the country.

She was buried in her Girl Scout uniform.

Hailey had heard so much about this woman since she'd joined the Scouts. She had celebrated both Juliette's birthday, which was on Halloween, and her founding of the Girl Scouts. But she'd never quite understood what all the fuss was about until now. While she knew Juliette Gordon Low had founded the Girl Scouts, she had never seemed like a real person to Hailey, making it difficult for her to relate to Juliette's experience. But inside the house on Oglethorpe Street, Juliette's troubles were on display, like the tea sets, canopy beds, quilts, and sofas too pristine and delicate for sitting. More than a century later, there were striking similarities between Juliette's troubles and her mother's plight, her mother's struggle.

Giselle was not deaf, but she had perforated her left eardrum years earlier. Her epileptic seizures were debilitating. And while

Hailey had heard no stories about Willy Low physically abusing Juliette like Wally had harmed her mother, both men treated the women in their lives terribly.

Hailey could still feel the sweet southern air on her skin when she got back to the apartment on Maple Avenue. Since Hailey was a sixth grader, turning twelve that April, she could ride the bus to and from school by herself, and now, with Wally gone, her responsibilities stacked up. Judas and Gillesy could barely walk and talk. Nine-year-old Karina had not adjusted as well as her sisters to the return to New York. In addition to having to repeat the second grade, she was having trouble with bullies at school. And she had bouts of sullenness, even as she looked forward to the weekend Scout meetings. Six-year-old Christina had been diagnosed with epilepsy; she experienced the same staring spells that Giselle had suffered as a child, and could sometimes be distant.

Hailey was more than a big sister; she had become a caregiver, a mediator, a problem solver, and a kisser of boo-boos.

And she had to take care of her mother, too, whose seizures and trips to the hospital had grown more frequent. Giselle worked ten- and twelve-hour days, juggling her commute to the dental office in Manhattan with pickups from daycare and school. It was obvious to Hailey that Giselle's schedule was taking a toll on her.

Hailey was a sixth grader with the weight of her family on her slight shoulders, which were covered with a vest blanketed with badges.

# 4

# NEW BEGINNINGS

AFTER HAILEY'S TRIP to the American birthplace of the Girl Scouts, Giselle, who had been elevated to co-leader of the troop, and her three oldest daughters faithfully showed up for meetings at St. Sebastian. As winter moved into spring, it became even more of a family affair, with Evelyn often volunteering, too, since Miranda's interest in Girl Scouting had deepened.

Hailey could see that her mother was fragile both physically and emotionally. Her bout in the hospital the preceding fall had lasted a week. Giselle had developed a staph infection, which threatened her kidneys and heart, and Hailey and Karina understood the severity of the situation when they saw how debilitated she was. Christina, Judas, and Gillesy were not allowed to enter the intensive care unit because of worries about spreading infections, so a nurse wheeled Giselle out to the elevator bank to hug them. The nurse had rolled all of the IV equipment along with Giselle, and a trepidatious Christina recoiled at the sight of her, confused by the tubes that sprouted from her mother's arms.

"It's okay, baby," Giselle said gently, caressing Christina's face and kissing all of her children. Tears welled in her eyes.

It was a horrible week. Many adults pitched in to help, but

Giselle had concerns they just couldn't allay. Trapped in her hospital bed, she worried about her children and about the infection raging through her body. And she worried about the hospital bills. Mounting medical bills seemed to be a relentlessly persistent part of her life.

The children were split up for the week between Wally, who cared for Judas and Gillesy, and Chris, who attended to Hailey, Karina, and Christina. But Hailey was clearly in charge; she knew everyone's schedules and what homework was due when.

Once Giselle recovered, she jumped back into work, but it was becoming less and less satisfying. What kept her going was her prankster-like sense of humor. At the dental office, she sarcastically complimented her colleagues for looking so fashionable in their scrubs; she rigged the levers of chairs so that they would sink as soon as someone sat down; she wrote fake names on the lists of patients checking in so her colleagues would call out names in the waiting room to no avail.

The Girl Scouts also kept her going. A year after complaining about having to sell and drag cookies to her co-workers in the dental office, Giselle now proudly stacked three cases of Samoas, two cases of Thin Mints, two cases of Savannah Smiles, a case of Tagalongs, and a case of Do-si-dos in the kitchen of the apartment on Maple Avenue and began figuring out the orders she was taking for cookie season 2015. "Finally got the cookies!! Now time to seperate everyones orders," she misspelled on Instagram in a rush, adding cookie emojis and a string of hashtags— #GIRLSCOUTS #COOKIES #cookietime #girlscoutmom.

Giselle told everyone she knew that the girls' joining the Scouts and her stepping up to be a co-leader were the best things her family had ever done. The once reluctant chaperone had come to see that her initial assessment of the Scouts had been totally off base. The Girl Scouts were more than just cookies, field trips, and sleepovers. Selling cookies promoted self-confidence and improved math proficiency; volunteering encouraged compassion and a sense of community; the tasks required to earn badges taught a wide range of practical skills and discipline. Giselle also now understood that joining the Scouts was a real commitment of time and energy. For the girls, of course, and for their families as well, who had to buy uniforms, get the Scouts to meetings, and support their cookie-selling, badge-earning, and community service efforts. But Giselle was convinced that it was a worthy undertaking.

In September 2015, Giselle, Hailey, and Karina carefully wrote out the Girl Scout Promise and the Girl Scout Law in different colored markers on a sheet of white construction paper and taped it to the front door. Then Giselle took a photo and posted it on Facebook. "Everytime we leave our house we are reminded of the positive morals we live by," she wrote that month, leaving out the fact that her life was falling to pieces.

⸻

The email was curt: Giselle's services were no longer needed.

It was July 2015 and Giselle was expecting to be fired. She had already told her bosses at the dental office that she could not continue to work late nights—she couldn't do that to her children or herself anymore. On top of that, she was missing too many workdays due to illness and medical appointments, and while her employers were sympathetic, they were losing patience. They agreed that she would train her replacement and then the office would let her go, allowing her to collect unemployment benefits.

Now the email made it official. Instead of the relief she thought she'd feel, she was sickened by a sense of panic. The truth—that unemployment payments would not carry her family and certainly would not help Giselle whittle down the debt she had accumulated—was sinking in. At a loss for how to move forward, she confided in Meridith. The two had become good friends, bonding over their five children each and cheap wine on Meridith's deck, a modest seating area with old furniture that overlooked a cluttered backyard filled with toys, evidence of children given the freedom to express themselves.

Inside, Meridith's home often looked just as chaotic, like a daycare center at the end of the day before the children sang the cleanup song. But Meridith was organized when it came to her career goals, with a focus that Giselle had never seen in any of her other friends or family. Meridith seemed like a good person to ask for advice.

Meridith had grown up in Sullivan, Maine, a small coastal town dependent on lobstering. She was the youngest of seven children in a family that had abandoned suburban New Jersey in search of a simpler, less expensive life. Meridith's father was on the school board, and Meridith and her mother were both active in a local theater company called the Gilbert & Sullivan Society of Maine. They were also active in the Girl Scouts.

In addition to earning the Scouts' highest honor when she was seventeen—an honor bestowed on fewer than 6 percent of Girl Scouts nationwide—she was class president, she starred on stage as the resident theater geek, and she perfected her arguments as captain of the debate team. Her life seemed perfect, but like so many things that appear one way and are in fact another, the reality was quite different. Pain was driving her overachievement. When she was little, Meridith had been molested, and her family, perhaps not knowing how to respond to her disturbing revelation, or simply in profound denial about it, didn't offer her the comfort and support that she so desperately needed. Meridith took her trauma and turned it into something else—a drive to speak up for herself and others outside of her home.

When she was seventeen, she represented Maine at a Girl Scouts convention in Miami, where amid the palm trees and blazing sun she went rogue and led four fellow Ambassadors and Senior Scouts on an unsupervised and flagrantly unauthorized whistle-stop adventure.

She shepherded the small group to a performance of *Godspell,* then convinced them to go to Dick Clark's American Bandstand Grill, even as the other girls, still wearing their royal blue uniforms ablaze with badges, begged to return to the hotel before chaperones figured out that they were missing. Amazingly, the legendary music host himself was in the restaurant, and he could not believe the mettle of these teenage Scouts from New England. Dinner was on Dick Clark. Their complimentary meal was something that Meridith would brag about in the years to come.

When she had to face the Girl Scouts leadership in Maine to justify her insubordination, Meridith calmly explained that she was not about to spend her convention watching chaperones drink at the pool.

Her confidence carried her to New York with savings from waitressing and dreams of working on Broadway. She landed a job in the theater merchandising industry—it's related to Broadway, right?—and rose through the ranks until she was vice president of Max Merchandising LLC, which created T-shirts and other paraphernalia for shows like *Rent* and *Phantom of the Opera*.

She and her husband, Dan, moved to Sunnyside, Queens, and had a daughter, Dorothy, in 2003. Dan quit his job to become a full-time stay-at-home father so Meridith could focus on work. Their family kept growing: after Dorothy came Vivien, Veronica, Natalie, and Marlene. And when each girl reached Daisy age, she joined the Sunnyside & Woodside troop that Meridith started when Dorothy was five years old. The troop had thrived in the years when Meridith and Luana were co-leaders. In fact, with its diversity and activism in the community, membership was so sought-after that parents from other communities signed a waiting list for their daughters to join.

The more she volunteered with the Scouts, the more Meridith felt that her particular talents might be put to better use in that organization than by figuring out new ways to merchandise T-shirts and key chains for Broadway shows. She left the job she had succeeded at for nearly sixteen years and applied for a position as vice president of multistream product and retail sales at the Girl Scouts of Greater New York. She had to take a pay cut, and she and Dan relied on credit cards to buy groceries, but she wanted to have more of an impact on girls and strongly believed joining the staff of the Girl Scouts was the way to achieve that goal.

It was October 2015, and Meridith was on her way up. Giselle seemed to be headed in the other direction. They were the unlikeliest of friends. Giselle had grown up around gangs and had a high school equivalency diploma. Meridith was college-educated and her knowledge of gangs was limited to *West Side Story*'s Jets and Sharks.

Meridith initially eyed Giselle with skepticism when she was dropping off the girls at the meetings. She wondered if Giselle was getting her nails manicured on Saturday mornings while she and Luana were teaching girls life lessons.

Giselle's beauty was striking, and she offered her smiles as naturally as offering a handshake. Giselle seemed so mature. She was youthful and moved with vigor, yet she carried her life experiences in her face. Meridith couldn't tell how old Giselle was, even speculating for a short while that they might be the same age. But they were thirteen years apart. Meridith was too young to be Giselle's mother yet old enough to have been her babysitter.

As much as Meridith was intrigued by Giselle, though, it was Hailey who had convinced Meridith that Giselle was the kind of mother she wanted to befriend. At Camp Kaufmann, Hailey approached Meridith not to tattle but to share her concern that other Scouts could be more thoughtful, more sisterly, to a Scout who had special needs. Meridith thought Hailey's stepping forward took not only maturity but a compassion that she had to have learned from someone.

When Meridith landed the job at the Girl Scouts of Greater New York in October 2015, she learned that the nonprofit had an opening for a recruiter. *Why shouldn't Giselle apply?* she thought. Giselle needed a job, having been out of work since late summer, and she needed a change.

Candidates for the position—it was called "community development specialist"—were preferred to have an associate's degree or a bachelor's degree; Giselle had neither. But she had a high school equivalency diploma and both the get-up-and-go and poise that came from juggling a never-ending stream of phone calls from patients who needed their teeth cleaned and their cavities filled. Having arranged files in dental offices for so many years, she was supremely organized. Plus, she had Meridith's support, and Hailey pushed her to apply. So apply she did.

Giselle had scored an interview and was awaiting news about the job when the Girl Scouts of Sunnyside & Woodside were asked to help serve a Thanksgiving lunch to women who were homeless and staying at Pam's Place on Twenty-ninth Street in Long Island City, a Queens neighborhood just across the East River from Manhattan. What started out as a single troop for Brownies had grown into several troops for different age levels as interest increased and the girls grew up: Daisies, Brownies, Juniors, and Cadettes, and Jimmy Van Bramer, a local member of the city council, asked all of them to pitch in.

Jimmy's lunch was intended to serve two purposes. Most simply and straightforwardly, it would give the homeless women living at Pam's Place a good meal. Less measurably, though, it might also start to change public opinion about them. The city did not have enough shelters to address the explosion of homelessness it was facing, and so it was turning hotels into shelters, either by temporarily renting blocks of rooms or by renting entire hotels outright. At Pam's Place, the city had entered into a long-term agreement to turn what was once the Verve Hotel into a shelter that housed 196 women. The community had been caught off guard by the city's decision, and its response had been resoundingly negative.

Concerned that so many of his constituents were vitriolic in their opposition to the possibility of shelters being placed in their neighborhoods, Jimmy had written an op-ed in the Sunday *Daily News.*

A young father enters a colorless room holding his infant son while his wife sits nearby trying to believe this isn't

happening. Their older kids, not much older than the infant, stay close. They are all tired and they are all homeless. The father tells the intake worker that they had been
staying with friends but had to leave and now have nowhere else to turn. He asks for help because they have no
money and his baby son just needs a bottle of milk.

The father is 25, it is 1970 in New York City, and I am
that baby boy.

The op-ed went on to describe Jimmy's father's alcoholism
and the despair and desperation of his family. To Jimmy, any
one of the women at Pam's Place could have been a member of
his family. He always tried to remember that truth even when
political pressure bore down on him. He surveyed the community room at Pam's Place and was in awe of the kindness the
Scouts were showing the women at the shelter.

"Thank you, baby," an elderly woman told Christina as the
Daisy handed her a Styrofoam plate filled with turkey, dressing,
green beans, macaroni and cheese, and cranberry sauce. Christina wore thin latex gloves, like a cafeteria lady, which made the
slippery Styrofoam harder to grip. But she went back and forth
carefully from the buffet line, where Giselle and other troop
leaders filled up plates for the tables of women, most of whom
were elderly, mentally ill, or struggling with drug addiction.

Jimmy laughed and talked with Giselle that day. He had met
her through Meridith, whose troop had made a name for itself
in the community. Jimmy was small in stature and had a baby
face despite his prematurely white hair. He was gay, white, a
college graduate, and in a stable relationship with his husband.
But if you looked below the surface, there were surprising similarities between his life story and Giselle's. He held elective office now, and had even been a Boy Scout, but as he had detailed
in his op-ed, he had been homeless as an infant, and his family
had always straddled the poverty line, shifting back and forth,
rising just above it and falling way below it. As he scooped green

beans and dressing onto plates and chatted with Giselle that afternoon, he took an immediate liking to her. He didn't know that she was unemployed, struggling financially, and hoping to get the new job with the Girl Scouts.

Days after the lunch, Giselle was at her mother's apartment when the Girl Scouts human resources representative called. Her pulse pounded as she left her mother's bedroom to answer the phone in the living room.

When she hung up, she burst into tears. "I got the job! Mommy, I got the job!" she screamed, running back into Evelyn's bedroom and into her arms.

Evelyn screamed, too, and then started crying. She was so thankful that finally her daughter had some good news—a job that she really wanted, one that she was excited about. Evelyn held her and they grew silent.

"God is good, baby," Evelyn finally said, rocking her daughter. "I knew you had it in you. God loves you."

When Giselle got home to her Maple Avenue apartment that night, she rested her phone against the printer on the coffee table so she could record a video of the moment when she shared the news with her children. She had bought the printer with money they didn't really have so that Hailey could complete her homework assignments without having to go to the library to print them out and then return home alone late at night. Giselle was sometimes exhausted by the number of choices she had to make about the allocation of her limited money. This choice had been easy, though; her daughter's safety was paramount.

Giselle sat on the floor and pulled the email up on Hailey's phone. Three-year-old Judas sat on the floor next to her and babbled. Karina was slumped on the couch. Plastic blinds, so crumpled and worn that light shone through even when they were closed, covered a window behind her. Hailey and Christina sat on the couch upright as if they were at their desks in school.

"So I got this email and, um, I got us all together so we can read it together as a family, and I'm recording to see everyone's reactions to what we're about to find out," Giselle said into the camera. "So here we go."

She handed the phone to Hailey to read aloud.

"We are pleased to announce that we have closed our search for community development specialist in the Queens service centers. Giselle Burgess is joining Girl Scouts as of Mon—

"Mommy!" Hailey yelled, leaping from the couch and into her mother's arms. "I told you! I told you!"

Giselle wept tears of relief and rejoicing.

Hailey, Karina, Christina, and Judas surrounded her. "I wuv you," Judas said, snuggling into her.

"Thank you, Papi," she said, hugging him.

"And thank you everyone who prayed and was there support- ing, keeping me in your thoughts," she said into the camera. "I'm super grateful, and, um, new beginnings," she added as if singing. "Let's do it!"

She smiled wide into the camera and then pressed stop.

In seven months, the family would be homeless.

# 5

# PATH

HOMELESSNESS RARELY HAPPENS overnight, save for a natural disaster or a fire. Losing a home is a slow process, often years in the making, with stretches of living right on the edge punctuated, perhaps, by brief, rare periods of being able to save a few dollars. One small mistake or poor decision can ripple out and be felt indefinitely. One accident or health crisis can set a family back for years. Giselle had been living in a one-step-forward, two-steps-back situation her whole life.

She was so grateful to Meridith and to the Girl Scouts of Greater New York for hiring her and putting her on a new career path, but months after she was showing off new business cards emblazoned with her name and fancy title—COMMUNITY DEVELOPMENT SPECIALIST—Giselle was $8,552 in arrears on her rent and owed close to $10,000 in medical bills.

When Giselle had signed her lease in the fall of 2014 for the apartment on Maple Avenue in Flushing, the one that Hailey had called a dump, she'd looked like a solid tenant with decent credit and a steady paycheck. She had carved out a career for herself as an office manager for dentists, working for three different ones—two in New York and one in Florida. But she always came up short on the $1,650 monthly rent. She began giving the landlord partial payments, and then she didn't pay at all.

At the Manhattan dental office where she'd been working after her return from Florida, she'd been bringing in more than $50,000 a year. At the Girl Scouts she was making $37,500 a year, about $18 an hour. That was more than New York City's minimum wage, which was $11 an hour at the time, but it was not nearly enough to support a family of six. She decided that if she worked hard, she could get promoted and would eventually make more money.

But that wasn't going to happen fast enough. Her landlord hired a lawyer and took her to housing court. Giselle couldn't afford a lawyer, so she represented herself. The judge issued a warrant for her eviction in March 2016, three months after she'd started her job at the Girl Scouts, but stayed the removal to give Giselle more time to figure things out. In yet another appearance in housing court on April 28, 2016, Giselle drafted her request in neat cursive writing but ran out of space, so she wrote the last sentence in smaller cursive and just under the lines allotted for answers: "I have been unsuccessful in finding an apartment. Either no response back, scam, I have too many tenants or my credit is too low. Also I am applying for a one shot deal landlords don't accept." A one-shot deal was an emergency grant tailored by the city to try to keep potentially homeless tenants in their homes.

Giselle attached photocopies of real estate listings to prove that she had been searching: a two-bedroom in College Point for $1,450, another in Rosedale, a couple more in Astoria. The competition was cutthroat. There were estimates that the city had lost more than four hundred thousand apartments renting for $900 or less since 2005. Now rents for an apartment large enough to accommodate her big family were out of Giselle's range.

She was not alone. In 2016, 22,089 residential evictions took place in New York City. The city had already started a program to provide free legal assistance to some tenants and had greatly expanded the service the previous year. But the initial focus was on fifteen zip codes that had a significant number of rent-regulated apartments, evictions, and people entering shelters. Giselle lived just outside one of those zip codes.

The housing court judge was unconvinced by Giselle's plea and ordered the warrant to be carried out by a marshal. Because Giselle knew that one of her options would be going into shelter, she tried to plan in advance by taking the subway to the Bronx, where the city's intake center for homeless families, PATH, was located. She traveled there in May and June, only to be told that a marshal would have to physically remove her family before they would be allowed to enter the shelter system.

That day came on July 7, 2016.

Giselle had prepared her children like a teacher giving instructions for a tornado drill. She had bad news, she'd told them the day before: They were going to have to leave their home. They had packed up whatever they couldn't put in storage and slowly made their way to Evelyn and Manny's apartment with their few belongings spilling out of garbage bags.

Evelyn had hung on to the same apartment in Woodside for twenty years. It was on the fourth floor of a walk-up, an inconvenient and unwanted daily workout, but it was affordable—a rarity—and the kind of apartment that families forced to be frugal clung to. There were only two bedrooms, and the house was stuffed with knickknacks and clothes and furniture that made it look even smaller. Giselle's stepfather, Manny, was an incorrigible collector of stuff, particularly anything Mets—even the front door was painted in the team's classic colors of blue and orange.

Giselle felt a deep sense of failure and shame. Here she was, back in her parents' home, but this time with her children. Ten people—Evelyn and Manny, Giselle's much younger siblings Mateo and Miranda, plus Hailey, Karina, Christina, Judas, Gillesy, and Giselle herself—were now crammed into the two-bedroom walk-up.

For her part, Evelyn questioned whether she was somehow to

blame for her daughter's homelessness. She thought about those times she had physically assaulted Giselle, which pained her deeply now. Evelyn had gotten sober; she and Manny had been married for fourteen years. Somewhere along the way he had told her he would leave her if she could not learn to stop hitting. She had learned.

Now Evelyn felt guilty about not being in a position to help her daughter more. No matter how hard she tried, though, everything she said came out sounding accusatory, like Giselle was to blame for everything when she really wasn't. Evelyn knew that.

Giselle couldn't listen to Evelyn's ear-piercing lectures without hearing her mother's disappointment and feeling disappointed in herself and devastated that she had let down her family.

Evelyn wasn't the only one nagging Giselle. Her brother Mateo, who collected figurines just like his father, complained that Judas, still a toddler, was touching his toys.

"Stop letting him in your room then!" Giselle yelled at Mateo as if he were her son and not her brother.

"This is exactly why I need to go. I can't be here anymore. You need your space, and I need mine," Giselle said to her mother in the living room. "My kid is stuck in a car seat all day long because I don't want him to touch anything in your house."

Evelyn tried to assure Giselle that they could work it out. "He can move around. You can stay. You don't need to leave. The baby just needs to play with certain toys that Mateo gives him."

"You make excuses for him," Giselle said.

She stomped into the bathroom, the only place where she could get any privacy. She slammed the door, yelling so her mother and everyone else could hear. "I can't fucking be here anymore! I'm tired of this. I'm done. I'm out of here!"

When Giselle emerged from the bathroom, Evelyn told her, "Okay, if that's what you want to do, but I'm not putting you out."

Giselle turned to her five children and said, "We have to go."

She studied their young faces and tried to convince herself that she'd made the right decision, that everyone would be better off out of this overcrowded, tense apartment. It was for the best, she repeated silently. It was for the best.

The next day they officially entered the New York City shelter system.

Giselle had never really known anyone who was homeless; it was something that happened to other people. Strangers. Street homelessness was a fact of life in New York, and she would give a dollar or two to people panhandling on the sidewalk— disheveled men and women with cardboard signs, curled up on subway grates, huddled on park benches.

That was the face of homelessness she and most New Yorkers knew, not this. Not her. Not her children.

Most homeless people, especially the families, blended in with everyone else.

Many, like Giselle, had jobs. They were men and women sitting quietly in the library. They were mothers and fathers carrying strollers up and down subway stairs. They were children walking to school. In 2016, the year that Giselle and her family became homeless, an average 36,000 adults and 23,000 children were living in the city's main shelter system each day. That did not count an estimated 11,000 other people who were in specialized shelters, like mothers and their children escaping domestic violence or runaway teenagers with nowhere else to turn. Another 2,800 people lived on the street.

With the explosion of homelessness in New York, the city was desperate to find housing for those seeking it. PATH—the acronym stood for Prevention Assistance and Temporary Housing—was the city program tasked with finding shelter for the homeless. It now tucked families into not only shelters but also hotel rooms that were not conducive to long-term residence and private apartments that were never intended to be used as shelters.

There were, in fact, homeless people everywhere. In 2016, there were at least 287 traditional shelters; at least another 265 private buildings with apartments being used as shelters; and 84 hotels being used as shelters citywide. When a hotel went into service as a shelter, neighbors were often unhappy, and they were vocal about it. Pam's Place, the shelter where Hailey had been interviewed by a NY1 reporter, had been a budget hotel called Verve until October 2015. When it transitioned into providing rooms for single women who had nowhere else to turn, the neighbors had made their displeasure known in ways both subtle and overt. That had been one of the reasons for the Thanksgiving lunch organized by Jimmy Van Bramer.

---

The PATH building, where Giselle and her kids headed with their backpacks and garbage bags after leaving Evelyn's, was in the South Bronx and seemed out of place in its immediate surroundings. It had brightly colored bricks in two different shades of red, a modern design with rectangular windows, and an impressive, postcard-worthy view of Manhattan. Under the administration then led by Mayor Michael Bloomberg, the city had spent $65 million to build it, replacing the Emergency Assistance Unit, a decrepit building and an embarrassment to the city where children had slept overnight on grimy floors while their parents tried to catch a few minutes of rest on uncomfortable plastic chairs. That building had been torn down in 2006 after years of outcry and litigation by the Legal Aid Society.

PATH had seven stories and was open seven days a week, twenty-four hours a day, though it had fewer staff between nine P.M. and nine A.M. A long ramp at the entrance made the building accessible for disabled people using wheelchairs, parents pushing strollers, and children rolling suitcases decorated with cartoon characters. During the summer, the lines snaked down the ramp, as families left the temporary arrangements they had made with relatives and friends. Families saw the summer as the best time to go into shelter, hoping to make transferring from one school to another less disruptive for their kids. Around July, the staff braced for the flood, but the city still aimed to get families in and out of PATH in six hours. Giselle and her children got there at eight-thirty on a humid Friday morning. Expecting a long wait, she took the children to a bodega to buy drinks to keep them quiet. A splurge, perhaps, but it would be money well spent.

The gleaming building may have been new but it still had an ominous presence. Security was similar to TSA at the airport. Belongings moved along a whirring conveyor belt and were scanned; guards waved wands around bodies. The children didn't quite know what to make of it all—the jostling crowd, the grim-looking officials, the long, long line. Giselle saw a sign: Food and liquids were prohibited except for baby food, breast milk, or formula. Hailey gasped when the security guards took away their drinks. Giselle tried not to show her dismay. Fifteen dollars wasted. Fifteen dollars that she didn't have to waste. The knot that had been in her stomach for days twisted a little tighter.

They were processed quickly, but then the wait began. The architects of the building had bragged years earlier about how the specially designed windows captured natural light and bounced it throughout the floors to save energy. But there was no sunshine in the basement, the last stop for families as they bided their time.

Giselle and the children sat beneath fluorescent lights, saying little and watching PBS programming that repeated on a loop for hours. Giselle tried to keep her thoughts from repeating on a loop, too, but she couldn't help wondering again and again what kind of life she was giving her children, who were sitting bored out of their minds in a sterile, dark basement, with no sense of what the next day—or for that matter, the next hour—

would bring. She did her best to cheer them all up with her ready smile, trying hard to keep her fears hidden, but it was difficult to stuff down her panic. The knot in her stomach just kept tightening.

They were waiting to be placed in what the city called conditional shelter: For ten days, before putting any family in permanent shelter, investigators would call landlords and relatives to verify whether applicants for housing were actually homeless. For years, advocates and attorneys for homeless people had complained about this intrusiveness, treating homeless people as if they were trying to steal something, as if everyone was a liar until proven otherwise. In the past, the definition of overcrowding varied from investigator to investigator, with some even asking relatives whether a person might sleep well on bedding in a bathtub. Acceptable long-term sleeping options included air mattresses, even if they took up all the floor space in a room.

About 58 percent of those vying for a place to live were initially found to be ineligible either because they had no documentation that they had been evicted or because relatives, unsure of what to say, would convince themselves or outright lie to investigators that ten people could comfortably and happily live in a one-bedroom/one-bathroom apartment. This meant that many people seeking shelter had to apply all over again after incorrectly being found ineligible; others just gave up in frustration, returning to crammed apartments or enduring family strife for the sake of a roof over their heads.

The day dragged on. Judas and Gillesy were antsy—they got up and then sat down and then got up again. Hailey, Karina, and Christina were anxious, distractedly watching the television, checking on their younger siblings, occasionally pretending to nap.

Finally, Giselle and her five children were called up. For whatever reason—because of all the filing she had done for dentists or because she had trained herself to be organized—Giselle was meticulous about her record keeping. She had assembled all of her paperwork and placed it in a blue plastic accordion

folder—birth certificates, proof of eviction, her driver's license—
and she was found eligible almost immediately. The top reasons
for homelessness, among the ones that could qualify people to
get shelter from the city, were domestic violence, eviction, overcrowding, and family discord. Giselle had hit an unfortunate
quadfecta.

They were put on a school bus and dropped off at a Quality
Inn on Queens Boulevard. The conditional shelter was only a
twenty-minute walk from her mother and stepfather's apartment, which was comforting.

The room had only a single king-size bed, but Giselle and the
children were so exhausted that they fell asleep piled on the bed
in the clothes they had worn all day and slept soundly. Giselle
was surprised when a social worker showed up the next day to
tell her they had to leave.

"Why? Why are you moving us?" she asked. "We slept fine
last night."

The social worker told Giselle that the city could not, in good
conscience, allow six people to sleep in one bed, and that they
were being moved to a shelter in Brooklyn.

They once again loaded up their belongings in backpacks
and garbage bags, and the social worker put them all into a cab,
where they huddled together. Giselle wrapped her arms around
as many of her children as she could reach and wondered when
this ordeal, this miserable odyssey, would come to an end.

The cab pulled up to a shelter in Brownsville, Brooklyn, that
looked like a big pink apartment building. On the ride over,
seven-year-old Christina had become nauseous. The medication
she took for her epilepsy sometimes made her sick. As the family
got out of the cab, she vomited. Giselle held back her long strands
of coal-black hair and tried to soothe her.

"Oh my God, that's disgusting!" a woman standing outside
the shelter screeched, and other people milling around nodded
in agreement.

Giselle ignored them and shepherded her children through
the front doors. They checked in and lugged their things into

their efficiency unit, where there were two twin beds and two sets of bunk beds, a kitchen with a few pots and pans, and a care package of towels and sheets. Everyone sighed with relief. "Mom, this is nice," Hailey said, not really meaning it but wanting to say something positive.

Giselle looked around and nodded. "It's not that bad, guys," she said optimistically.

But it was far from perfect. The floors were stained by wear and tear. The surfaces were covered with the kind of thin, mucky film that lingers when dozens of families have stayed in one place, going in and out and never treating it like home. The air smelled of sickly sweet lavender cleaner.

Giselle decided to try to get to know the neighborhood. The shelter was just a twenty-minute drive from the Maple Avenue apartment they'd been evicted from, but Brooklyn felt like a world away from Queens. She googled a nearby supermarket, and she and the kids headed over there. The weather had turned from sunny to overcast, and the high reached only seventy-two degrees that day, which made it feel more like gloomy autumn than summer.

"Hey, shorty, what's up?" two men catcalled as Giselle and her family reached the store, yet another reminder that Hailey had developed ahead of her years. Karina shot them a look; Giselle yelled at them.

"She's only thirteen years old!"

The men laughed, and one quipped, "Oh, Mama can get it, too."

Giselle pushed her kids into the store and rushed in behind them. She spent what she had on chicken cutlets, a box of rice, a can of beans, and a bag of ready-made salad. The girls wanted mashed potatoes so she got those, too, and milk and butter to make them creamy.

They returned to the shelter as two ragged-looking men were walking in. Giselle gripped her keys, fashioning them into a weapon. *I'm swinging these keys if I have to,* she thought as all eight of them got onto the elevator. The men got off on the same floor; Giselle and the kids went one way and the men went another. The family coolly walked into their unit and Giselle put down the bags of groceries before opening the door and peering back down the hallway. One of the men stared right back at her.

"Are they there?" Karina asked from inside.

"No, we're good," Giselle lied, pushing the door closed. "Let's make the best of the night we have."

Giselle cooked dinner, and for a few hours, the family forgot where they were. They played cards, War and Crazy Eights and Spit and Pig. Giselle loved games, and her children always had someone to play with. Judas was about to be four years old, but he loved screaming out, "I declare War!" even if it wasn't his turn.

While the shelter seemed like a good solution—everyone had a bed, it was comfortable, and they could cook for themselves—Giselle knew they couldn't stay there. The two men, the unfamiliar surroundings, her mother too far away to easily babysit: Living in the big pink building just wasn't going to work.

Giselle turned to Hailey and Karina. She was the mother, the adult, but she had had the girls so young that she often included them in her decision making. "Do you want to stay here or go back to PATH?"

"PATH," the sisters said in unison.

|||||||||||||||||||||

"Excuse me, are you going to sign out?" a clerk at the door of the shelter asked Giselle the next morning.

"No, I'm not coming back."

Leaving without checking out was against protocol. The shelter system was full of rules and protocol. Sign in. Sign out. No alcohol. Curfew at nine P.M. Children were to be accompanied at all times. No guests without approval.

Giselle and her five children made it to PATH in the Bronx by ten o'clock only to learn that if you improperly check yourself out, there's a forty-eight-hour waiting period before you can re-apply. In city records, Giselle was listed as "MOA," or "Made Other Arrangements."

She felt as if she had been dealt a body blow. In distress and with nowhere to go, she called her mother.

"Come home. Manny says come home," Evelyn pleaded. She really meant *Manny and I want you to come home,* but for some reason she just couldn't say it.

And then, after all she'd dragged her children through over the past couple of days, Giselle was back where she started on Sixty-fourth Street in Queens. Needing a few minutes alone, she left her children with her mother and stepfather and walked to a nearby bodega where she bought a loosie and a beer. She took a draw from her cigarette—a habit she'd picked up when she was thirteen years old, right after her parents split up—and began to cry. How had this happened? How had she worked so hard to provide for her family, landed a job that made her happy, and still ended up homeless?

She sensed her children's confusion. Being evicted, spending the night with their grandparents, going to PATH, then a hotel, then a shelter, then returning to PATH, and now back with their grandparents all within four days. Of course they were con-fused. So she tried to maintain the family routine. She and the older girls were scheduled to pass out cookies at Pam's Place that second week of July, and so just days after their eviction, that's what they did.

When the time came, Hailey smiled on NY1, talking about homelessness and women who struggled and making them feel better with cookies. Everyone told her what a good job she'd done. But there was one thing she couldn't do and she knew it. No matter how much she wanted to, she couldn't alleviate her mother's pain.

For the next six weeks, ten people negotiated the use of Manny and Evelyn's one bathroom and tried to give one another space, even though there was no space to give. During the day, Hailey, Karina, and Christina spent time with Chris at his job while Evelyn and her parents took care of Judas and Gillesy. Meridith and Dan's home wasn't too far away, and since it was summer and they often went camping, they offered Giselle and her children use of their home as a getaway. But traveling back and forth between Sunnyside and Woodside was unsustainable. Giselle knew that, so she prepared for a return to PATH to find housing. She pulled out a worn black suitcase that she had bought when she was seventeen years old and pregnant with Hailey. She charged everyone's electronic devices so that they could ward off boredom, and stuffed the suitcase with Cheez-Its, Chips Ahoy!, Nutri-Grain bars, crackers, and potato chips. Then she covered the snacks with clothes so they wouldn't be confiscated. She knew she would need the supplies.

Once they arrived she began her campaign. "I have to be in Queens," she begged social worker after social worker, her voice quavering somewhere between anger and despair. The building's open office plan created a maze of cubicles so that Giselle felt like a hamster trying to find her way out, moving backward and forward and back again.

Once more they were sent to the holding area in the basement with its dimmed fluorescent lighting. The children read, played games, and napped. Giselle sat in a plastic chair gripping her blue plastic accordion folder and worrying. She and her children had been placed in a shelter, and she had walked out. Now she dared to specify a placement. Beggars were not supposed to be choosers.

Finally, after several hours, Giselle's number was called. She went to the window, where a man told her she would be going to Thirteenth Street in Long Island City. He started to describe the location. "I know where that is!" Giselle beamed, feeling something close to happiness.

"Not everybody gets that lucky," the man told her.

At last, at four on a Sunday morning, fifteen hours after they had arrived for another ordeal at PATH, Giselle, Hailey, Karina, Christina, Judas, and Gillesy—rumpled and haggard and utterly exhausted—dragged themselves and their stuffed backpacks through the lobby of their new temporary quarters.

It was called the Sleep Inn.

The room on the fourth floor was the size of a standard hotel room. It had two double beds, one bathroom, and a miniature refrigerator barely big enough to hold six water bottles. An accent wall was painted a sunset orange, which matched the décor in the lobby and brightened the otherwise nondescript room, where the color of the rug looked gray or brown, depending on the time of day or who was looking. Giselle could not get over the view into Manhattan. The sun was rising, and clouds danced in a blue sky mixed with shades of pink and lavender. Christina crawled into the windowsill. Giselle looked at Christina in the dark, the illumination from Manhattan's skyscrapers pouring over her. They could see the Queensboro Bridge, its lights stretching across the East River from Manhattan to Queens like a string of Christmas bulbs.

*Inside their room at the Sleep Inn, Christina loved looking out the window at the bright lights of the Manhattan skyline.*

How could the city be so beautiful, Giselle wondered, when it was also crushing them?

Giselle unpacked the wrinkled clothes from the kids' backpacks and laid out the few pants and blouses and skirts that looked most decent. She was planning on her family attending an eleven A.M. service at Evangel Church, where her mother had worshipped every once in a while, and where Giselle had accompanied her a few times. The sprawling church and school were the landmarks she'd remembered when the man in the basement at PATH had given her the address of where she was being placed.

"What are you doing?" Hailey and Karina asked.

"We're going to church. It's four blocks away. There's no reason we can't make it to church."

Giselle looked around the tiny, sterile room piled with her belongings, and although she was exhausted, she struggled to fall asleep. She had not slept in hours, having made the trek the previous morning from Evelyn's in Queens to PATH in the Bronx and then back to Queens. The day had been filled with back-and-forths, like her life had been, between jobs and apartments and men. She couldn't help but think she was a failure.

After the good jobs she'd had and the decent places she'd lived, here she was, thrust with her children in a homeless shelter. The terror of the eviction hadn't subsided; now it was just a new kind of fear. At least the Sleep Inn, in the familiar surroundings of Queens, brought some relief. But what on earth would ever pull her out of this mess? Had she hit bottom, or was there another rung on the ladder even lower than this?

For Giselle, it had been a long, slow decline to this moment, a life punctuated by failed romances, jobs won and lost, and a childhood filled with darkness. But it was also a life that had contained a few undeniable moments of light, she thought, as she looked over at her sleeping children.

She prayed that morning. She pledged to be a better person, to be a better mother, to go wherever she was led, to trust.

"I promise you, God," she said softly, not wanting to wake those tender beings sprawled around her. And she meant it.

# 6

# PROPERTY OF DHS

**THE SLEEP INN** may have sounded like a cozy place to spend the night, but in reality it wasn't an inn and it wasn't cozy. It had been designed for budget travelers—investors had bet that those looking for cheap stays would ignore the fact that the hotel was next door to a giant public housing project and care more about how easily they could get to Manhattan on the subway. And tourists came, but the rise in homelessness offered an alternate business plan. All around the city, especially in the outer boroughs, hotel owners were turning their buildings into shelters, generating a surprisingly robust and never-ending stream of income.

When Mayor Bill de Blasio took office in January 2014, he vowed to reduce the number of people in shelter. But his solutions, like increasing the minimum wage and creating affordable housing, were not generating results fast enough or did not actually have a significant effect on the homeless population. He had also told the Department of Homeless Services to stop opening shelters, as elected officials around the city complained to the mayor that shelters were popping up in their communities with no notice. The delay in opening shelters forced the city to lean more heavily on hotels.

New York City was under a legal mandate to provide shelter to anyone who was eligible. It could not allow people to sleep on the floor at PATH. But the city had never built a shelter system that complied with its legal obligation, so by late 2016, there were 7,500 people living in hotel rooms.

The hotel accommodations were often on the fly. Homeless services workers started cold-calling hotels around six P.M. to ask if there were rooms available. Some hotels would decide that they did not want to risk tainting their brands by renting rooms to homeless people. Others took advantage of the city's dilemma, charging more for a room rented to the city than for one rented to a regular guest. In 2016, the year Giselle became homeless, the total tab for housing people in hotels was running about $400,000 a day. To lock in rooms and rates, the city began signing long-term agreements with some hotels, transforming them into shelters outright, as when the nearby Verve Hotel became Pam's Place.

The Sleep Inn was still a hotel in name at least, but it did not treat the homeless people who stayed there at all like guests.

Instead, life there was a series of indignities. For example, the sheets were made especially for homeless people and delivered to rooms twice a week wrapped in cellophane. The words PROPERTY OF DHS were stamped in black ink on each fitted sheet, top sheet, and pillowcase, as if anyone would want to steal the incredibly scratchy bedding. Giselle called them prison sheets, often referring to the families in the shelter as "inmates." And the "inmates" were supposed to use these rough, chafing sheets rather than their own.

Giselle hid the linens and blankets she'd brought with her in the small closet stuffed with the rest of their belongings. She quickly learned a routine. When she thought an inspection was coming, she'd rip her own sheets off the beds and hide them. At night she'd put them back on. She refused to let housekeeping in because she found staffers always moved things around and she feared they might find her hiding places. Plus, she didn't want vacuum cleaners that had been used to tidy up other rooms to be used in hers, in case any of those rooms were infested with bed bugs.

Microwaves and hotplates were considered contraband, but no matter—nearly every room had one or both, which kept shelter workers on their toes. They soon gave up on Giselle. She kept cooking oil out in plain view, yet the inspections never discovered her electric skillet.

And oh, how Giselle learned to work wonders with that skillet. She put it on the dresser, where she would dip chicken cutlets into flour and then gingerly fit them in to cook. She would discard the excess oil in the toilet, saving just a little in the pan to fry up canned corn, mixing in scallions that she cut up on a plate on the desk that doubled as a countertop. Hailey and Karina would dampen towels and place them under the door to keep any smoke from seeping into the hallway. They would wet a washcloth and stuff it around the smoke detector to keep it from erupting into a series of beeps that would alert the hotel that they were breaking a rule. Then they would help their younger siblings with homework while the room filled with an aroma that reminded them all of the apartment on Maple Avenue, the last place they could truly call home.

While cooking conditions were far from ideal, the children looked forward to the meals. Otherwise they would be forced to eat what social workers doled out three times a day in a room that served as a pantry and a take-it-or-leave-it take-out joint for breakfast, lunch, and dinner. Breakfast was school cafeteria–style: a small container of juice, cereal in a plastic square bowl that opened by tearing paper off the top, maybe a pastry enclosed in clear plastic, and a mini carton of milk. The items were often carelessly tossed into milk crates that resembled bins at a discount department store on Black Friday after frenzied customers had rummaged through them but before store clerks got around to straightening up. A certain discourteousness seemed to apply to the mess. Giselle and her family were not the only ones who felt it.

Standing in her room in the Sleep Inn, thinking about those unappetizing meals and looking down at those scratchy stamped sheets, Giselle had never felt more like a second-class citizen. She remembered passing out cookies and serving Thanksgiving dinner at Pam's Place, and she remembered how she'd encouraged her daughters and the other Scouts to treat the women there with dignity and kindness. The women had returned the favor. She was grateful to have a roof over her head here, but she felt there was no dignity and no kindness.

The move to the Sleep Inn took some getting used to. Giselle had to learn different routes to and from work and St. Sebastian's, where the Scout meetings were held, and figure out which neighborhood stores had the cheapest prices. There was the whole surreptitious cooking routine, and curfews and signing in and signing out. But she was grateful that she didn't have to worry about her children's education. Evangel Church ran an all-grades school within walking distance of the hotel, and the pastors there offered scholarships to all five of her children. They also gave Giselle their uniforms for free.

On the first day of school in September, Giselle's children headed out the door to Evangel Church as other young residents of the Sleep Inn filed out of the lobby on their way to nearby P.S. 111 or to trek to their old schools. Federal law guaranteed that children who became homeless did not have to transfer, but many were forced to change because they had been placed in shelters long distances away from their old schools.

Each morning, the kids took turns washing their faces and brushing their teeth, put on their uniforms, ate cereal with milk, and walked to Evangel. Hailey usually held hands with Judas and Christina on either side of her while Karina held Gillesy's hand. Changing schools wasn't so bad, though Hailey decided they should not tell their classmates that they were homeless. They would just be regular new kids at school. And besides, they lived in a hotel, not a traditional shelter, so their situation wasn't completely obvious to outsiders.

But there was a drawback to homeless hotel living, and it was a major one: A hotel could decide at any moment that it needed its rooms back.

⁂

"Wait. Two entire floors of this hotel are for homeless people?" Linda Moore, a paying guest at the Sleep Inn, asked Giselle incredulously the week after the kids started school.

Linda was a fifty-something woman from a small town outside Columbus, Ohio. She had emerged from a deep depression and decided to treat herself to a New York City adventure, something she had always dreamed of; a poster of Audrey Hepburn as Holly Golightly hung on her living room wall. Linda's round face was pale, a telltale indicator of her years of being homebound. She thought she needed a motorized scooter to get around but was determined to make the trip to New York by herself. The Sleep Inn, she had thought, was a four-star hotel; it wasn't.

But Linda, who had worked as a customer service representative most of her life, liked the price. She made plans to see a Broadway play and go to MoMA and to have breakfast at Tiffany's. She also found herself spending an inordinate amount of time sitting on the bench, never using the scooter, in front of the Sleep Inn and watching the world go by.

Giselle poured out her heart to this stranger, Linda, who took a draw from her Virginia Slim. Linda stared in disbelief as Giselle explained that she was not a tourist but a homeless mother with a full-time job who lived in the hotel with her children.

"We aren't allowed to eat at the breakfast bar," Giselle told her. "We also have a curfew."

The day after their talk, about two weeks after Giselle's arrival at the Sleep Inn, the shelter staff came knocking in the middle of the night. The hotel needed more rooms for regular paying guests like Linda, so Giselle and the other families needed to pack their possessions and leave immediately, at least for a few days. The staff told Giselle that a bus would roll out first thing in the morning and that she and her family would be on it. They'd be delivered to PATH and reassigned to another shelter.

Back to PATH? She couldn't go through that again. And what about the children? They had to go to school. And what about her job? She couldn't miss work.

Weeping uncontrollably, Giselle called Meridith sometime in the hours between midnight and dawn. "They're moving us out!" she wailed into the phone.

Hearing Giselle so frightened upset Meridith, who had just been promoted to chief operating officer at the Girl Scouts of Greater New York. At a time when she was basking in a career high, Giselle was experiencing a personal low.

Meridith didn't fully understand how the city's shelter system worked and tried to wrap her head around what was happening. "Come here," she said, offering her own home.

"If I don't go to PATH, I'll lose my space!" There were rules and procedures that needed to be followed, Giselle explained, sobbing. Always rules and procedures.

Meridith called Jimmy Van Bramer, hoping he could use his political sway to do something. "This is ridiculous," she told him. "What is this? Parents could lose their jobs, could lose their salaries. There are kids who have to go to school."

Meanwhile, Giselle called her grandfather. Papi arrived at five A.M. in his old burgundy Yukon to load up her clothes, electric skillet, and other belongings. Giselle stuffed a few clothes into laundry bags, prepared to stay wherever else the city was placing her and her children. Papi and Lucy were upset about Giselle's homelessness, but they tried not to pry, thinking their concern would only add to her worry.

Linda, the hotel guest, was outraged and took to Facebook: "So at midnight the management told all of the people here that are residents being paid for by a contract with the home and help department or something like that that they have to leave in 7 hours. One of my buddies tells me that's approximately 10 to 15 families will be homeless in the morning. They said it's not because the contract ran out. It's because they're overbooked. So the freeloaders have to leave 'for just a couple of days and then they can come back.' "

Linda invited the families being displaced to eat with her at the buffet and dared the staff to refuse. "Come on. We've got to protest," she told some of the people waiting in the lobby for the bus that would shuttle them back to PATH. "Come on. Rise up. Malcolm X!" she said, thinking it was a civil rights moment and that shouting the name sounded like a pretty good rallying cry.

All she could think about was the time she was homeless. She had been twenty years old and pregnant with her son with nowhere to go; she remembered standing in a phone booth and finding help through a church.

Linda tried to stop the caseworkers by embarrassing them. "How are you able to do this?" she asked, getting no response. She watched the bus pull away, thinking she would never see Giselle and the others again, and wishing she could have done more.

Hailey, Karina, Christina, Judas, and Gillesy were dressed in their new sweatpants and sweatshirts with the Evangel Christian Church school logo because that was the easiest clothing to throw on in a hurry. The school bus bumped along, slowly winding from Queens into the Bronx to PATH. The shiny building, with its endless cubicles and fluorescent lighting and coldness, was both familiar and strange; Giselle and her children had thought they were never going back. Giselle tried to hold it together, lamenting the fact that her children had seen her calling Meridith and then Papi in hysterics. Hailey sat with her arms crossed and on the verge of tears the entire time while her siblings tried to ignore what was happening. Judas sat in Gillesy's stroller, even though he was too tall and his knees were scrunched up to his chest. He played a video game, and Karina did her homework on a computer. Gillesy squirmed on Giselle's lap and then on Hailey's.

Meanwhile, Jimmy had called officials at the Department of Homeless Services. Within three hours of arriving at PATH, Giselle got the word that she could return to the Sleep Inn. As she and the children gathered their laundry bags and backpacks, other families asked Giselle why she was being allowed to leave PATH so quickly. Giselle was vague, afraid to tell those left behind that she had called in favors to save her and her children.

"One person at a time," Meridith told her.

The next day at the Sleep Inn, Giselle ran into Linda, who was proud that the young mother had figured out a way to stay put. "You're back, kiddo," Linda said.

She was back, and that was a good thing. She was grateful for it. But it sure didn't feel like she was home.

<br>

While she had saved her family from being displaced, Giselle was overwhelmed with guilt. She had used her connections to help her family, and they were the only ones allowed to return to the Sleep Inn immediately. Her life was so full of secrets now. At the Girl Scouts, Giselle's supervisor, Alida, was the first to learn that she was homeless. Giselle, having to miss work, had to tell her boss why she would be absent. Giselle also eventually told Meridith, whom she was initially embarrassed to tell. So no one but Meridith and Alida knew that she was homeless and no one would ever think to ask. At work she operated under a don't-ask-don't-tell policy—until finally she had to tell her co-workers, who had to fill in for her. At the Sunnyside & Woodside troop meetings she kept the family's ordeal to herself, even as a handful of parents talked, mostly negatively, about the homeless shelters moving into Queens. The children's classmates at Evangel were also unaware, so Giselle helped her brood by playing along, never explaining to the other children's parents that they were new students because they had just moved into a hotel room being used as a shelter, and that Giselle had prayed to God and Evangel was an answer to her prayers.

After her family was allowed to stay put at the Sleep Inn, Giselle decided that if she was going to follow the teachings that she read in her Bible each Sunday, she should not look out solely for herself and her family. She needed to effect change for others who were in their same circumstances. She began to document all the wrongs she saw at the Sleep Inn, whether they affected her family or not.

First on her list was addressing mealtime. The evening meals were frozen microwavable dinners. Each family received one per person: a protein, a vegetable, and a starch, each item about the size of a fist or smaller. No second helpings were provided for adults or growing children who might have needed a larger portion. The food was bland and unappetizing, often so smashed under cellophane that it was unrecognizable.

Worse, the "use by" dates of some of the meals were expired. Giselle snapped a photo of Salisbury Steak with Gravy, Mashed Potatoes and Green Beans, still wrapped in its plastic, on September 24. People had refused to eat it because the expiration date was August 31.

The homeless services at the Sleep Inn were managed by a nonprofit called Childrens Community Services, a new provider that would amass contracts worth nearly $700 million with the city to furnish shelter. More experienced providers were stretched thin and refused to take on extra jobs because the city was notoriously slow in paying its vendors. They also balked at the idea of trying to deliver social services in an unpredictable setting like a hotel. So what was supposed to be a temporary fix turned into an unmovable necessity that was costing the city millions of dollars as it adapted quickly to house the thousands of people who were streaming into the shelter system.

Childrens Community Services hired staff quickly in order to keep up with the demands of its massive contract, but employees would burn out just as fast, rotating through the shelter like guests entering and leaving a hotel through a revolving door. They were frustrated by the never-ending work of signing people in and out, distributing food, and trying to help find permanent housing for families so they could move out of shelter, not to mention the tension of interacting with people who were frightened and sometimes angry, and certainly going through the worst times of their lives.

Giselle realized that if she wanted to get help in any substantive way she'd have to reveal her homelessness to a wider audience, as embarrassing as it was. She got up her nerve and asked Meridith to reach out to Jimmy again, this time about the ongoing problems at the Sleep Inn; after all, both the inn and Pam's Place were in his district.

That fall, with Queens becoming ground zero for a roiling citywide debate about shelters, Jimmy raised Giselle's firsthand accounts of some of the issues at the Sleep Inn at a public hearing with Steven Banks, the city's commissioner of social services. He pummeled Banks with question after question about where shelters were being placed and how people were being treated. Banks and his staff took notes and moved quickly to usher in some changes, particularly regarding expired and unappetizing food.

Giselle had gotten some concrete results just as the Sleep Inn was filling up with more homeless people. There were now more Giselles staying at the hotel than there were Lindas, and there were plenty of kids around. But it was hard to make friends there when you weren't allowed to visit each other's rooms. When Giselle and her family returned from PATH after being briefly evicted from the hotel, they'd moved to a room on the second floor. Caseworkers had turned another room on the same floor into an office, and that's where "residents" of the hotel had to sign in and out. It's also where they went to request passes for overnight absences—say, to go to a family's home for a holiday or travel out of town to attend a funeral. If a room was unoccupied for forty-eight hours without approval, a family could get forced out of the Sleep Inn and would have to return to PATH. The second-floor office was also where adults talked to caseworkers about cooperating with housing specialists to find apartments, and where families picked up their three meals for the day.

Giselle could see everyone coming and going. She could hear mothers or fathers calling the names of their children. A little girl named Sanaa, about the same age as Karina, looked so confident, Giselle thought. Few teenagers were chatty, but a girl named Genesis always said hello. Mostly, children and their parents stayed to themselves. They were not allowed to spend the night in each other's rooms.

Social disengagement wasn't limited to inside the hotel: The Sleep Inn itself was located on a weirdly un-neighborly block of Thirteenth Street. Around the corner, life seethed. Tenants of the behemoth Queensbridge public housing complex yelled to hear themselves over honking cars, the screeching brakes of MTA buses, and the rumble of the F train below them. A man hawked used books from tables on the sidewalk right outside the subway station. The aroma of beef and chicken broths from a sought-after ramen shop permeated the air.

But the turn onto Thirteenth Street brought only desolation. In early 2016, a fire had destroyed a furniture store across the street. A masonry shop for limestone and marble adjacent to the store was oddly quiet.

Getting to the East River, a few blocks away, meant walking through the Queensbridge projects, a tough challenge if you were not a resident. The children of Queensbridge outranked the children at the Sleep Inn in the cold hierarchy of poverty— they had homes, they had kitchens, they had their own beds, and they could easily walk to Queensbridge Park and look out at the panorama of the river and Roosevelt Island.

When it came to social interaction, parents at the Sleep Inn had it no easier than their children. What do you call the people living in the hotel room next to yours if the room isn't a home and you have no plans to stay? Can you call them neighbors? If you're not allowed to invite them into your room, can you become friends?

The small bench out front where Giselle had met Linda, who had long ago returned to Ohio, became the equivalent of a front porch for residents. It was a smoking area, a place to gossip, a place to complain about the shelter staff, the hotel staff, the inedible food, and the scratchy sheets. A sliver of sidewalk across the street in front of the burned-out furniture store and the masonry shop became a play area for children; after all, there was no playground on the block.

When Giselle wandered to the "porch" to get a bit of solitude and to smoke a cigarette, she left the children upstairs with Hailey in charge. She did not want them to see her smoking, even though they knew about her bad habit. Giselle would plop down on the black iron bench flush against the wall right next to the entrance.

And that's where she met Cori, who'd also started smoking when she was thirteen. At the time, Cori had been living in public housing in Sheepshead Bay, Brooklyn, and had stolen a cigarette from her adoptive mother's purse. Arrests for shoplifting had followed in a life beset by struggle.

"It's Corinthia, like the Bible, like First Corinthians," Cori told Giselle over that first Newport outside the hotel. She had on a jet-black wig with bangs that hung down to cover her eyebrows.

Cori had a son, Fernando III, whom she called Trey. By the time she ended up at the Sleep Inn she had few belongings beyond one extravagant and unlikely collection: Over the years since she'd been a teenager, she'd amassed no fewer than fifty wigs.

"You have five kids?" Cori asked Giselle incredulously.

Giselle nodded and turned away from Cori as she blew smoke out of the right side of her lips.

"Sometimes I can't take it, girl," Giselle told her. "I feel bad, you know, because there's nothing for them to do here." She explained that her three oldest daughters were in the Girl Scouts and that she also worked for the organization.

Upstairs, Giselle's children were trying to entertain them-

selves. The food, the curfews, the lack of privacy, and the boredom took a toll on them. Christina, Judas, and Gillesy sometimes
played hide-and-seek in the room, but there were only so many
times they could run into the bathroom and close the door,
squash behind the bins against the wall, or curl into a ball in the
nooks between the beds and a nightstand. Judas was four years
old and usually could be kept busy with a tablet or some paper
and crayons. Gillesy, who turned three that October, needed
more stimulation. So Hailey and Karina dressed her up in sun-
glasses, put a flower in her hair, and let her carry a purse. She
sucked on a pacifier and learned choreography that Karina and
Hailey had learned from social media for "Juju on That Beat."
The girls carved out a small patch of space in between the double beds to sing and dance. Gillesy wiggled and laughed, still
holding the pacifier in her mouth.

On Saturdays, Hailey, Karina, and Christina left the shelter
to attend meetings of the Girl Scouts of Sunnyside & Woodside.
Like their mother, they never told anyone at the troop that they
had lost their home and were living in a shelter. It wasn't that
hard to go to meetings and return to the hotel, and the other
Scouts never asked the girls where they were living, but even so,
they began to feel different. They had made a big show of host-
ing the sleepover at the College Point house. The Sleep Inn allowed no guests for homeless families. Where would anyone
sleep anyway? They only had two double beds between the six of
them.

The holiday season was especially hard. There were no ovens at
the Sleep Inn to bake sugar cookies for Santa. Money was tight, so
buying even modest gifts was a challenge for all the families
there. Giselle tried to bring some Christmas cheer into her family's cramped quarters by taping five red stockings to the bottom
of the television and stringing a red garland along the door. A
Santa with his arms open wide hung just below, with three pieces

of cloth made to look like ornaments. They read "Ho, Ho, Ho." The kids trimmed a small artificial tree with lights and a silver star. It was about as tall as Gillesy, a sad little Charlie Brown tree, but better than not having one at all. Evangel Church, where Giselle and the children were now active parishioners, had donated gifts. Those were the presents Giselle placed under the tree.

*Giselle tried to make the best of her family's stay at the Sleep Inn;*
*she asked her children Christina, Gillesy, Karina, Judas, and Hailey*
*to pose with her for a selfie in their room.*

Many homeless families living at the Sleep Inn had nothing.

At Pam's Place, days before Christmas, Giselle and the girls returned to help the homeless women build gingerbread houses; they wore latex gloves and welded the graham cracker–like squares together with a gooey sugar and decorated them with gumdrops and peppermints.

One night that Christmas week, Giselle was lying wide awake on one of the beds with Gillesy and Judas awkwardly splayed around her. Hailey, Karina, and Christina were in the other bed. Giselle rolled an idea over and over in her head. It had started as just a tiny thought but had grown over time.

A suffocating boredom had descended on all the children in the hotel. If you couldn't bring any guests to the Sleep Inn—

friends to hang out with or do homework with or play with—
and if residents weren't supposed to visit one another in their
rooms, what could you do?

Then it struck her. The answer was herself and the girls—
and the Girl Scouts.

"I think I should start a troop," Giselle blurted out as she lay
in bed, waiting for a response.

Hailey wondered if starting a troop in a shelter could work.
She hoped so, but she stayed quiet because it was bedtime and
every day seemed so long and she wasn't sure exactly what to
say.

Karina was more optimistic. "Go for it!" she yelled.

# 7

# HERE

**WAS IT JUST** too crazy? A homeless woman starting a Girl Scout troop for homeless girls in a shelter? Would families who didn't have a place to live, a roof of their own over their heads, have the mental energy to even have a conversation about the Girl Scouts? Giselle herself hadn't had that energy when Luana was constantly trying to engage her in a conversation about the Scouts after she'd moved back to Queens from Florida. And she hadn't been homeless at the time.

Still, it was a good idea, she told herself. Why shouldn't children be able to enjoy their childhoods wherever they were living them out?

With Karina's encouragement ringing in her ears, Giselle reached out to Meridith. "Do you think we can start a troop in a shelter? Here?"

In fact, Meridith had already been thinking along similar lines. Just weeks earlier, she and other representatives of the Girl Scouts of Greater New York had met with staff at several shelters to kick around ideas for giving the Scouts some kind of presence within the homeless services that the city provided. They hadn't gotten as far as thinking about starting a troop, but maybe they could find a way for girls to participate in a Girl Scouting summer program called Urban Day Camp, or they could get women in shelters interested in volunteering. You had to get the city on board, though, which was never easy. The Girl Scouts needed the explicit backing of the Department of Homeless Services, a cranky, slow-moving bureaucratic monolith where the simplest request seemed to disappear into a black hole for weeks or months at a time, before being rejected.

Now, however, Meridith had a secret weapon: Giselle Burgess, who'd already succeeded in getting a councilman to grill a city commissioner about shelters and who'd managed to improve, ever so slightly, her life and the lives of other people staying at the Sleep Inn. Meridith had come to realize that very little could stop Giselle once she got rolling.

But Giselle couldn't do it alone. There were going to be many layers of red tape to cut through and she would need all the help she could get.

Meridith told Giselle the idea wasn't crazy at all. In fact, it was brilliant. And then she told her the first person she needed to get in touch with was Heidi Schmidt.

Heidi Schmidt's fashion sensibility seemed out of place in the Department of Homeless Services. She kept her hair dark, though she sometimes added a color from the rainbow for funkiness. She showed up in African fabrics one day and outfits inspired by salwar kameez the next. She was a white woman from Lancaster County, Pennsylvania, best known as Amish country, but despite her rural roots, she was a world traveler. Although she didn't make a big salary, as a single woman with no children she had enough money and frequent-flier miles to sail the Atlantic Ocean, soak in hot springs in Portugal, and put her face up close to snakes in Marrakech.

Despite now being an unburdened free spirit, growing up Heidi had felt trapped, watching the adults around her descend into drugs, alcohol, and domestic violence. Her parents' loveless marriage fell apart when she was six years old, and Heidi and her younger sister had to hide the poverty and violence they were experiencing living with their mother, who was engaged in a bitter custody battle, and her alcoholic stepfather, who abused her.

As a girl, Heidi had loved Girl Scouting: loved the camping, loved the friendship, loved the fact that it gave her something positive to focus on. Her mother had been a Girl Scout and had made it all the way to Cadette. Later, as a single mother in Pennsylvania on food stamps, she had enough money to get Heidi to troop meetings, but not much more. For the longest time, Heidi didn't have money for a uniform. Still, her mother managed to find a vest and a sash at a Goodwill store.

In time Heidi left on a scholarship for the University of Pittsburgh, where she majored in neuroscience and women's studies. Then she went as far away from Lancaster as she could, joining the Peace Corps and being assigned to Limpopo, South Africa, where she educated people about HIV and AIDS.

After working in the Department of Homeless Services for nine years, Heidi had been promoted to director of government relations. As the homelessness crisis was ballooning out of control, Heidi was feeling more and more inadequate. And then she got an email that floored her. At first glance, she thought it was yet another New Yorker complaining about a shelter opening in their neighborhood. And then Heidi saw that the writer of the email seemed to be asking if the Girl Scouts could hold a meeting at the Sleep Inn in Queens. And then the writer, who happened to be Giselle Burgess, stunned Heidi: She wrote that every floor of the Sleep Inn housed homeless people. Heidi was a director in the department that was in charge of homelessness—surely, if this was true, she would have known. Nope. That just can't be right. The shelter filled an entire hotel?

Giselle insisted it was true. "I live here," she replied to Heidi's disbelieving email.

If Heidi had been shocked to hear that all of the rooms in the

Sleep Inn were providing shelter for the homeless, she was absolutely shocked to hear that the person proposing to start a Girl
Scout troop there was a *homeless* employee of the Girl Scouts.
She began to grasp something that not enough city officials
seemed to understand: Homelessness was escalating at such a
rapid rate that a hotel had been informally turned into a shelter
in a matter of a few months, so fast that a community development specialist at the Girl Scouts was now counted among the
city's most vulnerable. They started talking on the phone, and
Heidi's conversations with Giselle soon veered from professional
to personal, with Heidi sharing stories of her childhood, and
how she herself had found refuge in the Girl Scouts as a little
girl. They were different races, from different backgrounds, and
from different parts of the country—one deeply urban, one
semirural—and yet they had so many shared experiences. A
bond between the two women quickly formed.

Giselle next contacted Kafi Hadaway, the administrator for
the city who was in charge of commercial hotels that had been
turned into shelters. When Kafi saw "Girl Scouts" in the email,
she decided to open it right away; she received so many calls and
emails a day—an average of four hundred—from staff of nonprofit organizations operating shelter services at dozens of commercial hotels. At a peak, Kafi was overseeing about eight
hundred staff at fifty-one hotels that housed about three thousand families. She even received complaints from homeless families living in the hotels, hoping she could help them with
transfers or problems they were experiencing. She was excited to
read an email that was asking about starting a program at a
hotel. She thought a Girl Scout troop in a shelter was a no-brainer.
As soon as she got off the phone she jumped up from her cubicle
and ran to tell an administrator who had more clout than she did.

When Kafi and Heidi first talked with Meridith and Giselle,
who were representing the Girl Scouts, they raised the idea of
holding an initial meeting at a venue near the shelter. That
would make it all much easier on the city's end of things. But
Meridith was adamant about having the meeting *inside* the

hotel. Parents should not have to worry about leaving the hotel, finding the meeting, picking up their children, and walking back to the hotel. "That's the obstacle, that's the barrier. We are trying to remove the burden. It is our obligation to get to the girls and their parents, not their obligation to get to us," Meridith kept telling city officials.

Once the Department of Homeless Services was on board, they needed permission from Childrens Community Services, the nonprofit running the shelter, and the owners of the Sleep Inn.

A conference call was organized for the day after Presidents' Day, 2017. Meridith, Giselle, Heidi, and Kafi got on the line with a representative of Childrens Community Services who said there was concern that parents and children would think that participating in the Girl Scouts would give the girls license to break the rules by going to one another's rooms. Meridith tried to assure everyone that the Girl Scouts' mission was a positive one, not a disruptive one.

Meridith and Giselle were in Washington, D.C., at the time of the call, where they'd taken older Scouts from the Sunnyside & Woodside troops to visit the new Belmont-Paul Women's Equality National Monument celebrating the women's suffrage movement. The troop leaders had drilled facts about women in Washington and elective office into the Scouts' heads in advance of the trip: 73 percent of women in the Senate had been Girl Scouts; more than half of the women in the House of Representatives had once donned the Scout uniform; there were six women serving as governors at the time, and four of them had been Girl Scouts.

It was a strange time to be in Washington. Donald Trump had just been inaugurated as president after beating Hillary Clinton—who had been a Girl Scout when growing up in a suburb of Chicago—a surprise defeat so crushing to women and girls that it had sparked the worldwide Women's March just a few weeks earlier.

It was also a strange moment for Giselle and Meridith.

Giselle and her two eldest daughters did not have permission from the shelter provider to travel to Washington, hundreds of miles from the Sleep Inn where their room sat empty; Meridith and Giselle had been afraid that permission to leave the shelter would be denied for any one of a multitude of reasons. And they felt they couldn't take that chance. Giselle was by now a respected and valued troop leader. The loss of her presence as a chaperone would have a big impact on the success of the trip—and her daughters' disappointment, and hers as well, would be significant.

*Hailey, Giselle, Miranda, and Karina posed in front of the Capitol Building in Washington, D.C., on a trip with the Sunnyside & Woodside troops.*

Evelyn was babysitting her three youngest grandchildren while Giselle, Hailey, and Karina, along with Miranda, Giselle's half sister, were in Washington, D.C., learning about women and government and history with the rest of their troop. They were breaking the kind of rule that Meridith was promising on this phone call the Girl Scouts would adhere to. But Meridith, who so many years ago had led her fellow Scouts on an escapade through the streets of Miami, believed that some rules had to be broken in the service of a higher cause. And so here they were, standing on the steps between the Capitol and the Supreme Court, Giselle on her cellphone and Meridith on hers, several feet away from each other so that no one else on the call would know that Giselle was not in New York.

Finally, everyone agreed on the logistics; Childrens Community Services gave the go-ahead, and Giselle and Meridith jumped up and down on the steps just yards away from each other. Kafi, who had worked at homeless services for only about fifteen months, screamed into the phone with excitement before catching herself and dialing down the volume to a more professional level.

Now everyone was counting on Giselle.

She had a big challenge ahead of her. After all those emails, phone calls, and in-person discussions, she still had one more big push in front of her: She needed to recruit some girls.

# 8

# THE BREAKFAST ROOM

GISELLE FLASHED HER electric smile at everyone she met. In her arms she carried twenty-five flyers that she had designed featuring a brown-skinned girl with a round face and a smile who was wearing a Girl Scout sash.

She taped two flyers in the hallways on each of the ten floors of the hotel, in the elevator, in the lobby, and next to an ice machine. She put one in the office of the resident assistants who lorded over all of the guests, and one more in the office used by social workers. A resident assistant stopped her. "I'm going to have to make a call," she told Giselle, looking her up and down: Giselle wore an outfit like the little girl in the flyer, a crisp uniform of a navy polo with the Girl Scouts' trademark trefoil, a scarf, and khaki pants.

"I have permission to put these up," Giselle said sweetly but firmly.

More than half of the three hundred people who filled the hotel's one hundred rooms were children, many of them girls between the ages of five and eighteen; Giselle figured with a target audience like that she could surely get twenty or thirty girls to attend the first meeting. After all, she was employed as a community development specialist at the Girl Scouts of Greater New York and she had wowed everyone there with her recruitment numbers; she could sell the Girl Scouts organization the way some girls could sell cookies.

But the Sleep Inn was different.

Even if they recognized her, many parents ignored Giselle as she tried to hand them flyers. Or they nodded their heads yes, but meant no. They were just too busy, buried in worries and the endless paperwork required for public assistance, food stamps, job applications, transferring a child from one school to another, and documentation of continuing need for shelter. They were catching up on bills: ill-advised loans to attend for-profit colleges with no degrees to show for it because they had dropped out; inflated, predatory loans still owed on cars that had long ago fallen apart and been towed away; credit cards with exorbitant interest rates; invoices for medical costs that were probably padded—but who could understand the fine print? They were all just trying to make it through each day.

Giselle understood their worries; after all, she shared their challenges.

Even as she was running around the hotel like a door-to-door saleswoman, she was also hoping to get a coveted public housing apartment. Yes, the New York City Housing Authority—NYCHA—had a poor reputation for leaving buildings in disrepair, but many of the apartments were roomy and guaranteed to be within a family's budget; 270,000 families jammed the waitlist for subsidized housing. Just days before she started publicizing the Scout meeting, Giselle had added her name to the roll. She hoped to get a leg up by reaching out to Jimmy Van Bramer's office, specifically to the councilman's director of constituents.

She was determined to get out of the shelter as soon as humanly possible, but her priority as she walked the hallways of the Sleep Inn was getting girls to a Scout meeting.

Giselle had decided that the best way to introduce Girl Scouting to the Sleep Inn would be to start with a series of workshops, onetime events that usually teach skills through both discussion and simple hands-on projects. Over the course of her employment at the Girl Scouts, she'd held plenty of workshops inside community rooms in public housing projects and in churches. *What would be so different about holding them here at the Sleep Inn?* she kept asking herself.

When paying guests had stayed at the hotel, they'd enjoyed a continental breakfast in the "breakfast room," but as the inn filled up with homeless people, the buffet had been shut down. Now all that was in the area was a microwave for the residents to heat their mediocre dinners with, and the breakfast room otherwise sat unused.

That changed on the afternoon of February 24, 2017. It was midwinter school recess, and parents would be hard-pressed to find something for their children to do. Giselle figured she would have a captive audience. The breakfast room was not well lit and chairs were stacked around and on top of tables made of faux wood with a glossy, laminate finish. All of the tables wobbled—they needed napkins folded eight ways beneath a leg to keep steady—but they would do. Giselle pushed them together and covered them in green plastic disposable tablecloths. The bright cloths gave some life to the room, which was painted nondescript beige. The temperature in the room was uncomfortably warm despite the cold winter day, so Giselle had tried to open the lone window but could raise it only an inch. Then she'd turned on the air conditioner, and now its drone was the only sound in the room.

Hailey, Karina, and Christina wandered in, wearing their vests, happy to have something to do. Six months in a shelter had hardened Hailey, and she'd grown more cynical. *This is weird. This isn't going to work,* she thought as she eyed the drab surroundings. She longed for the familiarity of her old troop.

Five other girls showed up at the first meeting. Four of them, like Giselle's daughters, were sisters, ranging in age from six to thirteen. Each one seemed to be louder, brasher, and more outgoing than the one before. Their big voices were a welcome disturbance of the silence that had hung in the room.

Giselle explained to them that she worked for the Girl Scouts and she was a co-leader of a troop in Sunnyside and Woodside. "Hailey, Karina, and Christina are my daughters, and they are all Girl Scouts," Giselle told them. "I live in the hotel, too. We are going to make the best of our time here." She didn't spell out for the girls that she meant this on two levels: We are going to make the most of our time together at the meeting, and also make the most of our time here at the Sleep Inn.

The lesson she had imagined for this first meeting would be about building windmills, sculptures, and towers. This made it a STEAM lesson—science, technology, engineering, art, and math. Alida and two more of Giselle's co-workers came along to assist her. They were all on the same recruiting team assigned to Queens, and so Giselle had had to share her plight with them. Though happy to have their help, she'd also dreaded this particular moment—her colleagues *seeing* her as homeless for the first time. They were smart and supportive—the Scouts always tried to hire wonderful people—but still, here they were, witnesses to her life in this undignified, grim place. If they had any feelings or judgments about her situation, they hid them well. The moment passed and the meeting went on like any other.

Constructing a model of a building was a foreign concept to the girls, but all eight of them could look out of the windows in their rooms on the floors above and gaze at a city filled with skyscrapers. They dove into their task, fashioning their own high-rises, even windmills, with drinking straws, paper, and glue; they made sculptures out of lime-green clay. They talked

*Christina and Karina built models with other girls from the Sleep Inn during the first meeting, before Troop 6000 had a name.*

and giggled and helped one another. Residents passing by the glass door of the breakfast room to get to the microwave could see the girls working together and they could hear their laughter; some people smiled at this unlikely sound.

"Are we going to sell cookies?" the five potential Scouts asked Giselle. After all, wasn't that what the Girl Scouts were famous for? Cookies *were* the Girl Scouts. That's how Scouts learned to talk to strangers, to count money, to market, to sell, to compete. That's what alumni remember: friendships, cookies, camping, and meetings, usually in that order.

But selling cookies wasn't going to happen, at least not yet. Giselle explained that they weren't officially part of a troop yet, and it was too late to get involved in cookie season. This was only a partial truth. The fact was residents weren't allowed to sell anything inside the hotel. Giselle could envision the resident assistants chasing the Scouts down the hallways to chide them for knocking on doors. If the troop was a success and still existed next year at cookie time, this was going to be a problem. Well, she'd cross that bridge when she came to it.

Hailey shifted the conversation away from cookies and told the girls about all of the other benefits of Girl Scouting, like camping and friendship. At the end of the meeting, she held up her index, middle, and ring fingers on her right hand and led the girls in reciting the Girl Scout Promise:

On my honor, I will try:
To serve God and my country,
To help people at all times,
And to live by the Girl Scout Law.

Giselle didn't want the meeting to end, but the girls had to return to their rooms.

"See you at the next meeting!" she called after them.

She had pulled it off, and Hailey had stepped up to help. Though Giselle was worried that eight girls, including her own three daughters, was a poor showing for all of her work talking to parents and putting up flyers, it was enough of a turnout to give her confidence that starting a troop could work, and she experienced the glimmer of a feeling she'd never had before. She had earned her GED. She had built a career in dental office management. She had managed to convince the Girl Scouts to hire her. A string of accomplishments like these had boosted her morale. But in the last several months, she'd been on the receiving end of charity and kindness: Her mother had taken her in; Meridith had helped her; the city was sheltering her family.

On this February day she had succeeded in doing something for people other than herself and her children. She had touched the lives of these young girls. She had been on the *giving* end of charity and kindness. It wasn't much—a few girls in a room building models out of straws—but it was something, and it gave her an entirely new sense of accomplishment.

# 9

# 6000

AFTER THE FIRST meeting of just eight girls, the people backing the idea of the Sleep Inn troop started thinking bigger—Heidi and Kafi at the Department of Homeless Services; Jimmy, the Queens city councilman; and Meridith and Giselle at the Girl Scouts. These people were now the troop's key advocates, strategists, and cutters of red tape. At the same time, Giselle was wondering how they were going to build the Sleep Inn Girl Scouts into a robust troop, much less expand the concept to other shelters and even other cities.

There was so much that needed to be done. Parent volunteers were an essential element to any troop's success. It had been one thing to have her co-workers show up to help out at the first meeting, but having Girl Scout staff attend future meetings in support roles was completely unsustainable. At the Sleep Inn, parents were dealing with all the fallout of living in a shelter, so volunteers would be hard to come by. Because Giselle was acutely aware of this, she tried to think of ways to make Girl Scouting, and the volunteering opportunity, more appealing. She decided that meetings would be held on Friday nights so parents wouldn't have to worry about their daughters getting homework done on a school night. That made things a little easier, but it was still a struggle to convince parents to think expansively about the opportunities the Girl Scouts offered when they were struggling to get to and from jobs, care for their kids, pay off their debts, and keep body, mind, and soul together.

Financial support was not as much of a problem as it might have been, given that the Girl Scouts were so firmly behind this endeavor. All fees would be waived for the shelter troop, and their uniforms would be provided for free. This was no small investment. National dues were $25 per Scout annually, and vests ranged in price from $18.50 for a Daisy to $26.00 for a Cadette. Some patches cost $1.75 each. It didn't sound like a lot, but it added up. And that was just the beginning. If the girls stuck with Girl Scouting, camping and other activities could cost hundreds of dollars. A ski weekend at Camp Kaufmann cost $95. A week at the Urban Day Camp cost $450.

But the troop also needed booklets, certificates with the Girl Scouts insignia, and supplies like markers and construction paper to complete the projects that earned the badges, not to mention transportation to get Scouts to the places they needed to be to earn their badges.

First, though, the troop needed a name.

Giselle suggested Troop 11101, the Sleep Inn's zip code. Although clever and easy to remember, that name would conflict with long-held tradition: Girl Scout troops in the city were limited to four digits, and the numbers had always corresponded to the boroughs. In the Bronx, the troops were numbered in the 1000s; Brooklyn troops were 2000s; Manhattan troops were 3000s; Queens troops were 4000s; and Staten Island troops were 5000s.

But this new troop was unique. It belonged to girls who did not know where they belonged. It wouldn't make sense to use the numbers normally applied to troops in any of the five boroughs. Given that its members had no fixed addresses, wasn't this troop of girls, no matter where it was located, really like a floating borough in its own right? Or even a shadow borough, because the rest of society was ignorant of or didn't want to acknowledge its residents? At some point Girl Scout staff realized that the 6000s, designated years earlier for specialized troops, like those for girls with special needs, were no longer used. And so the Girl Scouts of Greater New York settled on the name Troop 6000.

"You realize this is big? This is going to be amazing," Meridith told Giselle. Giselle wanted to jump up and down, but as usual, worries dogged her—what if she couldn't recruit more girls? What if she couldn't recruit parent volunteers? What if she couldn't maintain the little bit of momentum she had already achieved?

Three days after the troop was officially named, Giselle hid her anxiety as she stood on a stage to accept a proclamation from Jimmy Van Bramer, who'd selected her to be honored at his annual Black History Month celebration. Giselle was proud of her heritage, which included her father's black southern roots. She was in esteemed company. The flyer for Jimmy's event included the faces of Martin Luther King, Jr., Malcolm X, Rosa Parks, Maya Angelou, W.E.B. Du Bois, Nelson Mandela, Bessie Coleman, and President Barack Obama.

The celebration was held at the Jacob A. Riis Neighborhood Settlement House, where a longtime nonprofit of the same name helped immigrants and youths. Giselle stood on the stage with her children and Scouts from the Sunnyside & Woodside troop. The proclamation made no mention of Giselle's homelessness or Troop 6000. But it was a reminder for Giselle that people were expecting her to be great. She had to make Troop 6000 bigger than eight girls.

WHEREAS: Giselle Burgess's work has had a ripple effect; the girls she recruits and mentors go on to build a better world and community. Ms. Burgess is an incredible role model to not only her five children, but to children across Queens; and

WHEREAS: Giselle Burgess has truly enriched all of us with her service, and she is worthy of the esteem of all New Yorkers; now, therefore,

BE IT KNOWN: That Jimmy Van Bramer, Majority Leader of the New York City Council, gratefully honors

Giselle Burgess

for her outstanding service and enduring contributions to the community.

Expectations were now in writing.

⁞⁞⁞⁞⁞⁞⁞⁞⁞⁞⁞⁞⁞⁞⁞⁞⁞⁞⁞⁞

Giselle gave herself two weeks to find parent volunteers and to recruit more girls, but by the date of the second meeting, a late winter Friday, she still hadn't found any other adults to help. As the small crew of girls gathered, she also learned that one from the first meeting would not be showing up because she was moving out of shelter. Now there'd be only seven members of Troop 6000.

But then five other girls walked into the room—Jessica, Tiana and Tanae, Kiara, and Sanaa. All told at that meeting there were twelve girls.

Giselle served two Entenmann's cakes, white with birthday sprinkles, as she talked to the girls about the origins of the Girl Scouts, which happened to have been founded almost 105 years earlier, on March 12, 1912. She placed numbered candles into one of the cakes to spell out "105."

Sanaa, a nine-year-old with her hair combed into a messy king bun atop her head, emerged as a natural leader, taking in what Giselle said and asking questions about Girl Scouts founder Juliette Gordon Low. Tiana and Tanae, two petite sisters who were five and seven but looked like twins, were shy but active. They wore gray tops and their hair was styled identically, in cornrows that cascaded into braids with white and pink beads.

Ten-year-old Jessica was also reticent but polite. Kiara was ten but looked fourteen and walked with the moodiness that sometimes comes with being a teenager; she refused to remove her coat.

But by the end of the meeting, when it was time to sing "Happy Birthday" and to blow out the candles on the cakes, Kiara's coat was off, draped on the chair where she was sitting with her elbows placed on one of the wobbly tables that Giselle had once again pushed together. The girls were laughing and giggling so much that the closed door could not contain the sound in the breakfast room, and their voices and excitement floated down the hallway.

In the following days Giselle kept putting up flyers, now promising food to parents who came to learn about volunteering at a pre-meeting in the breakfast room on March 17, before the Scouts' meeting began. She ordered chicken parmesan, pasta, and a salad—a gourmet feast compared with the barely edible shelter meals; the Girl Scouts of Greater New York would reimburse her at the end of the month. She bought two gallons of soda and a gallon of water and filled up an ice bucket. She had gone through the trouble of getting the Girl Scouts' special green tablecloth emblazoned with the trefoil logo, and she placed a box of Trefoil cookies upright in the middle as if it were a centerpiece. Recognized worldwide, the clover-like symbol with three leaves represented the promise that a Scout would honor her spiritual beliefs and country, would serve people, and would live by the Girl Scout Law. But even as the room filled with the scent of tomato sauce seeping from the foil pans, Giselle sat alone. Once again, her worries took over. What if all this food went uneaten?

There was one person she could call: Cori.

"Are you still coming?" she asked.

⁂

Cori's life had been all about running. She was just a little girl when her first foster mother, who was an aunt, dragged her from place to place because she was escaping an abuser. Trying to stay hidden, she kept Cori out of school for a year. Concerned that the kindergartner had disappeared from class, child welfare workers began knocking on doors. Cori's aunt would send her to friends' homes so that the authorities couldn't find her, but they eventually located Cori and placed her with a great-aunt who lived in Brooklyn.

That woman was Mama Eula, and she would later adopt Cori. When Cori moved in with her, she discovered she had three older brothers, and it wasn't long before a baby brother, who had been removed from her biological mother's care, showed up. Cori was the only girl.

"Going from one problem to another," Cori told Giselle. Life had never been easy for her no matter where she lived.

As Cori was approaching her fourteenth birthday, Mama Eula, who had worked for a telephone company, retired to Jonesboro, Georgia, a small town outside Atlanta, seeking a slower pace and cheaper cost of living. She packed up Cori and her younger brother, Anthony, who was disabled, and the family settled into their new home. Cori, once meek, was suddenly a disrupter at school. She masked her malaise by changing her hair from week to week. Her first hair color was a honey blond. Two weeks later, she dyed it red. Then the hot Georgia sun turned her dyed hair green, and she began wearing wigs to cover up her coloring mishaps. And so began her wig obsession.

She convinced Mama Eula to allow her to drop out of high school and get her equivalency degree, which gave Cori the freedom to hustle; her first foray into illegal entrepreneurship was stealing clothes from the mall where she worked at Aéropostale, a hip store for teenagers. Cori was fifteen, about to turn sixteen, when she landed the job. A friend worked at Macy's, and together they schemed to take clothes and sell them to students. Cori got caught, but a judge let her go after setting a date for her to appear back in court on the shoplifting charge. Cori promised she would return. She never did.

One day, Mama Eula called Cori telling her to come home

because there was an emergency. Afraid that something had happened to Anthony, Cori rushed home. Her body was weighed down by layers of stolen clothing, one of the ways she would sneak entire wardrobes out of stores. When she arrived home, the police were there.

"Corinthia Fludd. You're under arrest," an officer said.

"Ma, what'd you do?" Cori yelled at Mama Eula, who was so afraid of the police that she'd done exactly what they'd requested: told Cori to rush home without giving her a heads-up about the unwanted surprise in store for her.

The police were there on a bench warrant for her failure to return to court. Mama Eula hadn't fully understood that Cori would be arrested and was now crying at the thought of her daughter going to jail. Cori asked to use the bathroom before they left. She quickly ditched the stolen clothes so that she would not get charged with an additional count of shoplifting.

Mama Eula may have turned Cori in, but she also followed her to the police precinct and bailed her out. Rehabilitation was slow in coming, though. Over the next several years, Cori ran with a crowd that took illegal entrepreneurialism to another level. That included her boyfriend, a neighborhood teenager with whom she fell in love after he had returned from a juvenile detention center. He was shot to death in July 2006; police never found his killer. She fell into a depression, and a cousin in New York sent her a plane ticket to visit for the Christmas holidays.

Cori never went back to Jonesboro. She enrolled at a for-profit college that quickly went out of business, then began a string of disparate jobs connected only by her desire to make a living. She was a waitress at Applebee's—twice. An assistant at a bank. A dietary aide at a rehabilitation center.

Her housing was just as random, moving from one long-lost relative's extra bed one day to a new friend's couch the next. She moved in with her biological mother, a woman she had grown up believing was another aunt. But by that time, she had had

Trey, and she feared that living with her mother would expose her son to drugs and crime. And so she became homeless, eventually landing at the Sleep Inn the same summer as Giselle.

She and Giselle had little in common physically. Cori was tall, and her height gave her a natural, statuesque glamour that was amplified by her wigs. She had only one child. And while she had family, she always felt alone.

Some days, Giselle—who was quite pretty—could come off as frumpy; she spent what little money she had on her children, and Cori was always encouraging her to fix herself up. Her black faux leather flats had worn so far down that the outer layer was peeling off. Most of her pants were in need of tailoring; the bottoms had frayed from brushing the ground. Her clothes never fit quite right. Since the birth of Hailey, Giselle's weight had fluctuated between pregnant and not pregnant. Her best dress slacks were a pair of black maternity pants that she wore to work when she really needed to look nice. She wore long button-down shirts to cover the elastic that had once stretched across her bulging pregnant stomach. When co-workers would tell her that she really needed to get some non-maternity clothes, she'd tell them, "Why? You can't tell."

Giselle's five children had varying skin tones—from Gillesy, who was as beige as a manila folder, to Karina, who was milky brown like a Kit Kat bar. The children created a breathtaking rainbow, reflecting both the beauty of Giselle's own diverse heritage—her father was African American and her mother was Guatemalan—and the variety of her failed relationships.

Giselle and Cori became a natural yin and yang, so when Giselle called in a panic begging for help at her Girl Scout meeting, Cori showed up, even though she didn't have a daughter. While they ate the Italian feast that Giselle had ordered, Giselle showed Cori a video explaining the ins and outs of Girl Scouting and volunteering.

"You're trained!" a bubbly Giselle told her. "Sign here."

Cori filled out the papers and Giselle had her first parent volunteer.

Girls trickled into the breakfast room, and Cori introduced herself. There were some new faces, like Genesis, the svelte teenager Giselle had met in passing, and her sister Brithani, who was eight; both girls had deep chocolate-colored skin and Honduran accents. They spoke Spanish to each other but switched to English to talk to the other girls. Genesis was mostly quiet and reserved and watched while Brithani—pronounced Brittany—happily joined in all of the activities.

The lesson at that third meeting was about calling 911 and how to alert authorities in an emergency. The girls put themselves in different scenarios, figuring out how they'd call 911 under an assortment of circumstances. In one, Brithani and Kiara lay on the floor, as if they had fallen from an illness or accident.

Cori told the girls that there were different agencies they should contact for different emergencies: "Fire, police, ambulance, poison control." Saying "police" tickled her a little bit. Here she was, the girl who had started smoking at thirteen, who had been arrested at sixteen for shoplifting, telling the girls how to call the police.

Over the next week, Giselle and Cori made a display for Troop 6000, putting the girls' names on construction paper shaped like trefoils, along with the Girl Scout Promise and Girl Scout rules: "Be Honest. Believe in Yourself. Make New Friends." She and Giselle stood on wobbly chairs to tape green streamers to the wall. It made things easier for them that they were the only ones using the room now so they could leave the decorations up.

Cori hung the girls' handwritten safety plans on the wall behind the display; then she sat down and Giselle snapped her photo. This moment, they thought, had to be chronicled, even if

it was just a picture they kept in their phones. Giselle was grateful that Cori had shown up to help her when no other parents
would, and Cori, in turn, was flattered that Giselle would think
of her as a savior. Here they were—two high school dropouts
who were somehow starting a Girl Scout troop inside a shelter.
And people began to take notice.

# 10

# THE RIBBON

**THE FOLLOWING WEEK'S** meeting on March 24 was supposed to be just a regular one in the breakfast room when in walked Jimmy Van Bramer in a blue suit with his well-coiffed white hair. *He must be important,* Sanaa thought.

It was the one-month anniversary of the first gathering of the troop, before it was even a real troop, before it even had a name. Now the troop was off and running fast, and Jimmy was there to make it official. March was also Women's History Month, so he decided to mark the occasion by recognizing local women in politics. Heidi Schmidt came with a woman she'd invited from the Queens borough president's office and one from the local community board, so the girls could see women in positions of power. They discussed a wide range of topics, from racism to crime to gender equity.

A sense of quiet satisfaction bubbled up in Giselle as she leaned against the back wall of the room. This was what she had wanted for her daughters and the other girls living here—a chance to think differently about the world and their places in it. She looked over at Cori, who was listening so intently to the conversation, and said a silent prayer of thanks for everything and for everyone in the room.

Sanaa studied Jimmy. She listened as he said things like "Women can do anything" and "You can run for office" and "A woman can be president."

Sanaa raised her hand. "Then what about that woman who tried to be president and didn't become one?"

Though Sanaa's survival tactic was to be the smartest, most personable person in the room, her tongue sometimes lay too heavy in her mouth, threatening to jumble her words, to make her a mumbler, so she worked to enunciate every word with authority, even if she was unsure of its meaning, even if she was uncertain of the pronunciation. As a result, her question to Jimmy came out as less of a query and more like a declaration with just a smidge of sarcasm.

Giselle shook her head, a little embarrassed yet impressed. Cori laughed. Heidi was in awe. At nine years old and in the fourth grade, Sanaa could not remember Hillary Clinton's name. But she was well aware that there had been an election and that a woman had narrowly lost. Sanaa was smart enough to know that she had commanded the room.

Sanaa—full name Sanaa Nina Simone Angevin—was raised that way.

Her mother, Mickyle—who had grown up in Brooklyn and had fond memories of being a Girl Scout—had pushed her to master the alphabet and her numbers at an early age, playing Baby Mozart as Sanaa lay in her crib. Sanaa had been plucked for gifted and talented programs, stayed firmly on the honor roll, and strove to be the teacher's pet. Her discipline and amiability had helped her as she bounced from school to school as her mother moved her and her brothers from Atlanta to New York, back to Atlanta, then back to New York again.

Sanaa was the embodiment of the person Mickyle hoped she would have been if there had not been obstacles in her way, if she had only made good enough grades to get a scholarship to a reputable college, if she had only not gotten pregnant before she had planned.

By the time Sanaa was two years old, Mickyle was pregnant with her son Makhi and living in a shelter in Harlem. She moved to Atlanta, entering Georgia State University, juggling multiple jobs, hoping to make a little more money, trying to earn a bachelor's degree that kept eluding her as her family grew; her third child, Malaki, was born when Sanaa was five. Mickyle thought she was finally making it in 2016 when she began looking for a house to rent.

But then Mickyle was in a car accident. The driver did not have insurance. Mickyle's rental car money was running out and there was no public transportation to get her to the distribution center where she worked packing baby clothing; getting to her other job at a nursing home would also be a challenge using mass transit. With pressure mounting and time becoming a disappearing commodity, she began to fail her online college courses.

She decided to return to New York but didn't want to impose on her mother or other relatives by taking up more space in already cramped, overcrowded apartments. Mickyle drove her rental car from Atlanta to Staten Island and ended up at PATH in September 2016. The family of four was placed at the Sleep Inn a month after Giselle and her family had arrived.

Sanaa wasn't quite old enough to understand what was happening. They were in a hotel room with no stove, no privacy, no closet space. Mickyle told her children that their new surroundings and circumstances were not excuses to fail; they would have to step up. She used writing as a disciplinary tool. Every time her children misbehaved, did not complete chores, forgot to do homework, or were mean to one another, she made them write letters of apology. Sanaa hated composing those letters at first but soon learned that atonement expressed in writing went a long way.

Along with many other children of elementary school age at the Sleep Inn, Sanaa attended P.S. 111. The school did its best for

an increasingly transient student population that carried frag-
mented academic records and a defensiveness that could pop up
at any time on the playground or in the classroom. About one
out of every ten students was proficient in math and English. In
New York City school rankings, P.S. 111 hovered at the bottom;
in its number of homeless students, it was quickly rising to the
top. Because Sanaa's defense mode was affability and achieve-
ment, she was immediately propped up as a role model for other
students.

What the school could not accomplish in test scores it made
up for in heart and activities, like the step team, the choir, and
the library club. But Sanaa and other students who lived at the
Sleep Inn yearned for something more. Once they walked home
from school, they were required to go straight to their rooms,
coming out only to warm up food in the lobby's microwave.
Sanaa had no idea that many of her classmates were living practically alongside her in the very same hotel. After all, there were
almost no opportunities to interact: They weren't allowed to
play in the hallways; they couldn't play unsupervised outside;
they couldn't visit or have sleepovers in one another's rooms.
Mickyle felt her children's isolation every time they sat on their
beds to finish up homework.

Then she saw one of Giselle's flyers hanging by the elevator.

"Well, Sanaa, do you want to do Girl Scouts? I was a Girl
Scout."

Sanaa wasn't sure what being a Girl Scout meant. When
Mickyle explained to her that there were badges and patches to
be earned, she couldn't wait to get to the meetings.

Now Sanaa had a new goal. Her inquisitive eyes darted from
one patch to the next on Hailey's vest. What a rainbow of accomplishments! They proved that Hailey was not only a Scout
but a good one. That's what she would become, Sanaa decided: a
good Scout. Hailey's patches covered her entire vest, evincing
her worldliness. Sanaa focused on Hailey's favorite, a deep-blue
oval at the top of her right shoulder that depicted Juliette Gordon Low's house in Savannah, which was in Georgia, just like

Atlanta, where Sanaa had come from. Many of the patches were "fun patches" that were collected but not necessarily earned. The fun patches came in all shapes and sizes—rectangles, squares, big circles, small circles, a pentagon, a triangle—and commemorated participation in Urban Day Camp, sleepovers, camping, and caroling, and recognized Hailey's punctuality and her love of fashion. Of course, she had badges and special pins for selling cookies with the Sunnyside & Woodside troop.

After the meeting with Jimmy, all the Scouts lined up so that Jimmy and Meridith could pin them with the First Aid Badges that they had earned at the previous meeting, the one where Cori had taught them how to call 911. So now Sanaa had her first badge, and it was a merit badge—something she'd had to earn—rather than a fun patch; she only had a gazillion more to go to catch up to Hailey.

The Scouts all gathered around Jimmy in the dining area. Kiara's father, David, who had shown up at the end of the meeting, asked them to pose. A green ribbon was placed across the door of the breakfast room, along with a TROOP 6000 sign.

Sanaa placed her hand atop Jimmy's. Kiara, who'd been so sullen when she showed up at the second meeting, reached over behind Sanaa to put her hand in, as did Brithani and the other Scouts. Jimmy cut the ribbon with a pair of oversize scissors. Cori and Giselle laughed and clapped on the sidelines. David took more pictures.

Amid all the cheering, Giselle started to cry. She was overcome by a strange mix of emotions swirling inside her. Yes, she had accomplished something pretty damn impressive, but would she be able to maintain it? Troop 6000 may have grown a little each week, but the growth was incremental in a completely unpredictable way, because each week at least one or two girls who'd been there before failed to show up. A couple of them disappeared because their families had found housing and they'd moved out of the hotel, like other girls would be doing in the coming weeks and months. That was a good thing, but it was a reminder that Troop 6000 was not an ordinary troop. It had hurdles to overcome that other new troops did not face: What was good news for those in the Sleep Inn who'd now found homes was bad news for the nascent Girl Scout troop.

Amid the hugs and pinning, Giselle spotted Genesis lingering in the hallway next to the elevators waiting to pick up her sister Brithani from the meeting. At fifteen, Genesis was a little taller than Giselle, but she often dropped her head so that she looked shorter. She had a brown spot on the white of her left eye, more of a distinguishing mark than a blemish, enhancing her beauty. Whenever Genesis laughed, it was almost as if she did not think she should be laughing; she would stop herself and close her mouth as if holding a secret. She looked down at the hallway floor when she locked eyes with Giselle, smiling and then pressing her lips closed.

Recruiting older girls had proved just as difficult as finding parent volunteers. To begin with, they seemed to view the Girl Scouts just as Giselle had as a teenager—an activity that was a little corny, one for people with means and luxurious amounts of time to kill. And they had other obligations, adult obligations. They were responsible for younger siblings, getting themselves to and from school, helping with shopping or surreptitious cooking or laundry, all while trying not to be another burden on their parents. A study by the Institute for Children, Poverty & Homelessness found that in 2017 nearly half of all high school students experiencing homelessness said they were depressed compared to about 30 percent of students who had homes.

Genesis's biggest worry was finding a job for herself. It didn't matter what kind of work, all she cared about was the income she could earn. Her mother sometimes seemed paralyzed by the undertaking of caring for her family, and so her oldest daughter was in a constant state of uncertainty—about money, about her growing responsibilities, about whether the family would be able to stay in the United States. Genesis had come to the United States from Honduras later than the rest of her family. When she arrived in Miami in 2014, she was excited to join her parents and her two younger sisters, Brithani and Gianna. But she

learned her parents' marriage had soured, and Genesis was unexpectedly caught in the middle, struggling to learn more English while taking on the care of her younger sisters. After they
lost their belongings in a fire in Miami, family in New York
encouraged a move to the city, but they ended up at PATH, like
so many other families.

Genesis hated the word *immigrant*—to her, it was code for
*un-American.* "I have my papers," she would say whenever anyone used the word to refer to her. Genesis only knew that she
wanted to stay in the United States, she wanted to be a model,
and she wanted to go to college. As a high school sophomore,
though, she had never heard of the SAT even as she walked past
a standardized testing prep program on the way from the subway to the Sleep Inn.

She could only focus on the basics: family, high school, and
money. The other stuff would come once she took care of those
three things. Her mother had named her from the Bible—
Genesis, the beginning—but Genesis had no idea how to get to
the end, to get to where she wanted to go.

Her school, Long Island City High School, enrolled about
2,500 students, mostly first-generation immigrants just like
Genesis. It had a robust ROTC program and a culinary arts program with state-of-the-art equipment. The school was praised
for turning around students' lives, boasting a list of success stories who had won scholarships or made it into elite colleges. But
about 40 percent of students never graduated. For all of the students who left and attained the impossible, there were a significant number who did not and never would. About 250 children
per class would not get a diploma, and Genesis feared she would
be one of them. Homeless students scored worse on proficiency
exams, studies showed, and were more prone to absenteeism
than housed students. Their lag was a reflection of a deeply segregated school system.

Genesis faced classism and racism. How she talked, how she
looked in her cheap clothes, and her dark skin all made Genesis
feel inadequate. People were confused when she spoke Spanish-

accented English, not realizing that there were black Hondurans, too ignorant to make the distinction between an ethnicity like Hispanic and a race. It took Genesis a little longer than native English speakers to learn to read and write in her new environment.

Now she stood by the elevator on the day of the ribbon cutting. Giselle saw her and headed toward her.

"Hi," Giselle said, embracing her. Genesis even had her vest in her hand. "Why weren't you at the meeting?"

Genesis didn't answer at first. She looked apologetic, or maybe disappointed. "I'm sorry. I don't want to do this," she finally said, handing over her khaki vest. She hadn't even gotten it pinned with the First Aid Badge.

"Once you're a Girl Scout, you're always a Girl Scout," Giselle said, forcing a smile through her dismay.

Then she took Genesis's vest, holding it with the same care that she used when dressing a newborn to leave the hospital.

"You know what I'm going to do? I'm going to hold on to your vest."

Genesis nodded, and Giselle saw tears in her eyes before the teenager turned away.

# 11

# THE GIRL NEXT DOOR

"YOU CAN DROP us off at the store on Twenty-first Street. We have to get something first," Hailey told her classmate's mother, a nice woman who had offered to give Karina and her a ride home from an after-school program on a rainy day.

Other parents offered to give Hailey, Karina, and Christina lifts to meetings of the Girl Scouts of Sunnyside & Woodside—they were still members of that troop, too—when Giselle couldn't be there. Hailey always told the ride givers to pick them up at the subway near the Sleep Inn, as if she were saving them the trouble of driving far out in Queens to her imaginary home.

Hailey didn't want her classmates from Evangel, her friends, and her fellow Scouts outside Troop 6000 to know where she lived. She could do everything—help Gillesy and Judas balance their dinners on paper plates on the floor of their room, make sure Christina finished her homework, be a supportive sister to Karina, who needed to talk about bullies at school—but she could not bring herself to say "I'm homeless" out loud. Whenever another girl asked Hailey if she could spend the night at her house, Hailey was evasive, turning the question around—"Maybe I can spend the night at your house?"

Giselle learned to lie to shield her children, especially Hailey. She thought she knew exactly how her daughter felt. Before the launch of Troop 6000, Meridith and Giselle's supervisor, Alida, had been the only people at the Girl Scouts of Greater New York who were aware that Giselle was living in a shelter. As more staffers learned the truth, Giselle gradually became comfortable with it and her feelings of shame began to fade.

She was so proud to pose with Jimmy, Meridith, and Heidi when people living at the shelter offered to take pictures with their cellphones. But what Giselle did not understand was that Jimmy saw Troop 6000 as an opportunity to talk about something good that was happening inside a shelter, just like serving a good meal or delivering cookies to the women living at Pam's Place, something to combat all the negativity that had arisen around the proposed addition of new shelters.

That March, communities around the city were riled up about Mayor de Blasio's latest plan to open ninety new shelters and to expand thirty that were already operating. He called the strategy "Turning the Tide on Homelessness," but it was more focused on managing homelessness than on solving it, a Band-Aid slapped on a gaping wound too far gone to mend.

It had been a long slog up to this point. For years, the city had distributed vouchers that could be used toward rent through a program called Advantage, which applied state, federal, and city funding. Homelessness, an incredible blight in the 1980s, seemed to stabilize. But when the state had a financial crunch in the early 2010s, Governor Andrew Cuomo and the state legislature, with little desire to raise taxes, cut the program way back, and Michael Bloomberg, de Blasio's predecessor, refused to take up the slack, saying it was not fair for the city to shoulder all of the responsibility. And so the amount of money dedicated to the homeless plummeted, and the number of homeless people on the streets and in shelters began to steadily increase.

De Blasio was ushered into office on a campaign message that he would address the wealth disparities gripping the city that were squeezing low-income people out until it seemed that only the ultrarich remained. And at first he made good on his promise; the city opened sixteen new shelters in 2014, his first year in office. But 2015 brought an abrupt unofficial moratorium on the construction of additional shelters as elected representatives from one district to the next called de Blasio and other officials demanding to know why the city was opening shelters in their neighborhoods. The facilities had seemed to go up almost under cover of night, giving communities little time to react, and de Blasio decided that his administration needed to take a pause.

But in 2017, with people continuing to pour into the shelter system in droves, the mayor and his team doubled down, insisting that the city simply had to give people living in shelters more comfortable, efficient, and compassionate services than hotels and apartments could offer. Under a new five-year plan, hotels and apartments would be phased out and even more shelters would be built, though communities would now get at least thirty days' notice to allow time for their input on the city's decision. Because the city wanted to place families back in the communities from where they became homeless—as Giselle had begged to stay in Queens—the ninety new shelters would have to be built throughout the five boroughs.

De Blasio called it a "blood and guts war strategy," but it would help only a fraction of those in need: If everything went as planned, the city hoped to reduce homelessness by five hundred people a year—what de Blasio called an "honest goal." At the time, there were roughly sixty thousand homeless New Yorkers.

"Turning the Tide on Homelessness" dominated the news cycle as members of the city council questioned its fairness. But little was being discussed about the actual people who were living in shelters and hotels.

Just days after Jimmy cut the ribbon to christen the Sleep Inn's breakfast room as Troop 6000's meeting space, he decided he needed to publicize the troop somehow, especially since there was talk of expanding the Scouts' presence into other shelters.

Why not put a face on the homeless problem and show that real people, real girls, were struggling in these places? He kicked it around with his staff and they decided to aim high—*The New York Times.*

The pitch that Jimmy's aide emailed to the *Times* was short:

*This girl scout troop has a simple message to these girls—they are more than homeless, they are a valuable addition to this City.*

*The real leader of this effort is Giselle Burgess, a Girl Scout employee and a resident of the Sleep Inn. Giselle is an inspiration and while certainly down on her luck, is working daily to help out wherever help is needed.*

*Do you think you would be interested in writing this story?*

As the outrage of neighborhood associations and residents in all five boroughs grew in response to the mayor's plan for the construction of ninety new shelters, homeless people had become mere numbers on a sheet of paper. A story about a Scout troop for girls living inside a hotel transformed into a shelter would be a welcome break from the ad nauseam "Not in My Backyard"—NIMBY—letters to the editor that were appearing in newspapers across the city and continuing coverage of the mayor's clumsy rollout of his new plan. It was an easy pitch, a great story, and a reporter and a photographer set out to attend meetings of Troop 6000.

But it would mean big changes for Giselle and her children, especially Hailey. Meridith seemed to understand that more than Giselle did.

"It's up to you," Meridith said to Giselle as they talked over what it might mean to reveal that she was homeless and living at the Sleep Inn. "We can stop this whenever you want."

Giselle thought about it, how her homeless status—and that of her children—would be front and center in one of the biggest newspapers in the world, with online readers in every corner of the planet. When she traveled the city for work in a Girl Scouts button-down or polo shirt, people respected her. They sometimes did not when she was a homeless person out of uniform. She knew it was increasingly important that the public see that homelessness could affect anyone, and she tried to convey this to her children.

"Troop 6000 is probably going to be in more shelters," Giselle explained to Hailey, Karina, and Christina inside their room. "A news reporter is coming to the meeting." She went on to explain that *The New York Times* was a major publication, and a lot more people were going to know they were homeless once the story appeared.

Later Hailey confided in Karina, "I'm scared of what my friends will think. They're going to pick on me."

Karina had been living in Hailey's shadow, protected by her smart, assertive older sister. Reading and studying came easier for Hailey. Because Karina had been held back a grade when they returned from Florida, she was still in fifth grade, months from her twelfth birthday. At school, she was often in the out crowd, and she'd grown more and more comfortable with her position at the bottom of a social hierarchy based on cliques. At her previous school before Evangel, that didn't stop her from running for class vice president in fourth grade. She lost but never regretted going for it.

Karina was as embarrassed as Hailey about being homeless. She braced herself for the harassment of classmates who appeared to be so much wealthier than she was, but Karina was ready. She possessed a self-awareness beyond her years and was very much a rebel, a negotiator, and someone who spoke out when something was important to her.

"I'll do it. I don't care," Karina told Hailey as if they had switched places and Karina were the oldest.

Karina's fearlessness made Hailey reflect on how she had been acting, asking everyone to lie so that her friends would not know that her family did not have a home of their own. She was now embarrassed that she had been embarrassed. "If they care," Hailey told Karina, "they're not my friends anyway."

The reporter from the *Times,* along with a photographer, attended the April 7 meeting of Troop 6000. Karina opened by reading the roll and then she led the Girl Scout Promise as the whole room watched. She started at six P.M. on the dot. The meeting had to be perfect because it had drawn a crowd, including Heidi, Jimmy, and Meridith. Giselle and Cori scanned the room anxiously.

Eleven-year-old Karina had come to realize that many of the younger girls did not really understand what homelessness even meant, though their parents had signed permission slips that allowed them to talk to a reporter about their situations and to have their photos taken. They didn't talk about themselves that way, as homeless. They did not refer to the Sleep Inn as a shelter. When they did talk about homelessness, they talked about others, like the men and women they saw on sidewalks and subways; they said how they'd like to buy food and supplies for them.

The girls knew they were different because they lived in a hotel room instead of an apartment, but they did not understand what that really meant. In most cases, it was because their parents had tried to protect them from the reality that they were so deeply entrenched in poverty that they didn't have homes. Cori had told her son, Trey, who had just turned seven, that he was on vacation. Mickyle hadn't told Sanaa and her brothers the full truth, leaving them to draw the conclusion that they lived in a special apartment building. The younger girls, wearing their blue and brown vests, listened intently as Karina introduced the reporter and photographer and explained why they were at the meeting. Their minds seemed to grapple with the word *homeless* and what that meant. They were not on the street. They were not begging on the subway. They were not holding cardboard signs on the sidewalk. Their clothes were clean.

But it slowly dawned on the younger Scouts.

*They* were homeless.

Hailey took her cues from Karina, opening up and telling the reporter that the girls in the room—about twenty now—were just the beginning of Troop 6000. There was strength in numbers, comfort in knowing you were not the only one, she said. "We're starting a chain reaction. Hopefully, in the next couple years, there will be more Girl Scout troops in shelters."

Nearly two weeks later, after the reporter had attended more meetings, the story was posted on the *Times*'s website on Easter Sunday. It appeared on the front page of the paper the next day, so Giselle and Karina woke up early and scoured the bodegas around the Sleep Inn and the Queensbridge housing project looking for a copy. Mother and daughter went from store to store in vain. "Do you have *The New York Times*? Do you sell *The New York Times*?" They knew the newspaper was printed in Queens—Jimmy's father had worked as a pressman for the paper—but finding it around the Sleep Inn seemed impossible. Tattered copies of the tabloid *Post* and *Daily News*, but no *Times*. Giselle and Karina finally gave up.

Giselle headed to work, taking the subway to her office in the Financial District.

She had grown used to weaving between hordes of tourists all looking for the famous Wall Street statue *Charging Bull*, but now she was wading through women and girls forming lines to take their photos of a new sculpture that had been installed weeks earlier. *Fearless Girl* faced the bull head-on, hands on hips and defiant. Created to bring attention to a gender diversity index fund, *Fearless Girl* was a David at 4 feet tall and 250 pounds pitted against the Goliath bull at 11 feet and 7,100 pounds. Her dress and hair appeared to be blown by the snorting breath blasting out of the bull's nose. Sometimes Giselle felt as if she and all of the other homeless and vulnerable New Yorkers were like that young girl facing the massive bull.

It was good to have a regular reminder to be fearless.

The Girl Scouts of Greater New York was on the seventh floor at 40 Wall Street, just a few blocks down from the girl and the bull. When Giselle stepped off the elevator, one of her co-workers ran up to her. She had a copy of the *Times* and there, right on the front page, were Karina and Hailey with two other Scouts. Giselle burst into tears and pressed the folded newspaper to her chest.

The media storm had begun. Giselle was flooded with requests for interviews and appearances—*The Ellen DeGeneres Show*, *Today*, *Good Morning America*, *Teen Vogue*, CNN, every local television station and some international ones. The story would keep going for days, looping on radio stations and TV news shows pining for a narrative that could bring viewers together at a moment when the nation was still riveted and roiled by the outcome of the 2016 presidential election. Giselle did not want to let anyone down, and she accepted nearly all of the interview requests. She showed her room at the Sleep Inn to the world, and she helped her daughters put their vests on for the cameras, even though she never really did that because they could do it themselves. But it made for good TV, and Giselle wanted to show Troop 6000 in its best light.

***

New York's City Hall was grand, like the White House, the only other building Karina and Christina could remember seeing in photos that resembled it. The sisters scaled the stairs and entered the doors of the 205-year-old building into the rotunda, where they saw a marble staircase that twisted to the second floor. That's where they and other troop members joined Jimmy Van Bramer, their host for the day, who was presenting Troop 6000 with a special proclamation the week after the *New York Times* story propelled it into the national news. Hailey couldn't be there because she had tests at school that she couldn't miss.

The City Council Chamber was cavernous and ornate, the ceiling decorated with gilded moldings. The girls sank back into tufted, burgundy leather armchairs with wheels and turned their gazes upward. They swiveled in their chairs as Jimmy explained that they were in the room where the city's laws were made. They ate candy given to them by aides to Mayor de Blasio. They took turns banging the gavel.

Minutes later, council members began filing into the chamber until nearly every one of those plush seats was filled, and Jimmy rose to speak. He gathered Giselle and her two daughters in front and presented them with the proclamation. Christina gripped the oversize document, which was practically as big as she was; she awkwardly raised it and lowered it, raised it and lowered it; she rested her chin on it.

"They have literally changed history," Jimmy said of Troop 6000. "We love you so much and we are so, so proud of every single one of you."

Jimmy introduced Giselle, who wiped away tears. "Thank you. Thank you, everyone who made this possible, who believed in us. I'm really hoping we can make this possible for so many other girls who are currently watching TV and saying I want to do that too, I want to make friends, I want to help make a difference. Thank you all for your support. Hopefully, we can make this dream a reality and make sure we reach all of our girls and women as well to make them feel, to help them feel empowered and to let them know not to give up."

Jimmy handed the microphone to Karina to speak on behalf of the girls. "Just seeing them every Friday, it makes me happy because we're all a group. We're a pack," she said, gripping the microphone and looking around to get reassurance from nodding heads and smiles in the crowd. "Thank you, Mommy, for making this happen. None of this would have happened without you. It's all you."

That same day, April 25, Dan Rather, the former *CBS Evening News* anchor, posted a long note on his Facebook page for his 2.5 million followers:

> *We are a nation of over 320 million individual stories, and we should not forget that.... My mind goes back to an article I read a few days ago that moved me. It was about a girl scout troop for homeless girls in New York. It was what might*

*be termed a small little feature story, but in its seeming sim-*
*plicity it spoke volumes about the current state of our nation.*
*How many of us can truly understand the struggles these*
*young women face everyday? How hard it must be for them,*
*whose lives are beset by chaotic tides well beyond their own*
*control, to focus on the joys of childhood or the responsibili-*
*ties of being a young student.*

*How detached the debates in Washington seem from this*
*reality, and so many other types of realities in cities, towns,*
*and rural communities across the United States. . . . Maybe if*
*our president and Congressional leaders were watching and*
*reading more of this instead of the empty rhetoric one finds*
*too often wafting over Washington, we would be in a better*
*place.*

After reading the stories and watching the coverage, Hailey took the final step to full realization that she had no reason to be ashamed to tell people she was homeless: Troop 6000 had become a badge of honor.

Two days later, Jimmy introduced Hailey and other Scouts during a town hall meeting with Mayor de Blasio. Wearing a navy suit tailored to his nearly six-six frame and a genial smile, the mayor towered over Hailey, who for her part had paired her badge-covered vest with a pair of Converse sneakers. She sometimes shuffled her feet when she was nervous, but that night she planted them firmly on the gym floor as she stood up to ask the mayor the first question of the meeting. She was beginning to understand the magnitude of what was happening, and of her own power. "I wanted to know what are your plans for the women's initiative and how are you advocating for girls in New York City?"

De Blasio smiled the way politicians do when they hear a big question from a young mind: surprised and amused, with a touch of being impressed. He said his administration was improving education and investing in universal pre-K and after-school programs. Then the mayor commended the new troop.

"Some families have worked really hard, but they have a lot of trouble making ends meet. Some end up in a state of homelessness, but that does not rob them of their humanity, of their dignity, or their value, or their worth to our society," he said. "The Girl Scouts is an amazing American institution that should be available wherever they are."

It was a powerful moment, but not necessarily because of what the mayor said. Something about seeing all the girls in their vests of brown and khaki and blue and green upended people's thinking, creating an opening for understanding that the country's current economic state was affecting the girl next door.

And that next door was, in fact, a shelter.

# 12

# MAN ENOUGH TO BE A GIRL SCOUT

**THE WEEK AFTER** the *New York Times* article ran, with all of its ensuing publicity, the membership of Troop 6000 was growing, but Giselle was still having trouble finding adults to volunteer their time.

"Would you like to be a troop leader?" Giselle asked the parent of one of her troop members over roasted chicken and mashed potatoes at a Boston Market in Woodside in April.

There was a pause. The parent had never considered this possibility.

David Browne was the father of Kiara, the ten-year-old who had initially refused to take off her coat at her first meeting but then boldly put her hand into the photograph with Jimmy and the Troop 6000 banner. Kiara had reasons for her caution. Not only was she living in a shelter, but she was at a new school, she was in a new city, and she barely knew her father.

The Sleep Inn and the Girl Scouts had given David and Kiara some stability and consistency after months of uncertainty. David had not raised Kiara. He and Lanye, Kiara's mother, had met in a group home in Philadelphia when they were teenagers, and David had only had visitation rights for the first decade of Kiara's life. In the summer of 2016, Lanye was in a financial bind and was hunting for new housing. She told David she just needed time to get everything settled. Maybe he could help out and assume care of Kiara during the last weeks of her summer vacation?

"It's the least you can do," Lanye told him on the phone. "I need you to take her until I can get on my feet." She thought David was doing well, after all, because he was living in a new apartment in Harlem and had room.

He returned to Philadelphia, packed up Kiara and her belongings, and took her home to New York with him. But by the time September rolled around, David's roommate had had enough. He refused to accept their new surprise tenant and kicked David and Kiara out. Both of Kiara's parents were now homeless, and David entered the New York City shelter system with his daughter. He enrolled Kiara at a school in the Bronx near their new living situation. Lanye, though upset about being apart from Kiara, did not want to disrupt her daughter's schooling, so she stood down.

*David struggled to find childcare, so often took Kiara to work with him.*

David was thrust into fatherhood and tried bonding with Kiara the best way he knew how: food. Growing up in Philadelphia, David had struggled, but he'd earned the respect of his family by honing his cooking skills.

Now he was working as a line cook at Vapiano, a fast-casual Italian restaurant in Manhattan, trying to find a way to turn his talents into a career as a caterer or maybe even a restaurateur. He often took Kiara to work with him.

David was over six feet tall and heavyset; Kiara was tall for her age and plump. They had the same eyes, the same eyebrows, and the same lips. Kiara had a high-pitched voice, and when David got angry or excited, his voice moved up the scale quickly from bass to falsetto. When they were both in good moods and getting along, David and Lanye would jokingly argue on Facebook about which of them she most resembled.

The Sleep Inn was the third shelter David and Kiara had spent time in, and it was a delight compared with the previous one, the Quality Inn in Floral Park. That hotel-shelter had been surrounded by residential streets where longtime homeowners mowed the lawns around their modest houses, proud of new fencing or bushes that they had grown tall enough for passersby to understand property boundaries.

It had all looked peaceful enough, but beneath the surface this community was a war zone.

The Quality Inn was on Jericho Turnpike, so far from Manhattan that David could barely see the city's skyline. When he and Kiara were placed there in September 2016, they had no idea that they were landing smack in the middle of the continuing fight between Mayor de Blasio and residents determined to thwart the opening of new shelters, including the Quality Inn.

New York was legally obligated to provide shelter to residents who had nowhere else to go. The court case that had started it all was a successful class action lawsuit with a lead plaintiff named Robert Callahan, a homeless man who died sleeping on the street before a consent decree was finalized in 1983 that required the city to shelter men like him. Steven Banks, now the social services commissioner, was a lawyer and sued the city the same year, filing another class action lawsuit that applied the right to humane shelter to families. The plaintiff in that suit was Yvonne McCain, a mother of four children who had become homeless after an eviction. The city then placed her family in a decrepit welfare hotel in Herald Square, where, as she described it, she had to use newspapers to cover urine-stained mattresses.

The city needed to do better than that. Banks brought the class action suit with McCain as the lead plaintiff and won it in 1986, but because of appeals the battle stretched into 2008, when the city finally agreed to grant a permanent right to shelter for families with children and to create a system to provide it.

The quarter-century fight defined Banks's career as an advocate for vulnerable New Yorkers, and when de Blasio was elected mayor in 2013 he asked Banks to join his administration as social services commissioner, believing Banks could fix the overall system from the inside more effectively than he could from the outside.

Banks described the shift in roles as like taking a car for an oil change only to find out it needed a new engine. Looking under the hood proved challenging for an inside man. The burgeoning crisis led to the temporary solution of booking hotel rooms for the homeless and then converting budget hotels like the Sleep Inn into shelters. As an advocate, he had chided the city for using hotels in this way, concerned that the residents had no means to cook and were forced to live in close quarters; now, as a commissioner, he needed to use the hotels until he could marshal the resources to build new traditional shelters.

And so the demonstrations started up. They grew more feverish and began to break unwritten rules of civility and decency. NIMBYism mixed with racism as some residents shouted, "White lives matter!"

The day after Labor Day 2016, someone called Banks's house in Brooklyn at around ten forty-five P.M.

He picked up the receiver, thinking it might be an emergency. In his previous life with the Legal Aid Society, he'd seen nothing wrong with listing his home phone number. Why shouldn't vulnerable people seeking help be able to look him up and call him?

"Your work has had such an impact on a lot of people," the woman on the other end of the line said. At first Banks thought that she was someone calling to wish him well in the midst of all the protests and efforts to stop shelter openings.

But the call took an ominous turn as she began to talk about his "negative" impact on communities.

"Why didn't you pick your newspaper up in front of your house this weekend?" she asked.

Was he being watched?

"Give my best to Harry and Susanna," the caller then said, referring to Banks's adult children.

"Who is this?"

"You'll hear from me soon," the caller responded. Then she hung up.

Banks was shaken. He sent an email to the police commissioner, and detectives identified the call as coming from a cheap burner phone that could not be traced; suddenly, after decades of living a normal life, Banks was under police protection. He was ordered to stop taking the subway, something he'd done every day of his professional life, not only because he didn't want to waste taxpayer dollars on a car and driver but also because he wanted to experience New York as other New Yorkers did, and because he wanted to be a firsthand witness to the hardship of the homelessness he was trying so desperately to end.

The backlash against shelters was only getting worse. Early protests concentrated on hotels used to shelter men—men were seen as more likely to drink in public and to make trouble—but eventually the focus turned to hotels that housed families, and as one of the hotels used as shelter, the Quality Inn where David and Kiara were staying found itself in the crosshairs. Flyers posted throughout the surrounding area described in inflammatory terms the perceived decline in the quality of life since homeless parents and their children had moved in. A photo showed two small children running around in a driveway with the caption "Hotel resident's kids playing in neighbor's driveway."

A major protest march outside the Quality Inn was planned for September 24, 2016. A flyer advertising the demonstration pictured Uncle Sam pointing with the words "We Need You!!!" Busloads of protesters from Maspeth, where community leaders had convinced residents that they had to fight shelters on all fronts and in other neighborhoods, were to be brought in to vent their rage.

City officials grew concerned about what children living in the Quality Inn would see and hear during the protest, so they threw together a field trip to the Children's Museum of Manhattan. David signed on. He'd take Kiara and get out of there. He'd been sharing his experiences on Facebook, and that day he gave his followers a play-by-play of the situation.

"I'm currently getting assistance from the city of New York," he said, before turning his phone camera on the Quality Inn behind him. "So today, at 10 a.m., that building with lights on it will be protested." It was around six o'clock, and now he panned the camera at a stack of blue wooden barricades stamped with POLICE LINE—DO NOT CROSS.

"I never thought in a million years they would protest the homeless," he continued. "Women and children. Women, men, and children. Babies.

"I won't let my daughter be a part of that. If somebody says something to my daughter, that's it. Me and baby girl are going out for the day. I'm about to show her a good time."

A few hours later the father and daughter boarded a yellow school bus. The chants had already begun. "Why are they protesting?" Kiara asked. She wondered if it was something to do with civil rights or police reform. Her father had told her about the Black Lives Matter movement.

"They're not protesting you. They're protesting the situation," David said, comforting Kiara with a half-truth.

They took the bus ride from Floral Park to the red-brick Children's Museum on the Upper West Side of Manhattan, about an hour's drive with traffic. The entrance was bright orange and blue; walking up the ramp, you could almost imagine that you were heading into a rainbow. Inside, Kiara pretended to drive a bus, she slid down a short pole as if she were a firefighter, and she played in a sandbox indoors. She and David munched on pizza provided by the city and got lost in the exhibits. As they rode the school bus back to the Quality Inn, Kiara laid her head on her father's shoulder. The angry protesters had gone, but the barricades were still up.

On television that night, Kiara saw the protest on the news. "Are we going to get kicked out?" she asked.

"You don't have anything to worry about. Daddy has it under control," David told her, not so much a half-truth as it was a lie.

David had no control, and neither did the de Blasio administration.

The city released its own video that evening, showing children and their parents on the field trip juxtaposed against the protesters promenading along Jericho Turnpike. A man banged a drum as if going into battle. People waved signs that said DE BLASIO HAS GOT TO GO and FIRE THE LIAR, referring to Banks.

That video, however, did little to change the minds of residents around Floral Park and did little to persuade the owner of the Quality Inn and the nearby Bellerose Inn, which was also being used as a shelter, to continue housing homeless families. The hotel owner had already signed an agreement with elected officials to phase out families by January 1, 2017, but the mayor's administration was making every effort to change his mind. That didn't happen; the demonstrations had been effective.

De Blasio was enraged—at the hotel owner, at the protests, and at the implied threats to Banks and his family. He fumed at a press conference in early October.

"Some of them have said disgusting things," he said of demonstrators. "They've also threatened my social services commissioner and his family, which I find reprehensible."

He dared the public to continue protesting. "I welcome their pickets as many times as they want because I will happily stare them down. We are going to put a roof over people's heads."

With the Quality Inn out of business as a shelter, David and Kiara needed a new place to stay. The city moved them into the Sleep Inn just after New Year's Day.

The guilt of missing a decade of Kiara's life, only to have custody as a homeless father, weighed heavily on David. In the caseworkers' room at the Sleep Inn, where he had to check in and out, get updates on potential rental assistance vouchers, and pick up meals, David encountered the woman who would change both his life and his daughter's life.

"She should come to Girl Scouts," a cheerful Giselle said to David on the afternoon they met. Kiara was standing next to her father as if they were attached.

Giselle smiled at Kiara and asked her directly, "Do you want to join Girl Scouts?"

In the next few weeks David saw Kiara transform from a deeply guarded girl to an outgoing ten-year-old who could not wait to get to the breakfast room on Fridays. Lanye, who kept in touch with Kiara through video calls, could not believe how her normally withdrawn daughter had become so chatty. The Girl Scouts had been the first activity to interest Kiara since she arrived in New York—she was missing her mother and siblings in Philadelphia—so David had to see for himself what all the fuss was about. The hotel was so abuzz that David took a picture of Kiara's green vest the night before he attended his first meeting with her and posted it on Facebook.

At the meeting with Jimmy Van Bramer celebrating the one-month anniversary of the troop as well as local women politicians, David took photo after photo with the camera on his phone. His favorite was the one of his daughter with a big smile on her face getting her First Aid Badge pinned to her vest and reaching her arm around the other Scouts to share in the ribbon cutting.

The restaurant where David worked had closed for renovations, so when Giselle asked if he would help chaperone Troop 6000's trip to Yankee Stadium a little over a month after the ribbon-cutting ceremony with Jimmy, he said yes.

For much of his childhood, kids had teased David for being effeminate, deriding him for his love of cooking and sewing and crafts. David was bisexual, and one of his only heterosexual relationships had been with Kiara's mother. Girl Scouts made David feel that all of his hobbies and skills were appreciated. Giselle had grown into a master crafter, and they quickly bonded over the talent to turn nothing into something. David thought Troop 6000 needed to make a splash at the baseball game, so he and Giselle went to Michaels craft store in Woodside and bought a white satin sheet and alphabet letters and familiar objects made of felt.

Afterward, Giselle took him to lunch at Boston Market, where they talked about their childhoods and Troop 6000, and that's when she asked, "Would you like to be a troop leader?"

The national Girl Scouts organization had been encouraging troops around the country to enlist fathers, uncles, and male guardians to assume roles as troop leaders in a campaign called "Man Enough to Be a Girl Scout," which had given Giselle the idea of approaching David. David had never even thought about being a Boy Scout when he was growing up in Philadelphia. Now he would be a Girl Scout leader?

Well, yes. He decided he couldn't wait another minute to be more involved. Back at the Sleep Inn, he pushed two tables together inside the breakfast room and spread out the sheet, and he and Giselle worked on the banner off and on for the next three days.

Yankee Stadium could hold more than fifty-four thousand people. On Sunday, April 30, the Yankees were facing off against the Orioles, but more important than who they were opposing was who they were celebrating: It was Girl Scout Day. All of the Scouts in attendance would get to line up on the great green expanse of Yankee Stadium's field before the game began. There were so many Scouts it seemed that they took up the majority of those fifty-four thousand seats, and David could not stop smiling, even when he was trying to be stern with girls who were so nervous and fidgety that they could barely walk in a straight line. But their contagious giggles infected David, who tried his best to act how he thought an experienced troop leader would act. "Signs up!" he yelled out, holding up three fingers on his right hand to form the Girl Scouts sign, his voice screeching like a whistle. Kiara, Sanaa, Brithani, Tanae and Tiana, and the other Scouts followed his directions.

Troop 6000—twenty girls strong that day—lined up with other troops from all over the city and waited their turn to go out on the field. But the city's newest troop clearly stood out in brand-new kelly-green T-shirts with TROOP 6000 in white letters. And just as they walked out into public view, they unfurled their striking banner: TROOP 6000 SLEEP INN. When David and Giselle were creating the banner, they wondered what they could say with pieces of felt. They wanted to eradicate homelessness, and they wanted people to understand that families should not be stuffed into hotel rooms with no kitchens and no privacy.

Next to the words TROOP 6000 SLEEP INN was the image of a hotel with a wrecking ball swinging into it. The crowd cheered.

# 13

# RICH PEOPLE STUFF

**GISELLE HAD NEVER** attended an event that required "the perfect dress," but now she and several of the girls were going to the annual fundraising gala of the Girl Scouts of Greater New York. The invitation had come on short notice, a last-minute overture made as a result of the publicity swirling around Troop 6000.

It was to be held on May 1, the night after the outing to Yankee Stadium. When they all returned to the Sleep Inn after watching the Orioles beat the home team 7–4, Giselle spent the night online, studying photos from the previous year's gala. She couldn't afford a dress—every penny was being saved toward the rent of the apartment she envisioned in her future, the apartment about which she could only dream now. But the Girl Scouts had the answer: They provided a modest wardrobe allowance to employees who were asked to attend grand events like the gala but couldn't afford the proper outfit.

That day was a busy one. When lunchtime came, she rushed to the Dress Barn on Maiden Lane off Pearl Street, not far from the Girl Scouts office. Giselle didn't want to get too gussied up, but she did want her outfit to have some oomph. The weather was getting warmer, so she reasoned she could go sleeveless: She spotted the lacy pink, sparkly dress almost as soon as she walked in the store, and then spotted the shoes—a pale rosebud pink—at the register. Total cost: $120.

After work and back in Queens at the Sleep Inn, where the family's personal belongings and Girl Scouts supplies were stacked in plastic bins pushed against the walls, Giselle flat-ironed her frizzy hair into a sleek do that flowed below her neck. The singed aroma of straightening hair wafted through the room. Other parents pitched in, excited to see Giselle represent them at such a fancy soiree. Tawanda Brown, Tiana and Tanae's mother, lent Giselle her faux pearl necklace and bracelet, telling Giselle that sharp as the outfit was, it needed a little something extra. David corralled the Scouts who were going to the gala, distracting them so Giselle could finish getting ready. Then he gave Giselle some silver nail polish that he had bought for Kiara. Giselle balanced herself on the edge of the bed and propped her feet up as she painted her toenails. They'd hardly dried before she squeezed herself into the dress and slid on the shoes. She carried a pink purse, too.

Karina gaped at her mother. "Mommy, you look so pretty!"

"Your hair looks good," said Hailey, who had styled her own hair, shaping two tiny buns on either side in the front and then letting the back hang down.

Some of the girls' parents had groomed their daughters for the Yankees game the day before. Mickyle had braided Sanaa's hair into an elaborate series of cornrows, adding some weave so that it ran past her shoulders with gold beads for accents. David had twisted Kiara's hair into dozens of strands until his thick fingers had grown numb.

David was not going to let all of that primping go to waste. Buzzing around like a parent on prom night, he gathered Giselle and the half dozen Scouts in the lobby for a group photo. "Smile," he said, minutes before a black SUV pulled up to shuttle them to the event. Standing in a row, the girls looked like they were being featured on one of the posters in a hair salon that beauticians use to help customers pick a hairstyle. Kiara, being devilish, gave a half grin. David insisted on more pictures, making Giselle pose in front of the Sleep Inn and then taking still more photos as she climbed into the passenger seat and as the girls piled into the back. They all waved to David as they rode off in style, slipping on leather seats and enjoying the city views. The SUV dipped into the Midtown Tunnel beneath the East River and emerged on the other side into the bright lights of Manhattan.

ıllıllıllıllıllıllılıl

The Scouts stepped onto the inlaid floors of Cipriani 42nd Street and into glamour that they had only seen in movies. They posed for photos at a step and repeat, a red carpet ritual they'd thought was reserved for celebrities only. A bartender served them Shirley Temples—which they learned were ginger ales with splashes of grenadine topped with cherries—as big-money donors walked around with glasses of champagne, wine, and cocktails. Giselle had limited the event to the older Scouts because she thought they would better manage being in the middle of all the hoopla with adults. The girls tried to blend in, holding up their glasses to toast because they thought that's what they were supposed to do with cocktails. At each round table, boxes of cookies were assembled to look like pyramid centerpieces, and Kiara's eyes widened as she looked down at the place settings—there were so many utensils. Her most extravagant culinary outings had been to buffet restaurants with her grandparents, to chain restaurants like Red Lobster and Chili's with her mother, and to diners with David.

The room at Cipriani was cavernous; guests chatted, clinked glasses, bumped into one another as they jostled to the open bars for more drinks and then searched for their tables. To the girls, the marble columns seemed to ascend as high as the sky. It was a little overwhelming—the huge, elegant room; the well-wishers and huggers inundating them; the people who wanted to cuddle them or shake their hands, bending down to talk to them.

"Congratulations!"

"How old are you?"

"What grade are you in?"

"Are you having fun?"

"I saw you on TV."

"You're the girls I saw in *The New York Times*."

"Are you her daughters?" several asked Hailey and Karina.

A table for ten cost a minimum of $10,000. At one table, Giselle and the half dozen members of Troop 6000 took up seven seats; three women, strangers who Giselle assumed had money, took up the remaining three places. The table was not far from the stage but not in the front row either.

The next hour was a crash course in etiquette and rich people stuff. Salad, steak, desserts, this fork, that spoon, this knife, that glass for water, this glass for wine, a cup for coffee, this speaker, that speaker, this awardee, that awardee. People held up numbers to bid in an auction. An eager man excitedly paid $2,200 for a case of Thin Mints and a glass of milk, which were delivered to his table on a silver tray with fanfare. He threw in another $9,000 for Troop 6000. The girls kept craning their necks to see who bid on what, as numbers on yellow pieces of paper flew up in the air each time the auctioneer, a blond woman who talked so fast that she sounded like a rapper spitting rhymes, pointed to a winner and yelled "Sold!" into a microphone. Phoenix, a ten-year-old whose family had become homeless after returning to New York from Memphis, jumped up after each "Sold!" as if she had won something.

Troop 6000 was given special recognition as the first troop for girls in shelter, sending Giselle, Heidi, and Meridith into tears. At the end, the Troop 6000 girls joined all of the other Scouts who had been invited that night and together they took a collective bow on stage.

But they could not stay for the after-party; they had to make it back to the Sleep Inn as close to the nine o'clock curfew as possible.

In the last moments before their departure, Kiara ambled

around the tables, encouraging the other Scouts to join her in grabbing boxes of cookies that people had left behind. "We can sell these," Kiara said. Sanaa wasn't so sure they could do that, but she knew that they could eat them. They loaded them into the SUV that was waiting on Forty-second Street to shuttle them back to the Sleep Inn. After they piled in, there were so many boxes they could barely see above them.

As the SUV started its journey back toward Queens, back through the Midtown Tunnel and into the dark streets of Long Island City, the girls watched as the lights of Manhattan were replaced by the sheer tiled walls of the tunnel and then the familiar shapes and sights of their temporary neighborhood.

The $10,000 table, the man who bid all that money for the milk and cookies, the other Scouts, so alike yet so different, seemed almost instantly like a dream. For all the boxes piled around and on top of them, these Scouts couldn't even sell cookies where they lived.

Soon Giselle and the girls were back in their crowded rooms, back to beds with parents and siblings and sharing covers stamped with PROPERTY OF DHS. Back to being homeless and dreaming of a day when they weren't.

# 14

# LIFESTYLES OF THE POOR AND FAMOUS

EVERY FLOOR AT the Sleep Inn looked alike to Hailey. It was a maze of sameness. The carpeting was a deep brown, like the color of chestnuts before they popped open as street vendors roasted them. Troop 6000 Scouts had found camaraderie not only in being homeless but in living in the exact same rooms. No one had a nicer desk or a softer bed. The Sleep Inn had no class system. Everyone was the same.

Each floor also had an ice machine, and Hailey could hear the cubes dropping into a bucket when she spotted Genesis and started to approach her. Her mom had run into Genesis on the elevator the day of the Yankees game, and in their brief chat before the sound of the ding and the doors opening to the lobby, Giselle tried to persuade Genesis to return to the troop. "We are going on a lot of trips. We're going to the Yankees game," Giselle had said. "The meetings are more fun. We need you."

"Is Hailey going to be there?" Genesis had asked.

It suddenly dawned on Giselle that Genesis had been disappointed when Hailey had missed a meeting to babysit Gillesy and Judas. When Hailey was not at a meeting, Genesis was the oldest Scout by far. She was overwhelmed by the responsibility of not only helping her sister Brithani—answering her questions, rounding up crayons and other supplies for her—but juggling the similar requests from a half dozen other younger girls asking her for help at the same time.

And so Giselle had dispatched Hailey to find Genesis and explain to her the benefits of sticking with the Scouts.

"Are you going to be there?" Genesis now asked Hailey as they stood in the hallway.

Hailey assured her that she would be at the meetings and that Genesis would not regret coming back.

"Well?" Giselle asked Hailey later.

"She said she would." Hailey shrugged and left it at that.

Days later, there was an unexpected knock on Giselle's door. She rolled her eyes, scanned the room to make sure her electric skillet was hidden, and opened the door. But it wasn't an inspector; it was Genesis.

"I miss everyone," she burst out. Genesis tried not to cry, but she couldn't help it.

"You kept your promise!" Giselle said, hugging her. After the tears, she released Genesis from her embrace and waded through the supplies piled up in her room to find Genesis's khaki vest.

|||||||||||||||||||||||||||

The next weeks were filled with tumult and confusion, the growing pains of the poor and famous. Giselle was being praised as a leader but could not lead her family out of the shelter. In an attempt to get a coveted public housing apartment, she had gone so far as to ask Jimmy's office to put in a good word. But Jimmy's recommendations and Giselle's promise to be a model tenant could not overcome bad credit and the need to find an apartment big enough for five children that she could afford on her $37,500 salary.

She kept hunting for housing and kept showing up for events representing Troop 6000, as asked. Jimmy tapped her to serve on the community board for Long Island City. Giselle was now in a decision-making position, one in which she could help to shape the community's response to shelters. But she had to juggle the meetings on top of everything else. So she called in reinforcements for childcare: Wally, who had been released from jail, Chris, Manny, and Evelyn, were all happy to fill in as necessary.

Evelyn was in awe of her daughter. Almost a year ago Giselle had become homeless and now she was a superstar on television.

"How are you the way that you are?" Evelyn kept asking her. "I didn't teach you anything."

Giselle would reassure her, "Yes, you did. I could not have done this without you."

The pandemonium, however good most of it was, made it hard for Giselle to find time for herself; she realized she was starting to miss those moments when she and Cori would stand outside the Sleep Inn and just talk.

Cori was taking classes to get certified to care for adults with special needs and she sometimes had trouble finding a babysitter for Trey, which pulled her away from Scout meetings. She was searching for a more fulfilling job, and she was flattered and surprised—and a little suspicious, too—when in April Meridith asked her for her résumé the same day that a reporter from *The New York Times* first attended a meeting. Cori had received a voucher from the city to move out of the shelter, but she didn't want to look for an apartment until she had a steady job that would allow her to keep up with the rent.

The city's rental assistance voucher system, which was supposed to help more than sixty thousand people climb out of shelters, was a jumble of different initiatives. Steven Banks had adopted a philosophy that homelessness was not "one size fits all," nor were potential solutions: There were different city, state, and federal vouchers based on income, family size, history of domestic violence, diagnosis of AIDS or HIV, and whether a person was working, underemployed, unemployed, or a veteran. The vouchers had an array of names, most shortened into acronyms. No one could ever remember what they stood for.

In front of the Sleep Inn, people talked about their voucher status like they talked about the weather.

"What voucher do you have?"

"SEPS."*

"I've got FEPS."

"Do you have a housing specialist?"

"No, but I heard I can get a LINC II."

"Wait. There's more than one LINC?"

David still did not have a voucher; he was frequently calling Vapiano, trying to get clarity on which days he was supposed to come in now that the restaurant was finally ready to reopen.

But he was also facing a much bigger problem than settling his work schedule: Kiara's health.

On May 9 and 10, she woke up with debilitating headaches, unable to catch her breath. On the eleventh, a Thursday morning, David panicked, calling 911 and climbing into the back of an ambulance with his daughter as they raced to the hospital. They were rushed into the emergency room, where he held her hand and told her everything was going to be okay. A doctor gave her a steroid shot and a nurse hooked her up to a machine that pumped oxygen, and Kiara was finally able to breathe in and out, in and out. She looked up at David in fright and confusion.

"I wish I could just make all of this go away," David told her.

Kiara, who'd had health problems when she lived in Philadelphia, suffered from severe asthma, and it was going to be necessary to set up a monthly payment plan to cover the expense of her doctors' appointments. The ambulance ride and emergency room visit were already more than $5,000. David felt as if he were digging himself into a bottomless pit of debt.

Troop 6000 began to suffer as well, a victim of its own success. Fridays became mad rushes to get ready for the meetings because so many people who had read about the girls or had seen

* SEPS is the Special Exit and Prevention Supplement; FEPS is the Family Eviction Prevention Subsidy. LINC stands for Living in Communities and is subdivided into LINC I, LINC II, and LINC III.

them on Facebook or TV wanted to volunteer. They wanted to read books to the girls; they wanted to teach the girls about horses; they wanted to give them fancy shampoo.

The New York Liberty, the popular professional women's basketball team, hosted the troop for an action-packed day, showering them with swag—T-shirts, headbands, and wristbands—until the girls were covered in paraphernalia. The WNBA team treated them to lunch at Planet Hollywood, where Karina covered her plate with French fries and sat next to her idol Ta'Shauna "Sugar" Rodgers, a guard who had surpassed men's records while she played basketball at Georgetown University and shot her way to being the school's leading scorer of all time.

In between lunch and an evening game, the players also took the girls to see *Wonder Woman*. As he passed buttery bags of popcorn to the girls at the movie theater, David shook his head in disbelief at all of the gifts and the free food. The girls downed sodas at Planet Hollywood, at the movies, and then at the game, where the Liberty beat the Seattle Storm. By the time Troop 6000 headed to the Sleep Inn on the F train, some of the girls were complaining of stomachaches.

Giselle tried to juggle all the invites. But she started to experience a new emotion, one that contradicted all the good luck she seemed to be having, at least publicly: resentment. So many well-meaning people wanted to give the girls backpacks and school supplies and clothes, never thinking that the girls lived in crowded hotel rooms and had nowhere to put everything. Just how many backpacks did one kid need?

The one thing people didn't seem to be handing out was housing. Workers at the Sleep Inn became less and less cooperative, even a little annoyed at all the hubbub. And Giselle was dead tired: She had a full-time job with the Girl Scouts, a full-time job being homeless, and a full-time job talking about being homeless.

The meetings began to feel slapdash. David, in charge one Friday, had to think quickly when he could not track down the key to open the breakfast room. So he marched the Scouts to P.S. 111 to run around in the playground. The girls skipped through the desolate stretch of Thirteenth Street in front of the hotel and wound their way on more ghostlike streets until they got to the school, singing "There Was a Great Big Moose" along the way.

Now one of their biggest appearances was coming up: *The View*, the daytime talk show on ABC that drew nearly three million viewers each morning. A camera crew came to the hotel and taped hours of footage for a video that would be shown during the live taping at the studio. All of the parents could tell their families to tune in at eleven o'clock to watch their children on national television without worrying that they would miss the segment; no need to search on the Internet for the right link. For David, it was all about Whoopi Goldberg—he had watched *Sister Act* too many times to count. He made her a T-shirt with her face on it and planned to give it to her. He and Giselle would yell out "Whoopi!" every once in a while in excitement.

The girls were asked to give *The View* a list of their favorite celebrities, and maybe, just maybe, one of them would show up as a surprise.

Who was the special guest? everyone wondered.

"Shawn Mendes!" Karina screamed on the chartered bus on the way to the studio. Giselle and David led the girls in singing songs, including Beyoncé's "Run the World (Girls)."

Karina swayed her head and Brithani wiggled in her seat as the bus fought traffic to get to the studio off Central Park, not far from Columbus Circle. Genesis looked out the window but smiled whenever Giselle and David would pass her singing, "Who run the world?"

Genesis was a little worried because Hailey was not coming. Judas was graduating from pre-K that day, and Hailey, though disappointed to miss a visit to a television studio and a chance to meet celebrities, wanted to be sure someone from the family would be there for Judas in case there were any delays getting back to Queens after the taping. She thought it was important that they not forget their family obligations—their priorities—as they all got swept up in the publicity.

"Can I sit here?" Kiara asked Genesis, sliding into the aisle seat.

"Okay," Genesis said, laughing. She was beginning to notice that Kiara always wanted to be close to her. There were plenty of seats on the charter bus, and they were all luxuriously soft and roomy, but here was Kiara, sitting right next to her.

Kiara looked like a sophisticated Raggedy Ann doll. Her father had twisted red yarn into her hair to add some flair for the special occasion. David continued to dance through the aisle of the bus, belting out "Who run the world?"

"Girls!" Kiara sang back.

The studio was air-conditioned to the point of refrigeration, a temperature that took some getting used to, but the girls followed the instructions of directors and producers during a rehearsal. They were arranged on blocks in twos and threes and told to smile and act surprised when surprises were announced. That was easy, since they didn't know what was happening; they were already amazed at the lights, cameras, and bustle of it all.

Giselle was thankful to be sitting in a chair surrounded by a team of busy beauty experts. The hairdresser straightened and curled her hair into a classic Michelle Obama look—a part slightly off-center to the left, and then swept to the right—and the makeup artist painted her lips a translucent pink.

Giselle wore a navy dress, black leggings, and her best pair of black booties, her dressiest and least worn-out shoes. She topped the ensemble off with a green Girl Scouts scarf. Sitting with Karina on one of the blocks as Whoopi Goldberg introduced the segment, she grew misty-eyed when she saw herself appear in a pre-taped interview at the Sleep Inn. Onscreen, too, Giselle was weepy: "My name is Giselle Burgess, and I am the troop leader of Troop 6000. I'm scared myself. I don't know where I'm going to be tomorrow. I don't know how long it's going to take me to find a home. I know they must feel the same way. They're children. They kind of get dragged into this, and it's not their fault."

The segment showed the girls happily singing and marching through the lobby of the Sleep Inn to the breakfast room, and then becoming more serious as they talked about homelessness. Giselle and Karina answered a couple of questions from Whoopi and Sara Haines, the co-host. Karina, now a pro, was brief in her response to how the Girl Scouts had helped her and the other girls: "It gives us confidence. It makes us part of the group. They're all my sister Girl Scouts and I love them all."

The audience said, "Awwwww."

Then the fun began. Whoopi introduced Karen Ideno, a vice president of Toyota, who popped up in the front row of the audience and said the automaker would donate $75,000 for the troop to attend Urban Day Camp, a seven-week program that the Girl Scouts held each summer where Scouts from second to fifth grade learn about subjects like animals, plant life, first aid, and space. The audience applauded; the girls put on their astonished faces as they'd been told to do in rehearsal; and Whoopi continued to work the room. "Isn't there more?" she asked Ideno.

The camera cut to co-hosts Sunny Hostin and Jedediah Bila, who were outside with a white Toyota Highlander with a green ribbon on it. The girls clapped and grinned in disbelief. But Whoopi, hamming it up, told Ideno that she felt there was still more. Then Hostin and Bila opened the trunk of the car to reveal laptop computers for the whole troop.

*The View* had to break for commercial, but Haines promised one more "huge surprise."

The lights dimmed and an acoustic guitarist sat on a stool and entertained everyone during the break. Then they were back on air again, and in walked twenty-year-old Alessia Cara, a singer who had been topping the R&B and pop charts, and who also had a massively popular cover of the theme song from the Disney film *Moana*, so Troop 6000 was familiar with the young star, to say the least. The girls tried to control their excitement, jumping off the blocks and then immediately sitting back down, remembering the directors' instructions.

"You should know you're beautiful just the way you are, and you don't have to change a thing, the world could change its heart," Cara sang as some of the girls began crying. Genesis, thinking about how her family was so relieved to be in the United States yet so miserable to be homeless, buried her face in her hands. Brithani wiped her face with the sleeve of her sweat-shirt. Karina, so proud to be part of Troop 6000, wiped tears away with both of her hands. Sanaa held it together, though her eyes, too, welled with tears.

Giselle also held it together, but David was sobbing. "You were ugly crying," she told him, laughing and trying to lighten the mood once the taping ended. All he could do was shake his head and smile.

||||||||||||||||||||

The next week, David walked into work at Vapiano on Thursday and a manager told him that he'd been terminated. "No show, no call" was the reason given. That meant David hadn't called in to find out whether Vapiano needed him, nor had he shown up to check his schedule. David acknowledged that two days earlier, unable to meet Vapiano's on-call last-minute demands, he had simply not shown up to work as requested. David hadn't had time to figure out his schedule with Kiara. Before the renovations, David had arranged for a friend to pick Kiara up at school when he was unable to, and the friend was the one who first dropped her off at the Scout meetings. At other times, David left work, picked Kiara up from school, and returned to work, while she sat in the dining area and did her homework.

David had worked at Vapiano locations from Washington, D.C., to New York City, and he had never felt stable. His schedule was dependent on the whim of managers. As he was the single parent of a child with a health challenge, this uncertainty created conflicts that were sometimes unavoidable—not to mention a huge amount of stress and desperate eleventh-hour searching for childcare.

No rights, no health care, and little gain at minimum wage—these were the hazards of working in fast food and retail. Two weeks before David was fired, Mayor de Blasio and the city council signed a package of legislative bills to put an end to the unstable schedules and unsteady paychecks of fast-food workers. Under the new laws, employers had to give workers their schedules fourteen days in advance, end back-to-back shifts, and offer current employees shifts before hiring new employees. David would have had the right to object to his termination except for the fact that the laws were six months away from going into effect.

David had never been to culinary school, but after toiling for nearly a decade as a line cook at Vapiano, he'd aspired to move up to management and become a chef or a caterer. There was no way that would happen now.

"Mom, I'm not going to have any money for me and Kiara to eat this weekend," David confided in his mother on the phone as he moved chairs and tables to get the breakfast room ready for a troop meeting.

"What are we going to do?" Kiara asked.

David hadn't meant for her to overhear him. "Maybe this is what I needed," he said a little more optimistically. "What, was I was gonna work at Vapiano for the rest of my life?"

When David told Giselle the news she tried to encourage him, telling him that he would land another job, but she had her own problems. Her struggle to find an apartment wasn't getting any easier. Taking notice of her increased duties with Troop 6000, the Girl Scouts of Greater New York had given Giselle a $10,000 raise. She was now making nearly $50,000, but other potential tenants were beating her to apartments; they had better credit scores and more money saved. She sent her housing caseworker an email listing a half dozen apartments she had found, all of them out of reach for her income, with landlords refusing to take her LINC I voucher or flagging her low credit score. There was a three-bedroom apartment in Bayside for $2,200; a three-bedroom apartment in Elmhurst for $1,750; another three-bedroom on Forty-ninth Avenue in Hunter's Point for $2,200.

It was just a list to Giselle. None of these places seemed real to her. She fought to maintain balance: Troop 6000, the responsibilities of being a single mother, making appearances, and looking for housing within her budget. How was she supposed to do it all at the same time, especially when apartments kept falling through?

There had been close calls. One frigid Saturday in March she and her co-workers were unloading hundreds of cases of Girl Scout cookies from two tractor trailers that had traveled twelve hours from Louisville, Kentucky, to Our Lady of Lourdes in Queens Village; the parish generously offered its parking lot to the Girl Scouts every cookie season.

Temperatures were below freezing, but Shaquna Johnson, Giselle's cubicle buddy in the office, cheered everyone on. "It's cookie time!" Shaquna screamed. Enthusiastically, Giselle joined in. "Cookies! Cookies! Cookies!"

Giselle's phone rang. Her knit gloves were frozen to her numb fingers as she dug for it in her coat pocket. It was a social worker, who told her, "There's an apartment available, but you have to go see it today. Here's the address."

Giselle asked Meridith if she could leave work early.

"Go, go!" Meridith shot back.

Giselle jumped in an Uber, reasoning that the carfare that she could not afford would be worth it if she got the apartment. She and the driver raced across Queens. They were minutes away when Giselle's phone rang again. It was the social worker. Too late. "The apartment is no longer available."

Giselle heard nothing after those words, as if she had gone deaf.

The Uber driver glanced sympathetically at her in his rearview mirror and asked Giselle what she wanted to do. "Take me to the Sleep Inn," she answered, never even looking up, worried that she would start to cry if she met his eyes. They both worked their apps to cancel the ride and then order another one. Giselle had spent more than $100 on round-trip carfare for nothing. *If it's for me, God will give it to me,* she thought. *I'm not going to try to keep doing this on my own.*

# 15

# ANNIVERSARY

THE EARLY JULY weather shifted between warm and humid and damp and chilly, a back-and-forth that mirrored Giselle's up-and-down life. It had been almost a year since she and her family had moved into the Sleep Inn. Eleven months with six people jammed into one hotel room with one bathroom, one closet, and no kitchen. The apartment search was becoming increasingly frustrating even though a glimmer of hope had appeared recently.

Childrens Community Services had assigned a new housing specialist to Giselle's case. His name was Roger Prince, and he was stocky and solid, with a round face and a build like a football player's. He radiated enthusiasm and optimism for the task ahead. He was making promises to find her a home, but Giselle had already been so disappointed that she did not fully believe him.

Roger was a Guyanese immigrant who had stumbled into social services. When he first moved to the United States two decades earlier, he got a job mopping floors and taking out trash at an Au Bon Pain. He worked his way up to sandwich maker, crew leader, shift manager, and assistant manager. After years of toiling there, and working in demolition and construction with his brother, Roger took a job driving homeless people who were searching for apartments from place to place.

He learned more about the apartments, and how to connect people and landlords. Just like at Au Bon Pain, he worked his way from the bottom to the top, from driver to housing specialist, supervisor, and then director. Childrens Community Services had poached him from another nonprofit that would eventually lure him back with more money and a promotion.

He threw himself into the hunt. Giselle was special, he thought. He saw a woman who worked incredibly hard to get back on her feet and who'd done so much for others. But it was clear to him that she was getting discouraged by all the big disappointments she'd already endured, as promising lead after promising lead had fallen through. There was only so much disappointment one could bear and remain resilient.

As much as Giselle was heartened by his attitude and his efforts, she was frustrated with his demands that she go to see apartments during her work hours. People in the shelter were managing work, children, and the boundless reams of paperwork. Giselle felt that most of the shelter staff looked down on them, as if they were not working hard enough. "I have to work. I'm not sitting in my room on my butt collecting a welfare check," she told him.

In her darker moments, she wondered about the reasons behind the tremendous outpouring of attention Troop 6000 received. Was it because people felt better about themselves when they saw others less fortunate than them suffer? Donations flowed in to Troop 6000; the troop had even been given a car on television. But she wasn't driving that car. It had been a gift to the Girl Scouts of Greater New York, and the nonprofit still needed to work out how it would be used. All the while, Giselle still didn't have enough money to move her children out of the Sleep Inn. She resented her self-imposed selflessness, even as she recognized it as one of the Christian values her pastor espoused at Evangel Church. But she still felt sorry for herself. Couldn't she maybe be a little more selfish? Just this once?

The Scouts themselves, after all, were growing more and more unappreciative, she thought. The girls were going places she had never dreamed of; they were being lavished with praise and gifts, but she had to constantly remind them to say thank you. And they weren't even satisfied with all of the privileges coming their way. Cookies came up again and again. When could they sell them? Why couldn't they sell them in the very building where they lived? Somehow, they felt they weren't true Girl Scouts because they weren't selling cookies. Giselle grew tired of having to explain the rules.

Some of the girls showed up at events without wearing their vests yet dripping with attitude. They bickered constantly. Giselle had to remind them again and again to share, to be quiet, and to work together. An accidental bump in the hallway would become a bigger incident. There was an unspoken etiquette in the hotel—how you waited in line for the microwave, how you held the elevator doors for parents with strollers, how smokers didn't blow in the direction of others outside the hotel, how to borrow and pay back a dollar or two or a loosie. Acting as armchair psychologists, Giselle, Cori, and David wondered if the fights and arguments among parents had trickled down to their daughters.

Giselle worried about the girls who were just acting out their parents' frustrations, but she was also angry with them and angry with herself. She was beginning to wonder if she even wanted the girls' hugs anymore because she wondered if they were genuine. The girls, especially the younger ones, were always throwing their arms around Giselle and feeling her warm embrace in return. She was unsure of whether she deserved their affection given the resentment bubbling up inside her.

And all of these feelings were brewing as the troop prepared for its first visit to Camp Kaufmann—its first overnight trip ever.

The girls woke up to rain on the morning of their trip to the camp. *Fitting,* Giselle thought. *Perfectly fitting.* It was a year to the day that she and her family had been evicted from their Maple Avenue apartment, and tears from the sky seemed an appropriate response to an anniversary that no one wanted to celebrate.

The Scouts straggled into the breakfast room at different levels of preparedness and excitement. One minute they were eager and sisterly, the next minute they were fighting over crayons and markers and construction paper as they waited in line for snacks and for the chartered bus that would carry them out of the city. And true to recent form, too many of them weren't wearing their vests.

"Where are your vests?" Giselle yelled as David passed the girls the breakfasts that the shelter staff had given him to distribute—graham crackers and cereal in plastic disposable bowls. David was man enough to be a Girl Scout, but he wasn't woman enough to go on the trip. A male chaperone for an overnight trip was forbidden, so David helped out where he could, and that morning it was in the breakfast room.

"And where are your ANDI bags?" Giselle added.

A week earlier, Andrea Weinberg, a rising-star entrepreneur who had found a way to combine her love of the outdoors and fashion, had given each of the girls an ANDI bag—a stylish black waterproof backpack that could be reconfigured into a purse—after she'd spoken to them about creating their own businesses. The bags were sold in high-end yoga stores and boutiques, retailing for $188. The girls had earned Entrepreneur Badges at that meeting, and Giselle thought the least they could do was take pictures of themselves carrying the bags to send to the enthusiastic young businesswoman who had once been a Girl Scout herself.

That meeting with the entrepreneur had not started well. Some Scouts were tardy, and some had shown up without their vests. And all of them, or almost all of them, were rowdy that evening. It had taken Giselle, David, and Cori almost forty-five minutes to get the group to behave and listen. Once they calmed down the girls were as attentive as ever, but the fact that it had taken so long had deeply embarrassed Giselle.

"Hi, Miss Gigi," some of the Scouts called out, skipping the answers to the "Where are your . . ." questions. Like children naming a grandparent, the girls had come up with their own nicknames for Giselle—now she was Miss Gigi or just Gigi. Many of the young ones loved to run up and give her a hug whenever they saw her, wrapping their short arms around her waist and resting their heads on her stomach.

Now Giselle hugged back before gently extricating herself. "Go get your vests!" she instructed. "Where are your vests?"

Some of the Scouts were focusing on who wore a bathing suit beneath their uniforms and who didn't. Yes, they were going on an overnight, but a lot of the girls were more excited about getting into the pool at Camp Kaufmann. Hailey, Karina, and Christina, having gone there many times with their Sunnyside & Woodside troops, had bragged to the girls about how much fun the pool was. New York City's public pools were free, but they were crowded and had a reputation for rival gangs itching to turn a swim into a street fight—so much so that pools in the city actually had a dress code: white T-shirts only, no colors. Over the years, the city said the rule was not about gangs but about dyes bleeding into the pools. Regardless of the reason for the ban on colored T-shirts, getting to the pools could be a hardship if there wasn't one nearby. Phoenix and Jessica had once walked more than a mile, or something close to it, because they'd gotten lost even though Phoenix's older teenage brother was with them.

"If you don't have your vests," Giselle warned, "you won't go swimming."

Several panicked girls scrambled back to their rooms, returning with their ANDI bags and wearing their vests.

Ten-year-old Sanaa had everything ready to go, arriving in

the breakfast room in her Troop 6000 T-shirt and her green vest that was beginning to fill up with badges and pins and patches. She wanted badly to earn a camping patch, like Hailey. "I packed as soon as I found out we were going," she proudly told the others.

Sanaa loved seeing new places, and she yearned for open spaces. Whenever people asked her what she missed about Atlanta, she said the yard. There was nowhere to play right outside the Sleep Inn. Sanaa wanted grass and bugs. She didn't mind bugs.

She was also looking forward to getting away from her brothers. There was no privacy at all in their hotel room.

The breakfast room grew louder by the minute as girls and their parents came and went. Mothers and fathers had questions about what time they would return on Sunday and how they could get in touch with their children. These were legitimate questions, but they had already been answered in paperwork provided to all of the families, so Giselle's patience was wearing thin.

The camping trip was coming on the heels of back-to-back field trips and special guests at the troop meetings. The girls had visited Mastercard's headquarters in Manhattan. They'd spent an extravagant day with the New York Liberty basketball players. A benefactor sent them socks. The actress Jessica Alba sent them shampoo from her product line. An Olympic equestrian silver medalist talked to the girls about horseback riding at a meeting. The Troop 6000 Scouts were being heralded as superstars, and it seemed to Giselle that the girls were beginning to expect gifts, praise, and outings in the same way that children expect money from a grandparent who always gives them a dollar or two when visiting. The Scouts naturally wanted to know what was in store for them on the overnight trip—goody bags? camping gear? celebrities?—and their expectations were sky-high. Giselle didn't know how to express her uneasiness with the troop's response to all of the attention, so she sometimes came off as annoyed.

"You changed your hair!" one of the girls shouted to Cori,

who was wearing plaits woven into elaborate cornrows that formed a bun at the back of her head.

Cori laughed. "Girl, I change my hair every day."

The girls kept asking David when they were leaving. He was trying to focus on getting them fed so they wouldn't complain about being hungry on the bus. Finally he announced, "We will be pulling out in a second. Unfortunately, I'm not going."

The room let out a collective "Awwww."

When the bus at last pulled away from Thirteenth Street, Cori took one look at Giselle and could sense her frayed nerves. Immediately she took the lead and got to her feet. "Let's do some chants!"

"What day is it?" Giselle and Cori shouted.

"Camp Day!" the girls called out.

"What day is it?"

"Camp Day!"

After chants, they moved on to songs. Giselle had two new ones for the girls. "Shaving Cream" allowed the girls to almost say "shit"—but replaced the word with *shaving cream*. Another was simply called "Girl Scout Camp."

Girl Scout camp, Girl Scout camp,
Oh please, Moms, don't send me to Girl Scout camp,
The buses that they give you, they say they're mighty fine,
But when they turn the corner, they leave the wheels behind!
Girl Scout camp, Girl Scout camp,
The leaders that they give you,
They say they're mighty fine,
But when they take their makeup off,
They look like Frankenstein,
Girl Scout camp, Girl Scout camp,
The toilets that they give you, they say are mighty fine,
But when you sit upon them, a bug flies up your hind!

The songs helped to fill the hour-and-a-half trip away from the city's skyscrapers and into the quiet communities of Putnam and Dutchess counties, where a few modest family-owned farms opened their doors to tourists who drank cider, ate homemade ice cream, and rode horses. The bus passed Red Rooster Drive-In, a restaurant shaped like a barn and painted in candy cane stripes with a giant ice cream cone as a chimney stack. It looked as if it belonged in an amusement park. The girls screamed and jumped from their seats. The bus slowed down on the narrow roads and the air smelled of dampness and greenness, like a lawn that had just been mowed.

Cori, who called herself a "city girl" and like most of the girls on the bus had never been camping, was just as wonderstruck as her charges. "I don't see a corner store," Cori yelled as she leaned her arms on the headrest of a seat and gazed out the window. All of the girls got closer to the windows to catch a view of all of the trees.

"Look at the cows!" Kiara shrieked, practically putting her nose to the glass.

Hailey, Karina, and Christina were some of the quietest on the bus; they had seen the view before, the rolling hills and farm animals. They had felt the butterflies in their stomachs as the bus bumped along the road like a roller coaster. They watched as their sister Scouts, including Cori, experienced everything they already had for the first time.

"Guess what, you guys?" Cori screamed out. "We're not in Kansas anymore!"

Giselle had arranged for the Scouts to make one stop on the way to Camp Kaufmann. Even in the rain, the farm was picturesque—lush green rolling fields, a two-story white house with black shutters. Horses, cows, pigs, and chickens roamed everywhere. It was so quintessentially quaint that it had been used in films, but it also served as a getaway for countless children every year and as a place for local equestrians to train. The farm staff warned the girls not to run, and not to be surprised by one unavoidable product of farm life—poop. "It's natural. We all do it," said the owner to squeals of fascination mixed with disgust.

The farm staff gave the girls, Cori, and Giselle ponchos, and they roamed around, touching animals they had only read about in books. They explored a chicken coop, holding freshly laid eggs that warmed their hands. Almost two hours north of the city and in the woods, it was much cooler here at the farm than at home, and the rain made it feel cooler still. That just-laid eggs could warm your hands was a totally unexpected discovery.

In the stable, the girls took turns brushing quarter horses with names like Ladybug, Dusty, Amigo, Copper, and Cocoa, preparing them to ride. In another barn, girls took turns patting two calves so new to the world that they had no names. And in yet another, girls jumped back fast when the hogs grunted and ate slop. They watched two cows get milked, but it was kind of boring since they didn't get to squeeze the milk themselves; instead, a whirring machine pumped the milk out of the cows and into a steel container. But the girls laughed and gagged when one of the cows peed and pooped.

"It's all natural," the farmer reminded them again. More squeals.

In the pouring rain the girls rode the horses for about two minutes each. "Go, Miss Gigi," the girls yelled out as Giselle straddled one and threw her hand up as if she were in a rodeo. The girls stomped in puddles, mud and water seeping into their sneakers, and ran around the great expanse of farmland. But then Giselle remembered that she had told them that they couldn't run on the farm because someone could get hurt. And the farmer had said no running, too. "Stop running!" she yelled.

One of the farm staff chatted with Toni Ostini, a friend of Meridith's who'd volunteered to chaperone. In the middle of a pleasant exchange, the staffer said offhandedly that it was a shame that all of the Troop 6000 girls came from drug-addicted parents, adding that some of the others on the farm couldn't believe how smart they were. Toni, taken aback, patiently explained that the girls were homeless, they were not helpless, and that their parents were not addicted to drugs and many of them worked. The staffer, embarrassed but now better educated, nodded.

Giselle overheard the conversation and felt like crying. "That's what they think of us," she muttered to herself. "We're homeless so we must be stupid or drug addicts." It was exhausting having to explain herself, and her troop, and homelessness in general all the time. And on this day, she just didn't have the emotional strength to tell the staffer that she, the leader of Troop 6000, was homeless, too.

Giselle looked up and saw more girls running—Sanaa, Brithani, and Christina among them. Sanaa was not going to let an open space go unused and she wanted to traverse every inch.

"Stop running!" Giselle yelled again and again, embarrassed that the girls were misbehaving in front of the farm staff. "Or there will be no swimming when you get to camp," she warned. More than anything, Giselle, stuck in her own respectability politics, never wanted anyone to equate being poor with being unruly.

A little while later, Giselle told the girls, who were full from hot dogs and hamburgers that they'd eaten earlier for lunch, that it was time to go. She was agitated and unhappy with the Scouts' behavior, but she made herself put on her big smile the way she always did. "Everybody tell them how thankful we are," she said.

The girls yelled in unison, "Thank you!"

Once on the bus again, Giselle plopped down in her seat and listened to the girls argue about who was sitting with whom and how that arrangement wasn't fair and this person wasn't any fun. She closed her eyes and hoped she'd be able to make it through the weekend.

16

# UPHILL

**CAMP KAUFMANN WAS** only about twenty minutes away from the farm, but it seemed like two hours as Giselle listened to the girls squabble.

"Don't sit here."

"She's already sitting here."

"You're not my friend."

"Shut up!"

She rose out of her seat to peer into the back, but she just couldn't bring herself to go talk to the girls. She was pretty sure she'd lose it. She looked over at Cori and Toni, but they were not as perturbed as she was.

Finally the bus pulled into the camp parking lot and the girls piled off, pushing one another to get to the front. Giselle heard no one say "Excuse me" or "Sorry." She just heard "Move" or "I was here first." Her temper flared.

"I'm done," she told Cori. "I'm done."

Cori and Giselle had cried together in the past, ruminating about their lost loves, the mistakes they had made, how so many factors—some within their control, some important ones out of their control—had pushed them into homelessness. And they'd also laughed a lot together; Giselle had an incredible optimism and an occasionally devilish sense of humor. And while the past weeks and months had been unbelievable, it was clear to Cori that Giselle was losing her sense of joy.

She gave her friend a pull-it-together look.

Giselle took a breath and shouted out, "Girls, we're going to Cookie Hall first."

To get there, the Scouts would have to climb Purgatory Hill, a rocky knoll that should have been a cakewalk for girls used to hiking up subway stairs, but that afternoon the hill seemed insurmountable because many of them had tuckered themselves out running on the farm. Giselle and her daughters had warned the girls about poison ivy before the trip, and as they huffed and grunted, some of the younger girls began pointing out poison ivy that wasn't poison ivy, just a different green plant. No matter. They were excited to start identifying things in nature.

"What's that?" the girls asked as if discovering a lost treasure. It was an electrical generator sticking out of the foliage.

Camp Kaufmann, which hosted about four thousand girls every summer, was well maintained for its age; its cabins, from those with bathrooms and electricity to ones that were more rustic, were like permanent tents. Troop 6000 would stay in the more substantial Silverbirch and Carola cabins because Daisies, the youngest Scouts, were on the trip and needed more care.

They took small steps along Purgatory Hill, but the troop outpaced Kiara, who fell behind as the girls sang "You Can't Ride in My Little Red Wagon." Kiara was focusing all her attention on breathing, not singing.

Cookie Hall was a mess hall of folding tables and yellow, green, and orange plastic chairs. It was about two o'clock and other troops had just finished lunch. Troop 6000 could hear running water and clacking plates and clinking silverware, the sounds of the camp staff washing dishes. That's when they met Valerie Bell, a longtime volunteer with the Girl Scouts.

"Listen, my name is White Lightning," she said. She was in her fifties and she had a gruff demeanor that scared some of the

Daisies and Brownies. But White Lightning was actually a softy, and she'd fallen in love with the Girl Scouts when her daughter, now in her twenties and also volunteering at the camp, had been a Brownie in Queens.

Decorative gift bags filled with swimsuits and other goodies were set on one of the dining tables. Each bag had a Troop 6000 Scout's name on it and included a card from a Scout in New Jersey.

Most girls ripped into their bags to pull out the colorful swimsuits and flip-flops. They were all different—one-piece and two-piece, rainbow colors and pastels. But one of the girls flew into a tantrum. "I wanted a two-piece!" she sobbed.

Giselle told her, "Be grateful. Be humble. These girls didn't have to get you these things." Then she turned to address everyone in the mess hall. "You get what you get and you don't get upset!"

The older girls, Genesis, Hailey, and Karina, watched everything unfold but stayed out of it, like fans sitting in the stands at a game, too worried about the outcome to cheer or jeer. All three were usually responsible for their younger siblings. At camp, with adult chaperones, they were free to just be kids. They were excited to swim, row boats, and climb walls without worrying about runny noses or picking someone up from school.

The arguments all day had been among the younger girls. Sanaa shook her head, trying to tell the younger ones to stop misbehaving. Jessica and Phoenix, both ten, chimed in, as did Brithani, who was eight. But all Giselle heard were girls trying to talk over her.

"No pool!" she declared in their general direction. It worked: sudden quiet.

Now Giselle and Cori began marching them up another hill, deeper into the woods. Kiara once again dropped behind.

"Oh, shit. I forgot her inhaler," Cori panicked, and ran to get it from Giselle.

Cori rubbed Kiara's back and placed the inhaler in her mouth; she had to do the same thing with Trey, who also had asthma and had been hospitalized because of it six times. "Take a breath."

Kiara took three quick breaths, and Cori shook the inhaler and placed it to her mouth again. "You all right?" Cori asked. Kiara nodded her head.

At the end of the walk was a short, grassy hill sloping downward and opening to a pavilion and a pond. Life jackets on a clothesline made of yellow rope were tied around the pavilion. There were blue life jackets for the older girls and red ones for the younger Scouts.

"If you see a bee, don't scream. If you see a turtle, don't scream," said a friendly camp staffer.

The water was a still, deep forest green, and rowing it was the equivalent of stirring molasses with a tiny spoon. Unskilled and unfamiliar with how to hold the oars, girls in every boat argued over whether to row under or over. Some screamed that they saw a turtle. Others screamed because they didn't see a turtle. They screamed at splashing water.

"I see the turtle!"

"Where?"

"Stop splashing!"

Out of the water again, the girls migrated into cliques under the pavilion and continued to talk about one another. Then they split up in groups and experienced some firsts. Genesis hit a bull's-eye on the archery range. Hailey reached the top of a rock-climbing wall. Brithani roasted her first marshmallow over an open flame.

As the sun went down, hundreds of girls formed a friendship circle around a flagpole in front of Cookie Hall. Troop 6000 kept its distance. "I don't like those girls in the different group. They were looking at me funny," a Troop 6000 fifth grader said. She folded her arms and marched into Cookie Hall.

Despite all of the social media and the news, many of the Scouts they encountered around the camp, especially the younger Daisies and Brownies, hadn't heard of Troop 6000. But all of the girls that weekend were from New York City, either

Queens or Staten Island, so they knew that 6000 was an odd number. "Where is it?" girls would ask. Even troop leaders asked, "Where are you from?"

Giselle simply responded, "Troop 6000." She was not in the mood to give a speech about homelessness.

Cookie Hall accommodated three hundred girls and volunteers. The sound of chairs scraping the concrete floor as they were pulled out from tables blended with the clank of utensils in the kitchen and the giggling and grousing of hungry girls who had worked up an appetite. When most of the campers had finished eating, White Lightning announced that there would be dessert. "Ice pops," she said to a rush of Scouts heading her way.

An ice pop was just frozen flavored water in a plastic tube, but to a kid, it was an elixir. In bodegas, ice pops were a staple in frozen cases, an affordable treat familiar to the girls in Troop 6000.

Giselle looked up from her now lukewarm dinner of spaghetti and chicken and saw five girls, including Sanaa and Brithani, fighting, pulling at a lemon-lime ice pop. And not only were they fighting, they were fighting in front of hundreds of other Scouts. It was exactly what she hadn't wanted to happen.

Giselle's eyes welled up, and she turned to Cori. "They're taking it for granted now. All of it. If you can't be loving to each other, don't come back. I don't know what to do."

"Maybe we should hold a parent meeting when we get back," Cori offered.

"I'm done," said Giselle for the second time that day.

Troop 6000 was supposed to join all of the other troops in a group campfire, a major event of the weekend. Every troop would surround a giant campfire where they could all bond no matter their borough. Giselle had been looking forward to it as an opportunity for her girls to simply blend in. The girls in Troop 6000 had imagined the crackling fire in the darkness and eating s'mores.

Instead, Giselle yelled out, "We're not going to the campfire!"

Scouts from other troops looked up and whispered to one another. A hush fell over Troop 6000, and then the murmuring and yelling and crying started.

"We're going to the cabins," Giselle said decisively.

"See! Look what you did!" one girl said to another.

"Why can't you behave?" Sanaa asked as if she were that Scout's mother.

Hailey, Karina, and Genesis sighed, unsure of what to say.

Some of the younger girls complained as they scaled hills that felt like mountains in the dark. "Shhh!" came the response from others who realized they were already in a lot of trouble.

The darkness and silence made the uphill walk to the cabins longer, more arduous. Giselle and Cori stayed in Carola with the Daisies, Brownies, and Juniors, where they told the girls that their behavior was disappointing and that they would be skipping the campfire so that Troop 6000 could regroup. Toni stayed with the Seniors and Cadettes.

At the entrance to the older girls' cabin, Giselle stopped Hailey, Genesis, Karina, and a couple of the other Seniors and Cadettes. "Listen, I need you to come up with some team building exercises," she said, hoping to salvage something out of the trip. Toni said that she had a mobile Wi-Fi device so the girls could find activities on the Internet.

When they got inside, Hailey pulled out paper and pen and her phone to begin brainstorming. Then she paused and looked up. "I don't even understand what happened today," she said.

"They were fighting over the ice pop," Kiara said as she stretched out on the bottom of a bunk bed. Technically she belonged in the younger Scouts' cabin, but she'd always seemed more comfortable with the older girls, and she had stayed out of the spats that had bubbled up all day among the Daisies, Brownies, and Juniors, so Giselle had decided to reward her. She was also rewarding the well-behaved Tiana and Tanae, the sisters who were two years apart but looked like twins. They sat on a bunk and listened quietly.

Hailey went over activities they could do, like the trust fall.

"What's that?" Genesis asked.

Hailey explained that one girl falls back with the faith that the girls behind her will catch her.

Genesis looked skeptical. "I don't know."

"Have you seen this Shawn Mendes video?" Karina asked.

Hailey rolled her eyes at her sister.

"I know!" Kiara said. "We can watch a scary movie!"

Everyone laughed. "Are you allowed to watch scary movies?" Hailey asked.

Kiara paused a little too long. "Yes."

"No, she's not," Genesis interjected.

While the girls in Silverbirch brainstormed, the younger Scouts were still arguing inside Carola. When they'd entered the barracks-style room, they found brand-new purple sleeping bags on every bunk bed, and now they were fighting about who would sleep where.

"Put on your pajamas!" Giselle barked.

Although Giselle had been telling the girls all day that there was no showering at camp—only washups, they were supposed to be roughing it—she readied herself for a shower, needing the comfort of the cleansing water and a few minutes alone. She went through the toiletry bag stuffed inside her backpack and pulled out her epilepsy pills; she took two every morning and then two again at night. Then she stepped into the stall, where lukewarm water sputtered out of the nozzle, bringing some relief even if it did smell like rotten eggs. She'd learned by now that the smell was caused by sulfur in the well water and that it was common in this area.

Sanaa could hear the water running, and with Cori also out of the room, she decided she had to take action. She told the girls to look for paper and something to write with. "We have to write letters saying we're sorry," she said, thinking about how her mother always made her atone in writing to her teachers or her brothers when she misbehaved or hurt someone's feelings.

Somehow, that suggestion quieted the girls down and they all got to work. After she finished her letter, Christina and another girl wanted to show their fellow Scouts how to use their sleeping bags. After all, Christina had been camping before. "So you get in like this," she said, zipping the bag all the way around her head. But the zipper got stuck. Christina panicked and couldn't catch her breath.

"Miss Giselle! Miss Gigi! Help! Miss Cori!" the girls hollered.

Giselle, wearing only a thin towel, slipped her way on the tiled floor down a hallway to the girls' room. Cori, too, was half dressed as she scurried into the room. The girls were already pulling and tugging at the sleeping bag with the same force and fury that they had shown when they were fighting over the ice pop. Christina's brown hand poked out of a small hole at the top, and Brithani, Sanaa, Jessica, and Phoenix were among the girls who ripped it open. Jasmine and Juwanda, sisters just two years apart, stood with their mouths agape. Christina, her face covered in tears, gulped the air. Giselle embraced her.

In that moment, there were no cliques, just teamwork. Giselle rocked Christina in her arms, telling everyone to put on their pajamas because they were heading to Silverbirch to meet up with the rest of Troop 6000.

"We have something for you," Sanaa told Giselle.

One by one, the girls handed their notes to Giselle and Cori, most of them written in marker and crayon with misspellings and grammatical errors. Some were only pictures with no words.

Sanaa's letter was the most formal and was a sort of summary of all of their thoughts with her own personal plea. She addressed it to the "Troop 6000 Leaders." She said she understood why Giselle and Cori would want to quit. "I agree with it because there is a big amount of kids that do and makes it harder to lead Troop 6000 and I confess I am one of those kids that makes it harder, but please don't quit. It's my first year of Girl Scouts and I don't want it to end. Not now. Not ever."

Inside Silverbirch, all of the Scouts sat on a tiled floor in an imperfect circle. Under their pajamas, they wore remnants of the dirt and grime of the day, despite taking washups, all of the puddles they had stepped in, all of the perspiration from struggling with oars and bows and arrows. Giselle and Cori sat in folding chairs just outside the circle, and they watched Hailey, who resembled a preschool teacher with her glasses and authoritative tone, take charge. "Today was kind of a rough start to camp. Can we agree on that?" Hailey asked, as the girls quietly nodded their heads.

"Can we apologize?" Hailey asked, not knowing that the girls had already written the letters.

But the girls followed her directions, and a cacophony of contrition rang out.

"Sorry."

"I'm sorry."

"I apologize."

Giselle placed her head on Cori's shoulder. "Hold it together," Cori whispered to her, tearing up, too.

In the first team building exercise of the night, Hailey told the girls to share what they liked about one another.

"She's cute."

"She's smart."

"She's nice."

"I like everything about her," one Scout said, looking at Christina.

"I feel like she's my sister," another told Jessica.

Once they finished sharing with one another, they turned to Giselle and Cori. "What I love about you girls is you know how to come together. I want to continue with you girls to see you grow," Cori said.

All of the girls got up and hugged Cori and Giselle one by one.

Giselle composed herself. "What I love about all of you girls is how you are always together," she said. "It makes me feel like the whole thing isn't for nothing. We don't have our homes, but we have each other. We're kind of different than the other girls. You're all my daughters. You're all my girls."

She told them that their arguments made her feel that she wasn't doing her job properly, as if the morals of the Girl Scouts weren't getting through to them.

"Please, please, don't let me look bad in front of people," she said, asking them to come to the Scout leaders for help rather than bickering among themselves. "We will find out what's going on. I was so angry with you girls today."

And then she said she was hopeful when she saw the girls ripping into Christina's sleeping bag. "Christina. She could have been really hurt. You girls moved so quickly to help her."

Her speech rambled a bit, but it was all about love and the uniqueness of Troop 6000. Other troops didn't go on all of the extra field trips that Troop 6000 enjoyed regularly, she said. "You guys are like superstars. Be grateful. A lot of people had to go out and buy things. People are giving you things left and right.

"What happened today is going to stay in today. When we wake up tomorrow, we will try a fresh start."

The next day, everyone went to the pool.

At the flagpole, as the sun went down, Troop 6000 joined all of the other girls. No one, it turned out, was looking at them funny.

Make new friends,
But keep the old.
One is silver,
The other is gold.
A circle is round.
It has no end.
That's how long
I want to be your friend.

# 17

# KEYS

**FOR YEARS, NEW YORK CITY** mayors had used City Hall's Blue Room to make major announcements, its very elegance elevating the import of the news delivered. The blue was not quite the color of the sky on a sunny day or that of a tropical bay. The wainscot, the cornice, and all of the moldings were painted white, making the rich blue even more dramatic. The drapes were also blue, though a slightly darker hue, and accented with marigold tassels. In other words, the room was fancy even if it was smaller than the chamber where Giselle and Karina had addressed the city council three months earlier, just after the story in the *Times* ran. Now, in mid-July, as Sanaa, Karina, Christina, Tanae, and another Scout named Nyalynn entered the Blue Room, they knew what they were about to unveil was important: The city was planning to invest $1.1 million in the expansion of Troop 6000 to other homeless shelters in the five boroughs.

The reporters, camera operators, and city officials there to witness the announcement didn't know that Troop 6000 had been suffering from growing pains, or that Giselle had nearly given up on it a few days earlier during their trip to Camp Kaufmann. What they saw instead was a smiling, professional

Giselle sitting cheerily in the front row. Next to her sat the irrepressible Cori, wearing a black wig over the cornrows that had loosened with the sweat of camping.

Meridith was there, too, having been named chief executive officer of the Girl Scouts of Greater New York, effective August 1. When the president of the board of the New York organization publicly announced Meridith's appointment the following week, she said, "Meridith Maskara is a lifelong Girl Scout, and her daughters represent the fourth generation of Girl Scouting in her family. In her brief time as a GSGNY staff member—first as VP of Product and Retail Sales, then as COO—Meridith has made a huge impact in leading the council to record-breaking cookie sales, establishing additional revenue streams including our first-ever official council store, and making Girl Scouting accessible to more of NYC's young women through programs like Troop 6000, our new initiative that brings scouting to girls in the NYC shelter system. Meridith came to us after a highly successful career in branding and merchandising. She decided to pursue her passion of helping build a more just and equitable world where girls could grow up to be the great leaders they want to—and can—be."

Inside the Blue Room, the girls recognized Jimmy, a familiar face among the officials now streaming in, shaking hands and greeting one another. Steven Banks, the social services commissioner who had received the telephone threat the previous September, took the podium briefly to tell the crowded room that the Scouts would be in charge of the press conference. But before the girls approached the podium, Jimmy spoke, addressing them directly: "I hope that you know this and feel this: that what you've done is so powerful and is so, so important in changing our city for the better."

He then turned to the crowd. "Introducing the girls to make this announcement is perhaps one of my proudest accomplishments."

As he turned back to the girls once more, his gaze was proud, congratulatory, welcoming. "Here at City Hall, you're home.

Here you are to make the big, big historic announcement. Here they are—Karina, Sanaa, and Christina." The girls approached and took their places.

While Mayor de Blasio was not there, his presence could be felt at the podium, which had been specially made to fit his extra-tall frame. To accommodate other speakers, a stool was always placed underneath the podium. But even atop the stool Christina looked tiny as she stepped up to the microphone, squinting in the bright white glare of the television lights. She spoke so softly that the audience could barely hear her.

"My name is Christina," she murmured. With her head just peeking out over the podium, she was almost impossible to see.

"Down in front!" a frustrated cameraman yelled.

Christina took frequent pauses between words and phrases, giving her speech a staccato quality. She told the audience that she liked the environment and science and making new friends. "My favorite thing we've done so far is camping."

Christina meant that. At home, she was the younger sister of Hailey and Karina, both of whom possessed strengths and personalities that overshadowed hers, or at least that's how she often felt. In Troop 6000, she was a veteran Brownie. After their disastrous first day at Camp Kaufmann, Christina showed her fellow Brownies and the younger Daisies all the ins and outs of the camp, confidently demonstrating how to take shortcuts through the woods on trails. When Troop 6000 took field trips or went on *The View*, Christina was sharing the same first-time experiences as her sisters and everyone else.

In the big Blue Room, however, she was too young and too shy to explain all that, so she simply turned the mic toward Sanaa. Sanaa, she said, would tell the audience the rest. The group clapped politely.

As if taking a baton in a relay race, Sanaa stepped onto the stool with a toothy grin. As usual, she was super prepared, having gone over her speech the night before even as her brothers annoyed her in their room at the Sleep Inn. "Thank you, Christina. My name is Sanaa and I am a Girl Scout in Troop 6000.

You may have read about us in *The New York Times* or you may have seen us on *The View* or the *Today* show. We have been on TV a lot."

Sanaa paused as the audience laughed, and she giggled, too, before pulling herself together to continue the speech she had written.

"Troop 6000 started in February. It is the first Girl Scout troop for girls who are living in the shelter just like us. Being in Troop 6000 is great because we get to learn from each other, help each other, and learn a lot of things. We get to wear a Girl Scout uniform and earn badges.

"The most important thing I've learned in my time as a Scout is leadership. For me, being a Scout means to help everyone, and I am proud to stand here today with my sister Girl Scouts to tell you the best news."

The crowd applauded.

Karina was next. She was taller and stood straighter than the other girls, and the almost-twelve-year-old sounded like a pro. "Today we're here to share some good news. Thanks to Mayor Bill de Blasio, Troop 6000 is expanding. Working together, the Girl Scouts of Greater New York and the city of New York are going to make Troop 6000 available to five hundred more girls and women. Girl Scouts is great because we all get to support each other, share our experiences, and feel like we belong, learning new things and learning how to be fearless."

She continued her speech, thinking about the weekend at Camp Kaufmann, but she did not share any details about those two difficult days—the crying or the yelling or the trust building or the apologies. Karina, unlike Hailey and even her mother, had never been embarrassed to talk about her homelessness. But some things that happened in Troop 6000 were private, just for them, things that maybe they could share later but not now. She gave hints that only Sanaa, Christina, Tanae, Nyalynn, Cori, and Giselle would understand, as if she were speaking in code. "I feel very lucky that I have a chance to be a part of Troop 6000. It makes me feel special and proud. And I have learned the true

meaning of being a sister to every Girl Scout and how to emotionally support others."

She looked at Giselle. "I also want to say thank you to my
mom, Giselle Burgess, who was the first leader of Troop 6000,
and I am so proud of her because she is now the manager of the
Troop 6000 expansion."

The audience clapped.

"And all of us Girl Scouts in Troop 6000 want to say thank
you to Mayor de Blasio, Commissioner Banks, our friend Heidi
Schmidt at the Department of Homeless Services, and all of
those who support and believe in us throughout the city. You are
going to make so many girls happy and you are going to make
their lives better, too."

Then Karina introduced Steven Banks. This was a positive
moment in what had continued to be many rough months for
him. The mayor's shelter plan, "Turning the Tide on Homelessness," which had been announced with such fanfare after the
protests, was faltering. Residents in Brooklyn and the Bronx,
where the first new shelters were opening, wanted to know why
the city couldn't find somewhere else to place homeless people—
why did officials always pick *their* neighborhoods? The opposition, including a lawsuit to stop the opening of a men's shelter in
Brooklyn, had slowed everything down. The longer it took to
open shelters, the longer it would take to move homeless people
out of hotels, and the longer homeless children would be no-
mads, moving from one school to the next.

The commissioner had spent much of his life arguing cases
in court, always finding the right words, but now in the Blue
Room he was oddly tongue-tied as a follow-up act to the three
girls. "Well, there's nothing I can really say after that. When
people ask what motivates me to serve in government it's to be
able to work with young people like the young people we just
saw," he said. He turned to address the girls directly. "You have
shown us all a way forward."

Karina resumed her role as emcee, introducing speaker after
speaker with poise and assurance until finally she got to one

that made her pause, ever so briefly: her mother. Giselle took the podium to enthusiastic applause and explained that the money the city was allocating to expand Troop 6000 to locations city-wide would be stretched over three years, and that it would help pay for uniforms, field trips, and supplies—basically, anything the girls would need. But then a reporter asked her about her "personal connection" to Troop 6000.

Giselle froze, suddenly overtaken by the miracle of it all: Almost a year to the day earlier, she and her five children had first entered the shelter system, and now she was standing at a press conference in City Hall, a roomful of cameras and important eyes trained on her, revealing that the city was giving $1.1 million to implement an idea that she, a homeless person, had thought up while lying in a crowded double bed at the Sleep Inn.

She could remember holding her phone at just the right angle to take photos of Hailey one year earlier as her daughter sat on the sofa at Pam's Place and talked about helping homeless women on NY1. That was when homelessness had been a new and strange thing to her family; none of them could quite believe or accept it. And now here they were in front of a row of television cameras talking about homelessness to the entire world.

And none of this would have been possible without Meridith, she thought, starting to shake. "Meridith Maskara has truly held my hand throughout a lot of hard times in my life," she said, struggling to get the words out. "I can personally say how Girl Scouting has helped me as a woman, making me, helping to make me feel like I'm important, to be able to teach other girls amazing skills and watching them grow." There was more applause, long and loud and heartfelt.

The city had done everything except give Giselle keys to New York. Then again, that wouldn't have meant anything to Giselle.

What good are keys if you don't have a home?

# 18

# BE READY

**TWO WEEKS LATER,** early one morning, knocks rang out like gunshots, rapidly and unexpectedly, on every door on the ninth and tenth floors of the Sleep Inn. Parents getting ready for work or leaving to drop kids at day camp opened their doors to orders that they had to leave the premises within hours. Buses would be out front to meet them and take them back to PATH to await assignment to another shelter.

There was no fire, no disaster, just the sudden desire once again of the hotel owners to free up rooms for regular tourists. With the economy in full swing and tourists cramming New York City, the owners decided it was time to distance the Sleep Inn from the stigma of being a homeless shelter and start bringing back the paying guests for whom the place had been built in the first place.

Staff members passed out thin black trash bags for belongings, and families on the top two floors scrambled, stuffing clothes and toys into the bags until they bulged to the point of splitting open. The trash bags were supposed to be for families who did not own suitcases, but many had put their luggage into storage to free up space in their crowded hotel rooms, and so most of them ended up needing the bags. Bags, unlike suitcases, could be crushed, which allowed more of them to fit into one large truck, and as a bonus they were easy to throw around, like garbage being tossed into a dumpster.

The major flaw at the heart of the city's use of hotels as a stopgap solution to providing shelter for those in need of it—the fact that hotels could decide at any moment that they needed their rooms back—was, at this moment, glaringly clear for all to see. It had happened more often than city officials cared to admit, turning each day into a nail-biter for those who lived in the hotels.

Sue Seaman had just dropped off her daughter, Jessica, who was in the fifth grade, and her son, Mikey, at a summer day camp at nearby P.S. 111 when the fusillade of knocking began. As soon as she returned to the Sleep Inn, other parents rushed to her to deliver the news about the emergency transfer. A resident assistant working for the shelter was handing out pieces of paper in the lobby.

"But my kids go to school here. My daughter is in the Girl Scouts. We're not going anywhere," Sue said loudly. "I'm not going nowhere!"

"Be ready before four," the resident assistant told her.

The economic line between the people who worked for the shelter and the people who lived in the shelter was as thin as the PROPERTY OF DHS sheets. Job descriptions required a caseworker or a housing specialist to have a high school diploma or GED, and their annual pay could be as low as the mid-$20,000s. Many of the people living in the hotel were civil and even downright friendly with a few of them. But the shelter staff, often on the receiving end of parents' frustration, had a job to do and part of that job was carrying out orders. Their apparent lack of sympathy was experienced by many of the residents as an added insult.

Desperate and confused parents called Giselle, who jumped on the phone with Meridith, who called Jimmy Van Bramer. And the families and their advocates started to fight back.

Giselle thought about Linda Moore, the hotel guest from Ohio she'd encountered at the beginning of her family's stay at the Sleep Inn, and how at the time of the eviction the previous summer, Linda kept telling the residents to rise up, to protest: "Malcolm X!" At the time of that first expulsion, though, Giselle and the Sleep Inn families had felt powerless, unable to effect any kind of change. Now they realized they had to mobilize quickly and work together to inform all parents, even the ones outside the building working and running errands. After getting off the phone with Meridith, Giselle ran down to the lobby and out the front door, where she saw Sue.

Sue began hotfooting it through the neighborhood. She spotted Tawanda Brown, who had lent Giselle jewelry for the Girl Scout gala, and her husband, Gerard Bookhart; they were the parents of young Scouts Tanae and Tiana. Tawanda had roots in Queens and Long Island. The family had become homeless when they were evicted from an apartment in Newark, New Jersey, first moving in with Tawanda's relatives on Long Island and then making their way to PATH in the Bronx. Like their daughters, Tawanda and Gerard were quiet and usually kept to themselves, but that day, faced with another move, they talked incessantly to other parents, spreading the word about protesting the move. There was power in numbers!

Tawanda was panicked by the shelter staff's pressing words: "Be ready before four." Her daughters were starting school in a month and they loved the Girl Scouts. She regularly joked about how the girls used to fight inside their hotel room all the time, tired of each other, tired of being cooped up together in a small space. Being Girl Scouts had changed all that.

"I'm trying to use the Girl Scouts to help them get along with each other," Tawanda would say. Apparently, it was working.

Giselle had always felt guilty that at the time of the first eviction from the Sleep Inn, in the summer of 2016, she had saved only her family. That sense of regret was one of the things that had driven her efforts to look out for other families at the shelter by documenting any mistreatment. Now it was happening again, and there was no way she was going to allow officials to move dozens of families with children poised to start school in a few weeks. Not to mention that all of the girls were about to begin their first full year of Girl Scouting.

"Don't get on the bus!" she yelled to the Scouts and their parents who were dragging their belongings in the black trash bags to yellow school buses parked out front.

But some parents and their children had already boarded. "Get off the bus!" she shouted even louder.

Giselle kept calling Meridith with updates and Meridith kept calling Jimmy.

"This is inhumane," Meridith said to Jimmy on the phone. "I'm getting in my van—I will block the buses."

Jimmy called city officials again, and soon the shelter staff was doing an about-face and pulling the families of all Girl Scouts off the bus. After being briefed, Steven Banks decided that Troop 6000's success in giving the girls some stability was a vital part of improving the shelter system and could not be disrupted at that moment. The two top floors were cleared to appease the hotel owners. The Scouts and their families from those floors were moved into vacant rooms on other floors, and into rooms of families who had weaker ties to the hotel or who were interested in being transferred to be closer to their jobs or relatives. Somehow all of the room juggling worked, but it seemed so unnecessary. Bureaucracy and hastiness had trumped courtesy and common sense, as it so often did when it came to the actions of city officials and shelter providers—until people who were looking at the whole picture, and who had authority, intervened.

Giselle had helped save a dozen families from scrambling to find new schools and from upending their children's lives once again. She had forced the city to take the time to make more reasonable, logical decisions about how to transfer families, giving them an opportunity to have some input. The ordeal made her grateful. But even while she was standing out there, yelling at others to resist, she was keeping a secret. Only David, Cori, and a few other parents knew it.

Sometime after the trip to Camp Kaufmann and the announcement in the Blue Room, her housing specialist had called, practically giddy. Roger had found something, far away but still in Queens, with room for Giselle and all her kids. After a half dozen apartments had fallen through and twice as many landlords never returned her phone calls, she no longer believed in Roger and what he tried to offer, but it sounded like this time he may finally have come through for them. She prayed that there would be no paperwork or money hitches. She prayed that her credit score would not fail her again. She prayed that she could make the numbers work.

She hoped for the best, but even as she prayed, she was prepared to have her heart broken again.

# 19

# TUDOR VILLAGE

**THE JETS ROARED** low enough to cast moving shadows over the neighborhood, providing welcome, if brief, moments of shade on a stifling hot day. Giselle wore a sleeveless sundress that hit just above her knees, and her legs stuck to the orange subway seat as she and Hailey made their way from the Sleep Inn deeper into Queens on the F train, transferring to an M train and getting out on Woodhaven Boulevard, where they jumped in a cab. Worried about being late and unfamiliar with the route, Giselle decided the $20 cab ride was worth it. There was no air-conditioning, or it was barely blowing, and Giselle, as her legs clung to the seats, could not understand why the driver had only cracked the windows.

Once a mostly white community held together by solid union jobs and modest living, Ozone Park had been battered by economic decline and was now experiencing a generational shift. Italian, Irish, and German families who had lived there for decades had died off or moved away, replaced by an influx of families with Asian, Latin, and Caribbean roots seeking new American dreams. An old union hall for transit workers stood vacant, and a mural of American flags covering the exterior of the adjacent old union hall for ironworkers was faded and tagged with graffiti.

Gentrification had not yet arrived here. Maybe it never would. For those like Giselle, driven away from the city centers by out-of-reach rents, far-flung places like Ozone Park were looking more and more attractive for the simple reason that they were affordable.

Within Ozone Park there was a smaller community called Tudor Village, with a park called Tudor Park—redundant designations no doubt meant to confer a bit of elegance to this humble neighborhood that working-class families had long called home. That's where Giselle and Hailey were headed on this sweltering day.

Roger had been trying to manage Giselle's expectations. She wanted to live somewhere like Astoria or Woodside, neighborhoods nearer to Manhattan, closer to where they used to live. Roger didn't think that was realistic. "You know what? That's a little difficult in terms of the rent you are looking for," he told her again and again.

"They want me to take any kind of apartment. I don't want to raise my kids just anywhere. I need a safe place," she insisted.

He made his pitch. How about Ozone Park? It might be far away, but it was nice, safe, and affordable. "Do me a favor? Come and take a look," he almost begged.

Now Giselle and Hailey were approaching a Tudor-style duplex house that looked bigger and grander in person than it had in photographs. With a bay window and a wooden door topped by a half-moon of glass, the house outshone the unornamented one attached to it. A new red roof brightened the red brick and concealed its wear and tear.

Giselle and Hailey were instantly enamored, even after the broiling cab ride—so much so that they hardly noticed the patches of dead grass and dirt that pockmarked the yard as they hurried up the front walk to the door. Giselle wondered where the apartment was. In the basement, like two others they'd seen? Tucked away on the top floor?

Roger, with his bullnecked build and sweat beads on his head, was on the porch waiting for them. He wasn't alone. The broker was also there. So were the owners of the house, a young married couple who had just completed the purchase, paying $555,000 for it—an inconceivable sum to Giselle, but within reach as a possible source of rental income for solidly middle-class New Yorkers. A Manhattan apartment less than half the size would be at least double the price. For budding small investors, renting to a family coming out of shelter could be, if not profitable, a stable revenue stream for at least a year. The city guaranteed help with the rent, depending on a tenant's income and circumstances. Some landlords were paid three months, even a year, in advance.

Roger had said it was an apartment but as Giselle stepped onto the porch, a realization washed over her. Roger had misspoken, or maybe he'd wanted to surprise her. Or maybe Giselle had just assumed that she could never afford something this size.

"Is this a full house?" Giselle screamed with wonder, a little embarrassed to be so excited.

A house.

*Her family could live in an entire house.*

Hailey took out her phone to video the exterior of the house, and then the interior, too, so she could show Karina and her other siblings. She was so nervous, though, that nearly every frame of video showed hands and feet and the floor. The fourteen-year-old had grown used to room 207 at the Sleep Inn, where she had spent nearly a year of her life. She and Karina gave each other space in the bed, leaving enough room between them for Christina to squeeze into when she wasn't in the other bed with Giselle, Judas, and Gillesy. Christina wasn't the easiest bedmate, though; her long black hair would smack them in the face as she tossed and turned, and she snored like an old man. But the family had somehow transformed a small, drab hotel room into a home, swapping turns in the bathroom, arguing over unmade beds, and pushing those plastic bins filled with their clothes, Girl Scout vests, books, patches, and toiletries against the walls.

*Now her family could spread out in an entire house. Space. Privacy.*

Hailey and Giselle explored. The living room alone was twice as big as room 207, and the walls were freshly painted a bright white. The paint smell was overwhelming, but mother and daughter welcomed the odor as if they were lucky enough to have a new car and it was a new-car scent.

They couldn't stop smiling as they walked on the newly buffed wooden floors. The kitchen had white appliances and a breakfast nook with white pleather-cushioned seats beneath a Tiffany-style lamp. Giselle pointed the booth out to Hailey and gave her a look of astonishment. "Oh, that's so cute. Oh my gosh!" Hailey exclaimed.

She was the same height as Giselle now, but still had a baby face. Tiptoeing, they both peered from a window above the sink into the backyard, which was little more than a slab of concrete with slivers of grass. There was a driveway on the side that led to a worn garage.

Giselle climbed the stairs to the second floor, with Hailey following right behind. The bathroom door was just at the top of the stairs, so they opened it first. "Mirrors," Giselle whispered as she stepped onto the white tile. They were something to behold: Three of them in a row, each one with two panels, were adorned with vanity lights. Giselle was fighting back tears.

They had lived in a hotel room for nearly a year now, but she still remembered the Maple Avenue apartment with its narrow shower, and how she'd had to bathe Judas and Gillesy standing up. "There's a tub," she said softly.

She composed herself and she and Hailey walked into the first bedroom. It was small. That would be for Christina, Judas, and Gillesy. They walked into a second bedroom, where the walls were painted pink. Hailey wanted it to stay pink. "Look at the color," she said breathlessly. "Look at the color!"

Then they walked into the master bedroom, which faced the

street. Sunlight pierced the dark wooden blinds. "What! Get out!" Giselle shouted.

"It has so much natural light," the husband said. "In the morning, the sun shines right through and you don't need an alarm."

It was a dream house. More than a dream. But now Giselle needed money. The deposit was $4,680. She had just $2,000 in savings.

Giselle approached Meridith about her dilemma and learned that she could get a hardship advance from the Girl Scouts of Greater New York. She received $1,600, which she would pay back $200 at a time in her next eight paychecks. But she was still $1,080 short.

"G, I have it. I can lend it to you." Shaquna, a cubicle mate who worked as a retail manager for the Girl Scouts of Greater New York, made the offer in the office after Giselle told her about coming up short for the down payment. "Pay me back when you can." Shaquna had been unloading cases of cookies with Giselle on that cold day in March when Giselle had sped off in an Uber to see an apartment—in vain, as it turned out. Shaquna had the money and figured her co-worker needed it more than she did.

"Oh my God. Are you sure? Are you sure?" Giselle asked. "Let me see if I can get it first."

Giselle was expecting a $1,000 payment for participating in an advertisement for *Marvel's The Defenders,* a new show on Netflix. Giselle and three other New Yorkers—a poet who had started an improv group for disadvantaged youths, a nightclub promoter who created an app that connected volunteers with needy groups, and an artist who opened a free computer lab in Bushwick, Brooklyn—were hailed as "four real-life defenders, out to change the world" in the online ad that appeared on the website of *Complex* magazine. The tagline was "Not All Heroes Wear Capes."

Giselle was painfully aware that she lacked superpowers. Days went by and the check had not arrived. "Shaquna, I'm going to need that money," Giselle said apologetically as she walked into work.

Shaquna left the office and returned shortly with ten $100 bills in a Chase Bank envelope.

She gave Giselle a knowing nod, and Giselle mouthed a thank-you.

On August 9, 2017, a Wednesday morning, in the Flatiron District of Manhattan, Giselle passed vendors hawking cheap cellphones and entered the building of the Human Resources Administration, a name for the welfare office meant to convey a more positive message than the word *welfare*. It was one of the places people could go for food stamps and other forms of public assistance, and it was also the central location for lease signings and key exchanges for those moving out of shelters. In 2017, an average of more than twenty people a day signed leases there, cutting deals with landlords who received subsidies from the city in addition to $1,000 bonuses. The subsidies were a key tactic in the city's fight to get homeless people, especially families, into homes of their own. Knowing the city was putting up the money, especially so much in advance, gave many landlords the extra confidence they needed to accept tenants with poor credit histories.

The city paid the landlord of Giselle's house four months' rent in advance, along with her security deposit, and agreed to continue subsidizing her rent with $1,958.17 a month for the next twelve months. Giselle would be responsible for the other $1,487, and then, after a year, the whole amount. The city also gave Giselle a check for $2,300 for furniture. "Right here," a clerk told her, pointing to the *X* on page after page of a stack of documents that Giselle signed with painstaking care, though the pen kept slipping through her fingers, wet from the tears she'd wiped from her face.

Her landlord handed over the keys. "This one opens the front door," she said. "This one opens the back."

It had been nearly a full year since she'd moved into the Sleep Inn. Giselle and her family had a home again.

An hour later Giselle jiggled the keys as she walked into Meridith's office at the Girl Scouts. She flashed a broad smile and fell into Meridith's embrace.

A graphic designer for the Girl Scouts saw Giselle in the office. "I got something for you," he said. Giselle was surprised to get a gift from a co-worker she barely knew.

"Congratulations," he said, grinning, and he handed her a Wonder Woman key chain.

<hr/>

Giselle left the office and headed to Queens, where she borrowed Dan and Meridith's minivan to pick up her children from the Sleep Inn and head to BJ's Wholesale Club. They entered the parking lot as if it were Black Friday. Giselle pushed the big cart through the giant store, packing the top high and then stuffing the rest into the bottom: milk, bags of salad, lunch meat, tomatoes, limes, industrial-size bottles of olive and vegetable oils, vinegar, salsa, chicken, ground beef, a case of corned beef, microwavable popcorn, a ten-pound bag of rice, oatmeal chewies, graham crackers, pancake mix, syrup, green and red peppers, onions, potatoes, grapes, strawberries. The bill was more than $800, but Giselle could afford it because it was on an EBT card[*] she'd had for more than a year but had barely been able to use— because there had been nowhere to keep food in the hotel room and all cooking had to be done on the sly. The idea of once again

---

[*] Electronic Benefits Transfer card

being able to prepare fresh food for her family beyond what she could fit into her secret skillet—to send her children off to school after a full breakfast, or to make them the yellow deliciousness of her arroz con gandules—elated her. She'd felt so guilty about not being able to provide for her children, and now she'd be able to nourish and nurture them in the most basic of ways: home-cooked meals. The thought made her practically giddy. For their parts, the children were thrilled, squealing with delight as they bought snacks that there'd been no place to store in their limited space at the hotel.

A custodian in the ladies' room at BJ's stopped Giselle. "You were on TV? I saw you on TV," she said. "I heard your story. You're an amazing woman."

Giselle smiled. She couldn't stop smiling. She'd been smiling and crying—sometimes simultaneously—ever since the lease signing that morning.

"Have a blessed day," the custodian told her as she wiped down the counter.

"You have a blessed day, too," Giselle said, beaming.

Giselle had the key to their new home so they loaded up the car and dropped off the food, stuffing the refrigerator and cabinets, though Giselle was still unsure about how to arrange her new kitchen. She would worry about that later. She had plenty of time to figure it out.

When they were finally done unloading, Giselle took a moment to stand on the sidewalk outside and survey the block. She'd been in such a rush when she and Hailey had first seen the house that she hadn't bothered to study the neighborhood. There was a bodega at the corner and a playground not far away. She tried to map out in her head the distance from the laundromat because the house didn't have a washer and dryer. But in the grand scheme of things that was okay because she had done it—she had gotten her family out of the Sleep Inn. Now all they had to do was return to the hotel and start packing, this time with no marshal, landlord, or resident assistant hovering over them.

A little while later, as Giselle scanned the hotel room and wondered how they were going to pack everything up, she realized how her family of six had turned into hoarders. There were pages and pages of drawings—stick figures, flowers, and squiggly lines and imperfect circles that Christina, Gillesy, and Judas had scribbled. There were toys that they had outgrown. There were school uniforms and everyday clothes and shoes. The room had also become the de facto storage space for Troop 6000, and bins full of extra badges, vests, first aid kits, and gifts sent by well-meaning philanthropies and even celebrities lined the walls.

How had the six of them been able to live crammed into this single room for close to a year on top of all this clutter? How had they gotten up and gone to work or school each day only to return to this room to eat, do homework, and take care of the normal chores of life—and start a Girl Scout troop—without constant bickering and disagreement? Looking back now, it seemed like they'd accomplished the near impossible.

Giselle knew that they couldn't take all of the things in this room with them. She didn't want to. It was okay to give away the outgrown toys and to throw away the drawings—they would make more memories in their new home. She needed to finish before the movers, contracted by the city, showed up the next day, and so she and the children filled nine black trash bags— the same kind they had used to bring their stuff into the shelter—with things they could discard, and then she and Cori dragged them down the carpeted hallway to the elevator and through the lobby to the two dumpsters outside. Hailey and Karina kept packing.

Cori and Giselle had two major events to celebrate: Giselle was moving into a *house* and Cori had just landed a job at the Girl Scouts as a recruiter for Troop 6000. Her job would be going from shelter to shelter to convince more girls to join as part of the expansion that came with the city's $1.1 million contribution. But the celebratory feeling of the night was jumbled up with other feelings, too. While Giselle was thrilled and relieved to be moving out, she was also disheartened about leaving behind Cori, David, and all the Scouts. Even though they were moving a good distance away, she was still going to be a troop leader at the Sleep Inn and her daughters would remain in Troop 6000. Karina often said that she preferred Troop 6000 to the Sunnyside & Woodside troops because she shared a bond with the Troop 6000 members. They had all been through the same ordeal of being in shelter and watching as their parents tried to pull their families out of poverty. Cori and David and the others who lived in the hotel were their family, and the Sleep Inn, as awful as it was, had been their home.

Cori, Giselle, Karina, and Hailey were still organizing and packing long after Christina, Judas, and Gillesy had fallen asleep in one of the beds. At some point, Giselle noticed that she hadn't heard her phone ring or vibrate for more than an hour and began to hunt under the beds and covers for it.

"Maybe you threw it out," Cori said.

Giselle and Cori looked at each other, then hurried downstairs and outside to the dumpsters.

Black trash bags were stacked higher than Giselle. She searched for her bags, the ones she had filled with old drawings and McDonald's Happy Meal toys the children would never play with again. Cori used her cellphone to illuminate the bags.

"This isn't going to work," Giselle declared in frustration.

"Dump them on the ground," Cori suggested.

"I don't want to make a mess. Johanna works so hard." Johanna, the hotel custodian who spoke little English, had tried to make the breakfast room comfortable for Troop 6000 despite the reluctance of other staff and social workers. "I'm not going to do that to her."

"Forget it. It's not here. It has to be upstairs," Cori said, and the two exhausted women went back to the room.

At around one A.M., Hailey's and Karina's phones made a beeping noise. It was Life360, an app that Evelyn, Giselle's mother, insisted everyone get because she wanted to track whereabouts for emergencies. Evelyn set up the app so that the

Sleep Inn was not labeled SLEEP INN or SHELTER; instead it was called GG AND BABIES TEMPORARY HOME.

"What was that?" Giselle asked.

An alert on the girls' screens read: GISELLE LEFT GG AND BA-BIES TEMPORARY HOME.

Giselle grabbed Hailey's phone and watched a virtual version of herself moving away from the Sleep Inn. The phone *had* been in a dumpster, the contents of which had been picked up by a garbage truck that was now heading through Queens. Giselle and Cori ran downstairs and down the block. "Stop! Stop!" Cori screamed. Then she turned to Giselle. "I don't know how you're not crying right now."

"Because I'm leaving tomorrow!" Giselle said. While she was frustrated, her face remained dry. "Crying is not going to bring it back. We are packing and leaving tomorrow."

The next morning—which was really just a few hours later—David, who was in charge of chaperoning Scouts to the Urban Day Camp, was outside with a dozen girls when he saw Giselle, Cori, and Hailey frantically emerge from the hotel. Hailey had her phone in hand and showed the message on the screen to David.

GISELLE IS AT GG AND BABIES TEMPORARY HOME the screen read, with a map now showing the virtual Giselle inching closer and closer to the Sleep Inn. Everyone could hear the blue garbage truck as it lumbered down Thirteenth Street toward them. Apparently it hadn't yet dumped the load it had picked up the previous night.

"Wait! Wait! My phone is in there," Giselle called out to the truck, trying to wave it down.

Hailey started giggling. "It's funny," she said to Karina, who had joined them with her phone in hand, the same message flashing on its screen. "It's so funny."

And then the alerts disappeared. The phone was gone, crushed in the truck's compactor. Giselle started laughing with Hailey, and the others gradually joined in, perplexed at first but eventually getting it. Because it *was* funny. Losing a phone in a garbage truck was *nothing* compared to the joy of a family finally having a home. And that's where Giselle and her children were headed at last. To their own beautiful home.

⠿⠿⠿⠿⠿⠿⠿⠿⠿⠿

The refrigerator in their new house was stocked, and boxes and containers were stacked in the middle of the living room where the movers had left them. The family didn't have beds yet, so Hailey directed all of the children to roll out sleeping bags.

"I can't believe this is actually happening," Hailey said. "I think this is a dream. We're going to wake up and be back in the hotel."

The younger ones still felt the tug of the familiar. "I don't want to stay here; I want to go back to the hotel," said Judas, who could barely remember any other home. He folded his scrawny arms in front of his chest.

"We're not going back there," Hailey told him definitively.

Karina, who was on crutches after a fall at basketball camp, was quiet. She thought about how far they had come, how long they had lived in the hotel room. She was normally talkative and so optimistic about the future, but she hardly spoke the whole day because she was keeping her dread and her hope a secret, like wishes made when blowing out candles on a birthday cake or blowing the fuzzy seeds off a dandelion. You don't wish out loud, or your dream won't come true. Karina couldn't wish aloud that they would never be homeless again for fear that they would be.

As they settled into their new home, friends and family soon came over to visit. David had permission to leave the Sleep Inn for the weekend, and he and Kiara showed up on Friday afternoon as if they were a home makeover team. Kiara nodded approvingly as David helped unpack and took it upon himself to move plates and bowls and pots and pans. "These should go near the stove," he said, moving spices into a different cabinet. Giselle agreed to whatever he said, happy to have the company and still wanting to pinch herself to make sure she wasn't dreaming.

On Saturday, Judas turned five years old, surrounded by his siblings, his aunt Miranda, David, Kiara, and Cori, who had arrived that day. Giselle made certain that his birthday—the first celebration together in their home—was an occasion to remember.

David had traveled all the way to his storage unit in Harlem to retrieve a grill and special cutlery to make sure they would have the tastiest hamburgers and hot dogs. He set up the grill in Giselle's concrete-paved backyard and then moved into the kitchen, where he made potato salad and rice and beans. They managed to prepare a feast and serve everyone while still keeping within Giselle's limited budget. It wasn't a fancy party, but to those who were gathered there laughing and eating, it felt just as special as the magical Girl Scout gala at the extravagant Cipriani.

To top off the birthday festivities, Giselle had bought a cake at BJ's, and she had put up some decorations with Teenage Mutant Ninja Turtles on them.

"Blow out the candles, J," Giselle encouraged.

Judas grinned widely as everyone sang "Happy Birthday." He had a smile like his mother's.

Later that night the party continued, turning into a giant sleepover. Cori, whose son, Trey, was visiting his father for the weekend, was so tuckered out that she fell asleep on the floor with Miranda and Kiara. No one minded the occasional jet flying overhead.

In the morning, sunlight streamed in through the windows. One by one, everyone followed the smell of bacon, waffles, potatoes, and scrambled eggs into the kitchen, where David was preparing another feast. The children squeezed into the sunny breakfast nook beneath the brightly colored lamps.

"You're home," David told Giselle.

It was bittersweet, of course. He and Kiara still lived in the shelter.

"Dad, why can't we just move in with G?" Kiara asked him. "Me and Hailey and Karina can share a room."

"Where am I going to sleep?" David asked.

"On the couch in the living room."

"You have it all mapped out, huh?" he responded, but as much as he longed to give Kiara a real home, he knew it wasn't their turn yet.

A little later David and Kiara went back to the shelter. Cori left, too, Miranda returned home to Woodside, and Giselle found herself alone with her children. She tiptoed over to the window to look out at the backyard, where Christina, Gillesy, and Judas screeched in delight. Then she filled the kitchen sink with sudsy water and began washing dishes.

Washing dishes. Could there be any more mundane household task? Soap, rinse, repeat. But they were *her* dishes, in *her* sink, in *her* house, and the children were playing outside in *their* yard. She could have never imagined that the simple act of setting a plate to dry and picking up the next one could fill her with so much joy and gratitude.

"I'm home," she whispered. *Home.*

# 20

# GONE

THE BREAKFAST ROOM at the Sleep Inn was completely empty—no tables or even chairs. When Giselle had called everyone she knew to stop the eviction of families from the top two floors of the Sleep Inn nearly two months earlier, she had dared to challenge the authorities, from the hotel staff to the shelter workers employed by Childrens Community Services. Now that she was no longer homeless, she was not obligated to sign in and out with caseworkers, no longer under anyone else's purview or supervision. She had been living in her house for more than a month, throwing cookouts in the backyard, entertaining her family and friends. She was settling into her new role as program manager of Troop 6000, which was on its way to being established in other shelters, but Giselle's loyalty was to the OGs at the Sleep Inn and she was continuing as their troop leader. So here she was, back as a free person. She had no curfew, no rules—and no tables or chairs.

"Where are the chairs?" Cori asked, as she and the Scouts trickled into the room.

Giselle rolled her eyes, trying to hide her anger from the girls. Cori rolled her eyes back. It appeared to be a case of petty payback. Since the hotel had had to fight Giselle over the ninth and tenth floors, maybe it would no longer be so convenient for the Girl Scouts to use the breakfast room for meetings. For months there had been a sign reading WELCOME TROOP 6000 taped to the door. That was gone now. The message was clear.

"We're just going to sit on the floor," Giselle told the girls, who immediately plopped down without fuss, some crossing their legs, others sprawling out as if they were in a bed.

Giselle's new home in Ozone Park was more than an hour by train and bus from the Sleep Inn. Because Giselle did not want to disrupt their schooling again, especially Hailey's and Karina's, all of her children still attended school at Evangel, which made it easy for them to walk to the meetings after school on Fridays. This meeting was the first of the new school year, and all the girls were excited.

David walked in and lowered himself to the floor, crossing his long legs, unwilling to smile or be his normal, cheerful self. He looked uncomfortable in his homemade Scouts vest, a blue denim vest with patches affixed to the back. There were five now, including one from the first trip he chaperoned to Yankee Stadium and another for Urban Day Camp. He had a booming laugh that usually began with a "Ha!" But now he was so solemn that it was disconcerting. "I don't even want to be here right now," he said to Giselle softly enough that the girls could not hear.

Kiara was gone, no longer in his custody.

David had taken her to Philadelphia on Labor Day weekend to visit her mother. For years, he had resented his limited visitation rights, and he was determined not to do the same to Kiara's mother, Lanye.

"I love you. I'll see you on Sunday," David told his daughter as they hugged.

Days later, as David readied himself to return to New York City, Lanye told him that Kiara would not be going back with him. She said a social worker in New York City had called her and advised her to keep Kiara in her custody. How could David have left her alone in their room at the Sleep Inn for three hours while he smoked outside? she asked. *Three hours!*

David was blindsided. Yes, he had left Kiara alone, but it had only been for a few minutes while he went downstairs to use the microwave. Tired of being cooped up in the room, Kiara, being a typical ten-year-old, had snuck out—but the door locked behind her and she found herself unable to get back in. When she spotted a shelter employee, she had ducked into a stairwell, but the employee saw her and reported David to the Administration for Children's Services, New York City's child welfare agency. David was quickly cleared of any wrongdoing, so he was shocked to hear that a social worker from the child welfare agency had called Lanye directly about the incident. But legally, Lanye had primary custody, and the child welfare worker was, in fact, required to contact her. David had no idea where the allegation that he'd left his daughter alone for three hours had originated.

Homeless parents were under the constant threat of being reported to authorities. Shelter workers, afraid of being accused of looking the other way, were extraordinarily precautious and strict, holding homeless parents accountable for the kinds of choices that wealthier parents might not think twice about— *Sure, I left my son in the car while I ran into the store for a minute.* Once, when Giselle went to look at a prospective apartment, she left a sick Judas with Cori, only to be called by a shelter worker informing her that she could not allow Cori to babysit. Residents were not allowed to care for children other than their own and technically they were not supposed to be in one another's rooms, despite the difficulty of fully monitoring that rule and the impracticality of having the rule in the first place.

The bar for having cases "indicated" was low in New York, meaning that if an allegation merely sounded true, even if it actually wasn't, it could go on a parent's record with the Administration for Children's Services and into a state database that did not distinguish between a child left alone in a hotel room for a few minutes and a child who had been beaten. Under New York law, such incidents stayed on a parent's record until a child turned twenty-eight, even if the parent was never convicted on any child abuse or neglect charges, unless an individual took arduous steps to get the record expunged; it was one of the most stringent child welfare laws in the country. Between 2014 and 2017, the number of investigations in New York City increased from about fifty-five thousand in a year's time to about fifty-nine thousand, a rise that city officials correlated with the growth of homelessness. Shelter workers and teachers were "mandated reporters," meaning that if they saw something, they had to say something. A child's coming to school on a chilly day without a coat could be investigated—and even indicated—as neglect. Black and Hispanic parents were more likely to be reported, another form of discrimination called Jane Crow by advocates for parents. Parents at the Sleep Inn had been "indicated" so often that Giselle had difficulty recruiting troop leaders because volunteers could not have such records. The Girl Scouts had a rigorous selection process to weed out parents who could be deemed dangerous to other children, even if the evidence was only an allegation in a database.

"Do you have an ACS case?" Giselle hated to ask parents. She feared the answer.

Fortunately, David's case had not been indicated. If it had been, in addition to the other problems it would have caused him, he wouldn't have been sitting in the room with Giselle and Cori and the rest of Troop 6000.

On the Sunday evening of Labor Day weekend, David had called the police in Philadelphia to see if they could intervene so that he could take Kiara back to New York. He was told that the police could not get involved because it was a custody matter. David then had to make a snap decision: stay in Philadelphia and fight for Kiara, or return to New York City so he would not lose his bed at the Sleep Inn.

David reluctantly got on a bus by himself, staring at Kiara's picture on his phone and sobbing for the entire two-hour ride. He had taken a photo of her at Philadelphia's City Hall, just a few blocks away from the bus station and the drop-off point where they'd met her mother. Kiara was wearing a T-shirt that read LEX PARTY 5-9-15, and while its written message held no personal meaning for her, she thought it made a statement with its bright pink-and-white lettering. She had bought it with Monopoly money at a pop-up boutique of donated new and gently used clothing that a nonprofit had set up for the troop in the breakfast room; Giselle had used the charitable event as a way for the girls to earn their badges for budgeting. Out of all of her T-shirts, Kiara thought that was the one she should wear to Philadelphia to show off to her mother, whom she missed, even though she also loved her father. And her mother missed her deeply, too; she'd raised Kiara without David for ten years. Lanye reminded David that the arrangement with Kiara was only supposed to be temporary, and she regretted that it had turned into an entire school year. She tried to assure David that Kiara's returning to Philadelphia, instead of some shelter in New York City, was for the best. She was close to getting a home.

"Where's Kiara?" a couple of girls asked.

David sat silently on the floor. There was plenty of excited chatter as Cori welcomed returning Scouts and some new ones, too, so it was easy to miss the question or simply not answer it immediately.

"We have another new Scout!" Cori shouted like an elementary school teacher on the first day of class.

"Awesome!" Giselle said.

Girls continued to pack the room until there was a full house: Hailey, Karina, Christina, Sanaa, Tanae, Tiana, Genesis, Brithani, Jessica, and other founding members of Troop 6000, the ones Karina affectionately called "the OGs," were all there.

"Where's Kiara?" another girl asked.

Sanaa knew where she was. David and her mother, Mickyle, had grown close, and Mickyle had shared the news with Sanaa. Now she couldn't help expressing her disappointment out loud.

"I feel alone without Kiara. I'm the only Junior here," Sanaa said, crossing her arms.

"It's all right, Sanaa. You're going to hold it down," Giselle said.

Tears began to stream down David's face. He jumped up and left the room, swinging open the glass door, frightening Sanaa and confusing all of the other Scouts.

"Girls, signs are up." Giselle and Cori raised their hands to show the Girl Scout sign. "I need you all to focus and pay attention. I need you to listen for a second."

Giselle had been wondering how she could possibly explain Kiara's absence. The idea of David's daughter not returning and of his loss filled her with uncertainty and made her want to weep. "So—um, a lot of you know—may know—or not know that Kiara is not with us anymore." Her words had a halting, jerky quality.

The girls audibly gasped, a few of them covering their mouths in disbelief. Kiara was back in Philadelphia, Giselle explained.

"I know that many of you have been asking where she's at. She's not here right now. We can only hope that she'll be back soon. We don't know when she's going to be back, but Mr. David needs us. Mr. David needs all the love and hugs and appreciation that we can show him and support him in every way that we can.

"So you know Kiara's always going to be with us here in her own way, right, but while she's not here, everything that we do, I need you guys to keep her in mind, okay, and we'll send her positive thoughts, and if you guys want to work on something, we can put that together, okay," Giselle said, knowing that the girls loved making cards and writing letters.

Cori felt like weeping, too, but now she chimed in, "I think that would be great!" What else could they offer the girls? They needed to do something.

And what could they do for David? Cori and Giselle just didn't know. In a few short months the three of them had grown tight, connected through the bonds of homelessness, parenthood, and the Girl Scouts. They borrowed a few dollars here and there from one another, they shared food, they broke the rules and watched one another's children, sometimes in each other's rooms. When David lost his job, Cori and Giselle joined him on the "porch" one evening. They shared Barton vodka and Coors beer and managed to scrape up enough change for four loosies, trying to turn David's latest misfortune into some kind of celebration. He would get another job, Cori and Giselle assured him, but David just kept shaking his head. Their normally upbeat friend wouldn't even crack a smile.

"I'm going to cheer you up," Giselle declared. "I'm going to make you laugh."

Giselle suddenly snatched Cori's wig off her head. That night, Cori was wearing one of her long brunette specimens. "Giselle!" Cori yelled, both embarrassed and angry. She tried covering her unkempt hair with her hands but realized she needed them free to grab the wig from Giselle, who was now swinging it over her head and running in circles. Cori finally wrestled the wig from Giselle's grip, all while cussing her out.

*Cori, Giselle, and David were inseparable, holding one another up in good times and bad.*

The gambit worked: David let out a deep belly laugh that went on and on. Every time he regained enough control to stop, he started again.

Losing a job was one thing; losing a child was another. Giselle knew that there were no pranks or jokes that could possibly cheer David up or fill the void created by his daughter's absence. But now in the breakfast room she could try to comfort Kiara's fellow Scouts by continuing the meeting and moving forward.

Giselle told the girls about some of the great things planned for the troop over the course of the upcoming year. There were discussions about playing soccer, attending a dance camp, and organizing other activities.

"But what do you *most* want to do next?" Giselle probed.

"Coding?" Sanaa said.

"Cookies," another girl said. Immediately a chorus of "Cookies! Cookies!" filled the room.

"Cookies," Giselle said, nodding. "We're trying to figure out how we're going to do this."

Giselle began rehashing the mechanics of cookies sales, explaining that every troop has a bank account, but Troop 6000, because it was a special program spread across several shelters, did not. This was not the entire truth. When she realized her partial explanation was going over the girls' heads, she moved on.

Eventually the Scouts' laughter began to fill the emptiness of the room, which now had no chairs and no Kiara. The girls were accustomed to loss—to missing their old homes with their familiar beds, missing their mothers' good food cooked in a kitchen, missing their old neighbors and neighborhoods, missing friends and teachers at their former schools. They would miss Kiara, but they were resilient and they would move forward in spite of their loss.

David returned to the meeting in time for the veteran Scouts to teach the new ones the tradition of the friendship circle. He nodded solemnly to all the OGs and took his place in the circle between Christina and Jessica, crossing his right arm over his left. Jessica and Christina grabbed his hands, petite Christina's face coming just to his elbow. Then he looked down at Giselle's middle child, with her long dark hair and her brown skin still kissed by the summer sun, and she looked up at him, squeezing his hand with her tiny fingers and not letting go.

# 21

# "YOU ARE A POWERFUL WOMAN"

THE JACKSON AVENUE Family Residence in the Bronx looked like a school building, red brick with green trim. When it opened in 1988, the shelter was so shiny and new that it sparked jealousy among those who lived in the crumbling tenements around it. Children threw rocks; adults griped that they had worked too hard to see homeless families live so lavishly. But Jackson Avenue was not immune to wear and tear, and families living there through the years complained of mice and roaches and stuffy rooms made hotter and mustier by the lack of air conditioning and windows that would not open.

The physical condition of the building had improved thanks to a massive repair effort of all city shelters that began in 2014, but fixing a radiator was different from alleviating the pain of living in a place that is not your own home. There was no easy fix for that. Starting a Girl Scout troop there offered, as a baseline, some hope that the girls living in the shelter could find some joy when they walked through the doors.

As Cori approached the building, she mentally rehearsed again and again what she would say on this, her very first recruitment visit.

My name is Corinthia Fludd.
I work for the Girl Scouts of Greater New York.
Troop 6000 is the first troop for girls in shelter in New York City.
We want to start a troop here.

She chuckled a bit because she knew that she sounded like Giselle. Well, the professional Giselle who was now her co-worker, not the Giselle she'd smoked cigarettes with on the "porch" of the Sleep Inn. Cori could not believe that she, too, had landed a job at the Girl Scouts.

Following her gut instinct, Meridith had asked Cori for her résumé, but Cori's initial response had been perfunctory. Why would this stranger offer to give her a chance? No job had ever worked out long term for her. She'd finally set her sights on being a home health aide when Meridith broached the possibility of working for Troop 6000 with her. And Meridith, as first Giselle and then Cori had come to learn, was nothing if not persistent.

She had a plan to assemble a squad of bold women to jump-start the Troop 6000 expansion and that's what she did. Giselle became program manager; Cori became the recruiting special-ist; and Heidi Schmidt, who had worked for the Department of Homeless Services and who was a key early supporter of the cre-ation of Troop 6000, became the director. Meridith had seen Heidi at so many Troop 6000 events that she figured Heidi might be itching to do something different, and it turned out she was right.

Cori had been in awe the first time she traveled to Wall Street and entered the seventy-one-story building where the Girl Scouts of Greater New York was based. She'd done everything in her power not to laugh when Giselle greeted her—"Welcome. Follow me"—in a professional-sounding voice more like that of a telemarketer than her wisecracking friend from Queens. Giselle was sort of her boss now, or at least a colleague who had more experience and was higher in rank.

They passed the reception desk and a small store, a souvenir shop that sold all things Girl Scouts. The seventh floor was a

maze of hallways and glass-enclosed offices with a room of cubicles. One of those cubicles was Cori's, and from it she could see
Meridith's corner office, and what hung on the swivel chair behind the big desk: Meridith's vest from when she was a Senior
Girl Scout and Gold Award winner.

Most of Cori's work was done not in her cubicle but outside the
office. The plan was to extend Troop 6000 to at least fourteen
more shelters within the five boroughs. Cori had to go door-to-
door to shelters all over the city trying to solicit women and girls
to get involved with Troop 6000. Giselle became the unofficial
face of the troop and continued to do media interviews when the
Girl Scouts asked, but Cori, in her job as a recruiter, was the first
official from the Girl Scouts that many parents met face-to-face.

Cori had molded herself into a version of Office Giselle, at
least on the outside. On the day she visited the Jackson Avenue
Family Residence, she wore one of her brunette wigs, a button-
down shirt with the Girl Scouts insignia, and dark slacks. She
carried a handful of flyers with her name and contact information printed at the bottom. As soon as she walked in, she spotted
a petite woman who walked with a switch, as if she were itching
for a fight. No matter: Cori began giving her pitch in the same
voice that Giselle had used while taking Cori on a tour of the
Girl Scouts office.

"Hello, my name is Corinthia Fludd," she said smoothly, pro-
fessionally.

The woman's name was Ebony, and she stared blankly at
Cori, who quickly realized the problem: She was not being herself, and that was never going to work. She immediately dropped
her Giselle impression.

"Girl, I'm Cori," she said, going into detail about how she
lived at the Sleep Inn, got involved with Troop 6000, and now
worked for the Girl Scouts.

"You're starting a Girl Scouts troop here?" Ebony asked when
she realized that this stranger was not joking. "I have three
daughters. I know a whole lot of girls in here."

Ebony was a self-aware recovering bully who relapsed every

now and again. Tattoos snaked up her arms and down her waist, her way of making clear to everyone that she was not to be messed with. She had grown up in a foster home run by an older couple in Brooklyn—she called them her grandparents, but she was not related to them.

Well into her thirties, older than Cori, she was nevertheless willing to listen and to follow directions that day in the Jackson Avenue lobby. She offered to pass out flyers and to round up girls. And so she spent the next week selling other people on the idea of Troop 6000. She told anyone who would listen that Cori, that bewigged recruitment lady from the Girl Scouts, was "mad ghetto," a big compliment; it was Ebony's way of signaling to everyone that the Girl Scouts had employees who were down-to-earth and Troop 6000 would not be one of those programs that felt patronizing.

Ebony was what social workers would describe as "service resistant," but Ebony would call herself knowledgeable. She didn't trust any of the new voucher programs for rental assistance that the de Blasio administration had started, nor was she interested in jobs programs that wouldn't give her financial security. She told caseworkers she would work and wait until she could get a spot in public housing, which based a tenant's rent on income. Once you got a spot—and waiting could take years—as long as you continued to meet the income and other requirements, you could keep the apartment indefinitely.

Besides sparring with staff at the shelter, Ebony's main focus was raising her three daughters: twelve-year-old Lelilani, six-year-old Maliyah, and four-year-old Melanie. She'd been a single mother since she and her boyfriend had broken up earlier that year.

With Ebony and her daughters on board, Cori had already recruited four people for the Girl Scouts shelter expansion plan, even if Melanie wasn't quite old enough yet. On her second visit to Jackson Avenue, she brought Giselle along to hold an official meeting, and Ebony had found more than two dozen girls who were ready to join.

No two shelters were the same in a city that had more than four hundred of them, and the Ruth Fernandez Family Residence, also in the Bronx, was not as receptive as Jackson Avenue had been to Cori's Girl Scouts pitch.

After initially meeting a few parents and staff there, Cori knew she needed help; the vibe was hardly welcoming. She could not let Heidi and Giselle, not to mention Meridith, find out that she was failing to get Troop 6000 off the ground there. She needed backup. And she knew exactly who that was.

"What are you doing?" Cori said on the phone, without saying hello.

"I'm not doing nothing," David responded.

"Don't you want to go to this shelter with me?"

David, who'd been alone in his room at the Sleep Inn, agreed to meet Cori at Ruth Fernandez; he threw on his Troop 6000 blue jean vest and hopped on the train.

"So Ruth Fernandez doesn't have a troop leader," Cori told David once he arrived.

David shook his head, confused but flattered that he was being tapped once again to step in as Troop 6000 hit a bumpy stretch. Most of his focus these days was on finding a good-paying job, getting an apartment, and regaining custody of Kiara; a hearing was set in Philadelphia in October, just one month away.

"You didn't tell me you wanted me to take over. You told me to just come with you," he said to Cori.

She smiled sweetly in return.

Thirteen girls showed up for the meeting, and David and Cori had them participate in a team building exercise. David missed Kiara terribly; helping at Ruth Fernandez once a week, he quickly realized, might fill the void in some small way. He signed on.

Once David's cooking prowess became evident, the girls at Ruth Fernandez would come to call him "Chef D." He found creative and entertaining ways to incorporate food into lessons, testing the girls' senses, for instance, by using lemons, brown sugar, white sugar, and spices in a blind smell test. For a lesson on nutrition, he led the girls in a mock cooking show and judged their creations of sandwiches and salads.

David had once flopped at an audition for *MasterChef*, a competitive cooking television show; he had shown up unprepared, not understanding that he was required to provide his own equipment. The whole episode had been excruciatingly embarrassing. But at Girl Scout meetings he could make mistakes and prepare food knowing that the girls weren't judging him. He, too, was learning. The girls were just happy to be there, having fun with one another and attempting to slice, dice, and prepare whatever projects he cooked up.

By the end of September, Cori had managed to start Troop 6000, or at least meet staff and parents, in four shelters beyond the first two new ones in the Bronx: two on Manhattan's Lower East Side; one in Harlem; and another in Bushwick, Brooklyn. Including the Sleep Inn in Queens, there were now a total of seven locations for Troop 6000.

One Saturday morning, Heidi, Giselle, and Cori gathered all of the volunteers who were poised to become troop leaders at the Wall Street office for a training workshop. Ebony sat at a table with mothers from Jackson Avenue. Mickyle, Sanaa's mother, and Sue, Jessica's mother, represented the Sleep Inn, along with Giselle and Cori.

Other volunteers who varied in age, occupation, and income filled out the room. One was a teacher; another was a fashion stylist. And one was a statuesque woman named Jinji Nicole, who used a cane. A former model and dancer who had strutted alongside Diana Ross in the film *The Wiz* in her heyday, Jinji was regal. She was by far the oldest person there and made it clear that she was to be respected. She believed her purpose was helping others, having made a headline in *The New York Times* a couple of years earlier when she volunteered to help other low-income seniors, but then realized that she needed help herself in order to pay her rent. A nonprofit had helped her get back on her feet with rent assistance, so Jinji believed strongly that she owed something to the world. Volunteering for Troop 6000 was a way to give back.

With the exception of a male Girl Scouts employee who was in the office to take care of audio and visual, David was the only man present. Jinji took on the role of impromptu sage, sharing her opinions with anyone who'd listen. "I wouldn't want to see the world without him," she said, referring to men as if they were a single person. "But Lord, sometimes he gets on my nerves."

Everyone looked at David and laughed; they knew her remark wasn't aimed specifically at him. "What did I walk in on?" David said, laughing himself.

Jinji told him their work was all about guiding girls. "We're gonna lead these babies where they need to go."

The training session ended with a cryfest. Troop 6000 had started with Giselle, Cori, and David as the first and only troop leaders. They'd had victories, they'd stumbled, they'd had to learn on their feet. And now here they were talking to a room full of people about how to be troop leaders in other shelters. Heidi had been there every step of the way, too, and she understood what the moment meant. Overwhelmed by the significance of the day, Giselle looked out at all of the volunteers and just couldn't help herself. She started to cry, initiating a chain reaction that went from Cori to David to Heidi to all of the volunteers. Troop 6000 really *was* coming together. "It means the world to me," she said through her tears.

"I'm glad people are crying," Heidi said, with a big grin on her face even as tears welled in her eyes. "Success!"

⸻

The success would not have been possible without Cori's recruitment efforts. The weight of homelessness sometimes depressed Cori so much that she barely left her room at the Sleep Inn, especially on the weekends, when Trey left for visitation with his father. Now that weight seemed to be lifting. She was meeting people who respected her uniform and her hard work, who wanted to be part of the Troop 6000 that she was promoting. And that made her proud, and happy.

Two months after she started her job with the Girl Scouts of Greater New York, Cori was excited to represent Troop 6000 in Columbus, Ohio, where the Girl Scouts of the USA were holding their triennial national convention. For three days, about 10,000 of the 1.8 million American Girl Scouts and 800,000 adult volunteers would meet to celebrate one another, learn more about Girl Scouting, and plan for the future.

The Scouts poured in, disembarking by the busload, crowding the baggage claim at the airport. Trefoils dotted store windows. The area surrounding the epicenter of the event—the Greater

*Cori, Christina, Hailey, Giselle, and Karina*
*represented Troop 6000 at the Girl Scouts*
*Conference in Columbus, Ohio, October 2017.*

Columbus Convention Center—embraced the spirit: Nearly every hotel hosted Scouts and their parents and chaperones, with laughter filling lobbies and ringing out onto the streets. Green lights from the convention center illuminated the sky.

Giselle, Hailey, Karina, and Christina served as Troop 6000 envoys along with Cori. They were disappointed that the whole troop, especially all the OGs, couldn't attend; after all, many of them had never been on a plane before. It would have been one more life experience, one more badge to earn that they didn't even know they wanted until they were in the thick of Girl Scouting. But the Girl Scouts couldn't coordinate all of the logistics with New York City's shelter system, and the organization had to make a decision to designate a few girls as ambassadors. Giselle's daughters, who now had their own home and no longer needed permission to be absent from a shelter for more than forty-eight hours, were the obvious choices.

Attending the convention as a new employee of the Girl Scouts, Cori was an equally obvious choice as an ambassador. Leaving Queens had been complicated for her. She had to seek permission from Childrens Community Services, but she took care of it, providing her caseworker with a letter from the Girl Scouts.

When Giselle, Cori, and the girls arrived in Columbus wearing their matching pink Girl Scouts of Greater New York baseball caps on Thursday morning, they immediately headed to registration, where they were handed laminated name tags suspended from beaded lanyards. Their names were typed neatly, along with their age group and their council, Greater New York. The officialness of it all was thrilling.

The convention center was a whirlwind of colors and trefoils and vests and badges. An older Girl Scout leader from Illinois wore a vest that was so long it almost swept the floor as if it were a caftan, making room for what had to be at least two thousand badges, pins, and homemade trinkets that Scouts traded called SWAPS, Special Whatchamacallits Affectionately Pinned Somewhere. When Cori looked out at the convention floor, she saw an endless swath of vests that looked like badges on a single giant vest. Troop 6000's appearance at the Yankees baseball game earlier that year had seemed like a pretty big deal, but this was massive.

"I didn't know there were so many," Cori said to Giselle in a hushed voice as they made their way across the floor taking in all the people and paraphernalia. It was almost overwhelming.

They ran into Meridith, who had arrived days earlier for a meeting of chief Girl Scout executives from around the country. She hadn't been to a convention since she was a girl in Maine twenty-six years ago. Now she was a star on the rise, chief executive in the country's largest city who had helped create Troop 6000 and secured seven figures in government funding to keep it going.

It had been a busy few days, and not without controversy. The media attention received by Troop 6000 bothered some people. The Girl Scouts had long embraced girls who had been homeless or had lived in financially unstable households, sometimes even subsidizing their dues. What was the big deal about Troop 6000? some of them asked. The difference between simply subsidizing dues for a few deserving girls and founding troops in shelters and tailoring meetings for the girls who lived there was so huge and obvious that Meridith had to wonder what it was the naysayers were actually bothered about. She knew the sisterhood would overcome any animosity; the people she had to worry about were outside the Girl Scouts.

Just minutes before she ran into Giselle, Cori, and the girls, Meridith strolled across the convention floor through rows of tables and booths selling Girl Scout paraphernalia and mementos. A genial vendor chatted her up, and Meridith, in turn, talked about being from New York and bringing Troop 6000 to Columbus.

He said he had heard of them. And then he had a question: "Where are they sleeping? Outside the convention center?" He let out a prolonged belly laugh.

Meridith was shocked. Was he seriously making a joke about girls being homeless? She stared at him in disbelief. When she

From top to bottom: *Christina,*
*Giselle and Christina,*
*Cori, Hailey*

was finally able to speak she said, "You better not ever say that again."

The Troop 6000 contingent was happy to see a familiar face amid the sea of vests and badges. Someone handed them all foam headpieces that looked like the Statue of Liberty's crown. Meridith didn't want to ruin the moment, so she smiled as wide as she could while they posed in front of a display that read I AM A G.I.R.L., the Girl Scouts slogan, in which G.I.R.L. stood for

GO-GETTER

INNOVATOR

RISK-TAKER

LEADER

Strangers who recognized the distinctive number on the girls' vests and on the tote bags that Cori and Giselle carried approached them. "You're Troop 6000!" girls and parents shouted. Many people wanted to take selfies, and Giselle, Cori, and the girls obliged; they were proud that so many Girl Scouts from all over looked up to them. It was an amazing feeling, one that made them understand the idea of being a G.I.R.L. in a whole new way.

They spent the rest of the day wandering around the convention center and taking more photos with admirers. They attended a plenary session with thousands of other Scouts, joining in the loudest recitation of the Girl Scout Promise they had ever heard.

When they checked in to the Hampton Inn & Suites after ten o'clock, Giselle, Cori, and the girls couldn't get over what felt to them like pure extravagance. The rooms were much larger and plusher than the ones at the Sleep Inn, more like small apartments, really; the bedrooms were actually separate from the living areas, where the girls took turns plopping down on the couches. The five of them had been assigned two suites. Each had a kitchen area with a refrigerator, a sink, and a microwave. The only thing missing was a stove. This was the kind of room that homeless families should have been living in back in New York, they all agreed. Families would have had privacy, space, and the dignity of not sleeping on top of one another. Even though it was late, Cori told the girls to put on their bathing suits. The Hampton Inn had an indoor pool, and Cori insisted that they were going to take advantage of every amenity available, including eating at the breakfast buffet, something they had never been allowed to do when they lived at the Sleep Inn.

When they all finally crawled into bed that night, they had one final thrill. To anyone else, the sheets were nothing special—plain white linens, the usual hotel offering. To Giselle, Cori, and the girls, however, they were pure luxury because they were soft, not scratchy, and there was no trace anywhere of the words PROPERTY OF DHS.

The second day of the convention was just as frenzied. Instead of merely taking selfies, the girls began having conversations with Scouts from other cities. Hailey collected badges and SWAPS, stuffing them into a ziplock bag that bulged so much it began to look like a throw pillow.

By the end of the day, Troop 6000 was readying itself for special recognition, because it was considered to be one of the troops that fully symbolized a core belief of the Scouts: "A girl who meets or can meet membership requirements shall not be denied admission or access to [the] Girl Scout program because of race, color, ethnicity, creed, national origin, socioeconomic status, or disability." Equally important, its new model of what constitutes a troop was pushing the Girl Scouts into the future.

As they were walking into the meeting where they would be recognized, Cori's phone rang. It was the resident who lived next door to her at the Sleep Inn.

"What?" Cori said, waving Giselle into the room. She remained on the phone outside the doors.

Inside the room, Giselle and the girls settled into their seats and the lights dimmed. Juliette Gordon Low's words appeared on the screen: "Truly, ours is a circle of friendships, united by our ideals."

The first image was of Girl Scouts in Knoxville, Tennessee, singing the circle song. Three special education teachers had started a troop for their students. Andrea McCarter, one of the teachers, said, "I think that girls get to shine in any troop, and I think that troops take on a personality of their own. It's a small group of like-minded girls that get to shine with their own skills."

In Tucson, Arizona, a troop drew its Scouts from a predominantly undocumented Latino community. A nervous Scout swayed when she talked into the camera: "I love Girl Scouts 'cause it's fun to do and we learn a lot."

In Orange County, California, the council tailored troops to recognize the different heritages and religions of girls. One troop met at a Buddhist temple, and many of its members were Japanese. Another met at a school for students who were Muslim.

And then Genesis appeared, filling up the screen in her khaki vest. "You know, I'm fifteen. I'm a teenager. I see the girls in

New York, like how they are. And they'll, like, make fun of you 'cause your mom can't afford a pair of shoes."

Genesis put her head into her hands, her eyes watering. "With them"—meaning her fellow Troop 6000 Scouts—"it's different. When I'm around them, when I'm around them, like, I forget about all of that. And it's just, like, it's us."

At the same time Genesis was crying onscreen, Cori was sobbing outside the room. Her neighbor at the Sleep Inn had told her that a resident assistant was in her room packing up her belongings.

Cori had done everything right—seeking permission and getting a letter from the Girl Scouts—but there had been a miscommunication or someone had decided that the letter was not adequate authorization for her absence from shelter for more than forty-eight hours. According to Childrens Community Services, Cori was in breach. So now they were kicking her out.

After the special tribute, Giselle and the girls found Cori shaking in the hall.

"What's wrong?" Giselle asked, her own anxiety immediately skyrocketing.

"I just got a call." Cori shook her head in disbelief. "Why are they packing up my stuff? They're kicking me out."

"They can't do this," Giselle said, incensed. "I promise we're going to handle this!"

Cori called her caseworker again and again, leaving messages. Giselle pulled her cellphone out of her tote bag and started scrolling through her contacts. She began dialing numbers, too. "I'm calling Jimmy. I'm calling Heidi."

Within an hour, Cori received a call from a representative of Childrens Community Services. She would not be moved.

Cori turned to Giselle in disbelief. "You are a powerful woman."

The convention would always be historic for them. Meridith had learned that educating people about homelessness was harder than she'd imagined. Giselle learned that she had the heft and access to change the lives of other people, and her daughters came to understand that the Girl Scouts truly spanned the globe, and that they were worthy representatives. And Cori got confirmation that finally having a job that commanded respect could not shield her from experiencing all of the indignities and cruelties of homelessness. When she arrived back at the Sleep Inn, her room looked just like it had when she'd moved in with Trey: Their clothes and personal belongings, including food and her laptop, had been stuffed into clear plastic bags, which sat on the floor waiting for her to unpack them.

But no one could take away Troop 6000. It was now in six additional New York shelters because of Cori, and she would add seven more by the end of the year.

||||||||||||||||||||||

Earlier in 2017, in a coordinated count all over the country, the federal government had estimated the number of people sleeping in shelters, in their cars, or on the streets. Nearly 554,000 people were homeless, and that did not count the families who were on the brink, doubled and tripled up with friends and relatives. It was the first time in seven years that homelessness had increased in the United States.

In Nashville, back in April, Agenia Clark, the chief executive of the Girl Scouts of Middle Tennessee, was going through her routine of watching the news while working out on her treadmill when she saw Giselle on the *Today* show. Seconds after the segment ended, her cellphone rang. A board member was on the line: "Are we doing this?"

Nearly 1,900 Nashville students were considered homeless, a designation given to children who were also living in doubled-up situations. In New York, by order of the court, people could stay in a shelter indefinitely as long as they qualified, and the average families stayed for fourteen months. In Nashville, there was no court order, and families had only three months to try to pull themselves together before they had to leave. The shelter staff tried to help them to find homes or reconnect with relatives and friends who could make room for them. As those who studied homelessness had learned, three months wasn't nearly enough time to put a life back together. But in the Music City, with no court mandate and limited resources, three months was all families could get.

The Girl Scouts of Middle Tennessee could not solve that issue, so for now, they would have mere weeks to make an impact on the girls living in shelter. Under Agenia Clark, they did just that. As the new school year kicked off in August, the Tennessee council started a troop at the Safe Haven Family Shelter with fifteen homeless girls.

They called it Troop 6000.

# 22

# UGLY CHRISTMAS SWEATER

**ONE MORNING IN** December, Meridith called Giselle and said she missed spending time together. With the swirl of starting Troop 6000, expanding it, and publicizing it, Meridith and Giselle now had an increasingly clear boss-employee relationship and little time to socialize with each other. She suggested they go out that night. Dinner would be Meridith's treat, and then a little dancing at the Copacabana, the famous Midtown club. Meridith's kids had missed Giselle's, and Dan had volunteered to babysit, so all ten children could hang out together at their house; the matched set of playmates had always been a bonus.

Giselle had the day off, with nothing on the calendar except some errands and a routine doctor's appointment. The children, who were at home on winter break from school, were thrilled with the idea.

Giselle was grateful for the invitation. It would cheer her up. Christmas was just three days away, but it didn't feel like it. Even though they were no longer living in a shelter, a holiday with gifts and a tree and maybe a dinner fancier than beans, rice, and chicken—an inexpensive meal that she often fed her large family—was out of the question. Yes, they had a whole house in which to celebrate this year, not just a single hotel room, and they were all grateful and appreciative. But with the rent she paid and other expenses for the house, no matter how carefully she budgeted, there just wasn't anything left over. A year earlier, she had decorated their room at the Sleep Inn with a tiny tree. This year, there was no tree at all.

Later in the day, after Giselle had arranged to get the children to Dan and Meridith's place in Sunnyside, she realized she had to figure out what she should wear for a night on the town. When was the last time she had gone out dancing? She couldn't remember. After brief deliberation, she threw on a sleeveless black dress and black and gold stockings. And what should she do with her hair? Giselle decided she would wear it curly. She didn't put on any makeup, just the tiniest bit of lip gloss so she could avoid chapping in the winter air. After inspecting herself in the paneled bathroom mirrors, she decided that while she didn't look great it was good enough for a simple girls' night out.

She took the train to Midtown and met Meridith at an Irish pub, where she ordered bangers and mash and Meridith had a steak. They tasted each other's food and laughed over a glass of wine. Giselle had missed evenings like this, those rare occasions when they'd sat at Meridith's house drinking the cheapest wine that would not make them sick and talking about the Girl Scouts and raising children.

Because she had worked on Broadway for so long and had so many connections in the entertainment industry in New York, Meridith was always able to finagle a couple of tickets to musicals and talk shows. Near the end of the meal she had a surprise for Giselle.

"My friend got us some extra tickets to *The Tonight Show Starring Jimmy Fallon*," she said with a grin. "We're going to go there before the Copa."

"Really?" Giselle flashed one of her million-dollar smiles.

Giselle had been visiting Midtown Manhattan during the holiday season since she was a little girl, a treat her parents could afford because there was no cost to view the lights on display, the elaborate store windows, and the tree at Rockefeller Center. The giant tree had never failed to take Giselle's breath away. This year, it was a Norway spruce from Pennsylvania adorned with fifty thousand lights and topped with a Swarovski star.

Full from sausage, steak, and wine, Meridith and Giselle had to wade through shoulder-to-shoulder swaths of tourists to get to the studio at 30 Rockefeller Plaza, where Jimmy Fallon taped his talk show. Giselle had been holding a grudge against Fallon for a while. Like many talk show hosts, he had offered to donate something to Troop 6000, promising the Girl Scouts that he would pay for pizzas at a meeting, but he had never followed through. *The View* had arranged for Toyota to give Troop 6000 a car, and Jimmy Fallon couldn't follow through with a couple dozen pies? Whether it was forgetfulness or ignorance, Giselle took it as a slight.

Sometimes, when Giselle wanted to make a point, she would cock her head with attitude and blink twice. This was one of those times. "I hope I get a chance to talk to him so I can ask what happened to the pizza," Giselle said.

Just like the ABC studio where Giselle and the Scouts had taped *The View*, Fallon's studio was icy cold; if there was a "winter" option on the thermostat there, that's where it had been set. Giselle had worn an oversize taupe-colored sweater over her dress, probably best suited for wear only around the house, but she kept it on, even when she and Meridith were seated in the very front row.

Giselle remembered how there had been breaks between segments during the taping of *The View*. Her front-row seat could get her within earshot of Fallon. "I'm really going to tell him about those pizzas," she asserted.

Fallon's first guest would be Issa Rae, the actress, writer, and producer who starred in *Insecure* on HBO, and it would be the last night of a giveaway he called "The 12 Days of Ugly Christmas Sweaters." Fallon, good-natured and always laughing at his own jokes, had been rewarding one member of the audience each night for the past eleven nights with an outrageously awful sweater.

Now he went to the "Christmas cabinet," a stack of colorful boxes made to look like a bureau, and fished out a sweater. "That is *beautiful*," he said, holding up a truly hideous garment that made the audience roar. "Now, let's see who's going home with the last Christmas sweater." Fallon reached into a bag, pulled out a card, and called out the number 121.

He scaled steps in the stands to where a woman named Katie, who said she was from New Jersey, raised her hand and was announced as the winner. Fallon told Katie she looked great, and that the sweater, which had a shiny green lining, was actually more like a cloak or a cape. "Do you have anything like this?" he asked her.

"Now I do," Katie said, getting a laugh from the audience.

Giselle thought they were about to go on another break when Fallon said, "Hey, guys! I'm in the Christmas spirit. I don't want to give away one sweater. Oh, no! I want to give away two sweaters. That's right. I have one more Christmas sweater to give away."

A young guy in a suit appeared and ran up the aisle through the audience to give Fallon a lumpy black sweater decorated with Santa Clauses and bells and presents.

"Who wants it?" he teased the audience.

Giselle didn't know she wanted the sweater so badly, but apparently she did, and she waved her hands wildly like everyone else in the audience.

"Yes, right there, you in the front row. You can get it."

Giselle stood up, not caring anymore that she was wearing no makeup and her hair was a mess.

Fallon walked over to her and someone handed Giselle a microphone.

"What is your name and where are you from?" Fallon asked.

"Giselle, and I'm from Woodside, Queens."

"Do you have anything like this?"

"No."

"Let's try this. See how this looks. You want to try this thing on?"

"Will it fit me?" Giselle asked.

"It's more of a draping thing. Yeah, this is good. Everyone's wearing it in New Jersey. Trust me," he said.

Giselle dipped down and allowed him to enwrap her with it. "You look beautiful," Fallon said.

Giselle was blushing and gushing. "Thank you. Thank you so much."

Fallon kept talking. "Hey, you know what? I have to say something here. I know a little bit about you."

"You do?"

"You're a pretty incredible person," Fallon told her.

The realization washed over Giselle, slowly and then quickly—she'd been set up.

Fallon detailed her journey from single mother to founder of Troop 6000 to the expansion into more shelters. Giselle looked back at Meridith, whose eyes were glossy with tears even as a "gotcha" grin lit up her face.

Fallon was still talking. "Troop 6000 has done so much for others, and we wanted to help make the holidays a little brighter for you and your kids, so in honor of Troop 6000, we're giving you a check for six thousand dollars."

The same guy who had emerged with the sweater reappeared with a giant check. Giselle looked down and realized her name was on it. The check was made out directly to her.

She kept looking back at Meridith and then looking at Fallon. "That is not all," he told Giselle, who was getting more emotional and more confused. JCPenney, the department store, also wanted to make a donation, he said.

Seemingly out of nowhere, there were Hailey and Karina. They were holding another giant check—this one for $50,000 to Troop 6000.

"Do you know these girls?" Fallon asked.

Giselle buckled over and Fallon had to make sure she didn't fall. "Do you know these girls?" he asked again.

Giselle collapsed in her daughters' arms and the three of them put their heads together in an embrace that felt like it lasted forever, like no one was watching.

The girls got to go backstage and watch the rest of the show in the green room while Giselle and Meridith continued to sit in the audience. After the show, the Roots, the hip-hop group that was the official house band, joined Hailey and Karina backstage, along with Giselle and Meridith. Fallon's staff paid for Giselle, Meridith, and the girls to get home. Giselle forgot to ask Fallon about the pizza.

*Giselle backstage with Questlove,*
*the drummer in the Roots, the house band*
*on Jimmy Fallon's* Tonight *show.*

As they were leaving the studio at a very late hour, emotionally spent and yet energized at the same time, Giselle had a question for Meridith.

"Wait, we're not going to the Copa?"

# 23

# "LEAN ON ME"

DEEP INTO WINTER, the family was still stepping on the occasional pine needle from the huge tree Giselle had bought at the House of Holiday, a giant store in Ozone Park that prided itself on being New York's "ultimate Christmas shopping destination." Strolling through the sprawling market of lights and wreaths and ornaments and train sets, Giselle had felt the cheer of the holiday bubbling up inside her. The scent of Douglas firs and Fraser firs and Scotch pines filled the air, and her youngest children were eagerly awaiting a Santa sighting. Giselle had decided it was almost as nice as visiting Midtown on a crisp winter day to take in all the holiday decorations around Rockefeller Center. She bought her children a few things they needed—like a new iPad for Hailey so she could do her homework, and new shoes for everyone—and a few things they wanted—like a guitar and Shawn Mendes paraphernalia for Karina; a Nintendo handheld game for Judas; and arts and crafts kits for Christina and Gillesy. She also got one more gift—a Pandora ring—for Hailey. The check from *The Tonight Show* had brought some much needed joy at a time when Giselle once again felt that she had little to give to her own family, even as she was working so hard to give to others.

A complication had arisen during this holiday season, though, with the original Troop 6000's meeting place: The Sleep Inn had folded up its welcome mat. The hotel now had so many regular guests that rearranging and closing the breakfast room had become troublesome for the staff, and their chilliness was apparent to all. There were other problems, too. Formerly homeless people were not supposed to return to a shelter without permission. While Giselle was an employee of the Girl Scouts and could visit the shelter in her professional capacity, volunteers like Jessica's mother, Sue Seaman, were not allowed to come and go because the Seamans had moved into their own apartment in Ozone Park. Giselle and Cori had already been holding occasional events outside the shelter, and now it looked like they were going to have to make a formal move for the regular meetings.

Giselle had been talking to people at Evangel Christian Church about opening up one of its classrooms to the troop. Evangel was within walking distance of the Sleep Inn, which would mean that the Scouts could get to the meetings easily, an essential requirement for any new meeting space. While the inconvenience of an outside meeting place was something Meridith had been adamant about avoiding a year ago, before Troop 6000's very first meeting, it looked like now that was the only way this group could continue. Evangel agreed to welcome Troop 6000, and the Girl Scouts were grateful for their hospitality.

At the same time Giselle was focused on finalizing details with the church, she was also planning World Thinking Day, a day in February when Girl Scouts across the United States and Girl Guides around the world would reflect on their global link as girl leaders and future women leaders and learn about places they'd never been. The event was driven by the World Association of Girl Guides and Girl Scouts, which had formed in the 1920s to bring together Scouts overseas with American Scouts. Troop 6000's celebration would fall on the same date as the one-year anniversary of their first meeting, so in a way February 24, 2018, would be a grand fete for the troop.

The Sleep Inn Scouts would give a presentation on Guatemala—Evelyn's birthplace—performing a traditional dance that Giselle had watched on YouTube and then taught them; exhibiting pottery that they would make out of clay; and displaying a map of the country that they would color themselves. Giselle was so busy buying clay and figuring out the logistics of transportation for all of the different shelters that she kept putting off calling her gynecologist after her routine checkup the preceding month.

But then her doctor's office called. She had an abnormal pap smear. She needed to come in for a follow-up appointment.

"Can't we talk on the phone?" Giselle asked, irritated and frustrated because there were not enough hours in the day. "Is it good or bad?"

The caller told her she needed to come into the office.

Days later, after further testing confirmed her doctor's preliminary diagnosis, Giselle sat her children down in the living room. She had some news. The "living room talk" was always nerve-racking for Hailey and Karina. There had been the time Giselle told them she was moving to Florida, and the time she'd told them they were officially homeless and going into shelter. This was a new living room, of course, but it was still stressful. The children gathered around their mother and waited for whatever she had to say. Judas and Gillesy stretched out on their siblings' laps.

"I have cancer," Giselle told them, fighting to hold back her tears. It was cervical cancer. Then she did her best to explain what that was.

Hailey began crying. The others asked questions machine-gun-style.

Karina: "Okay. What medicine do you have to take?"

Christina: "Are you going to lose your hair?"

Karina: "I'll shave my head, too!"

Realizing she needed to be strong for her siblings, Hailey pulled herself together and tried to inject some levity into the despair that had enveloped the living room. "I'm not shaving my head, but I'll wear colorful scarves."

She and Giselle laughed through tears.

"I can give you some of my hair." Christina offered coal-black tresses.

Giselle explained that there was no need for wigs or shaved heads yet. She was going to undergo radiation treatment. It would last for about six weeks and then everything would be okay.

Hailey backed her up. "It's going to be okay."

In the next few days Giselle downplayed the severity of the situation as she let her family and friends know. She told Cori one day after work and smiled, her default response, as Cori burst into tears. Cori considered Giselle to be one of her best friends now, but she had no clue what to say. She definitely didn't want to make what was surely the most harrowing experience of Giselle's life any worse, so she made a joke.

"Bitch, you can't die. Who's going to watch all those kids?"

In the weeks to come, Cori called Giselle's mother several times to see how she could help, to find out if there was anything Giselle wasn't sharing.

Giselle's father, GWIZ, had cried and was nearly inconsolable when she told him. Her stepfather, Manny, clammed up in an awkward, perhaps fearful, silence while Evelyn pummeled Giselle with questions: Who were the doctors? What did this mean? How serious was this? What stage?

"I'm going to google," she said decisively. It had always tickled Giselle when her mother announced that she was on a mission to find answers online. Usually Evelyn's research involved the Mets, because of Manny's love for the team, or finding the perfect recipe, or tracking down something about the Girl Scouts. Giselle doubted that googling held the answer to the problem she was now facing.

Giselle was a walking billboard for the health problems faced by black women and low-income people, especially those who grew up in urban areas. Her childhood had been confined to a small, overcrowded apartment in which air didn't circulate. With the exception of her two years in Florida, she'd lived her entire life in a part of Queens that was known as an "Asthma Alley," because disproportionately high numbers of residents suffered from respiratory problems; more than half of the city's power was pumped out of plants along the East River, and air pollutants hovered over Long Island City and drifted to Woodside and Sunnyside. Influenced in part by the advertisements she saw on posters in the windows of bodegas all over her neighborhood, she had begun smoking at a young age.

Because Giselle had worked in dental offices for so long, she'd learned to take good care of her teeth and had had regular dental checkups. But she was not always able to make it to routine preventive doctors' appointments. That her cancer was discovered during a wellness visit was an amazing stroke of luck, given that routine exams were not routine for her. Nor were visits for small problems likely to happen, due to the high cost of medical care; problems usually had to become severe before a trip to the doctor—or the emergency room—ensued. Like a majority of black people in the United States, Giselle had had a serious chronic medical condition—in her case, epilepsy—discovered during a trip to the emergency room.

And living in poverty meant constant stress. Giselle could remember few times when she wasn't worried about money or keeping a roof over her children's heads. Hers was a chronic stress that was not going away anytime soon, and as Giselle would later learn, stress could produce chemical reactions in the body that directly and negatively impacted a person's health. The method she chose to manage her stress on her own—through smoking, which she felt relaxed her—only compounded her problems.

On the first day of her treatment, Giselle left the Girl Scouts building in downtown Manhattan, weaving through tourists and passing the New York Stock Exchange on the way to the subway. She was in a rush, never looking up to marvel at the palatial structure, with its white marble and colonnades and pediments. High above the street, the statue of a woman dressed in a long gown and flowing robe held out her hands as if protecting the world and fighting it all at the same time.

Giselle pounded down the station stairs, ran for the closing doors, then raced uptown on that train before burrowing beneath the East River on another one lurching toward Astoria, Queens, where she was about to begin treatments at an office there. She'd turned down offers from her family and friends to accompany her to treatments. Even though she was filled with an almost overpowering sense of dread and anxiety, she knew she needed to get through this alone.

In her darkest moments she let herself descend into a horrible eddy of imaginings. Round and round the chilling thoughts swirled in her head. Was Hailey ready to take care of the others if Giselle died? If she wasn't (and how could she possibly be old enough—she wasn't even fifteen), what would happen to the family? Would the children be split up? Would they end up back in shelter? Or worse: If she became so sick with cancer, if the cancer spread, what would happen if she could only lie there and waste away as her children watched helplessly?

It took all her strength—and earphones blasting a playlist of Beyoncé, Aaliyah, and Lauryn Hill—to chase these thoughts out of her mind as the train rumbled and screeched its way to Queens for that first treatment. She'd managed to live with epilepsy, she reminded herself. She'd managed to survive an abusive relationship. She'd gotten her career on track. She'd had the inspiration for Troop 6000 and with the help of the Girl Scouts and some amazing friends, she'd taken a crazy idea and made it into a reality. And, by some miracle, all five of her children were healthy and doing well. She could survive cancer, she told herself. She could do it. She had no choice.

Giselle expected the office to look fancier than it did, or at least more modern. She had worked in enough dental offices to know that this one lacked the trendy décor of newer suites where mood lighting and comfortable furniture were aimed at trying to make people forget they were sick. She had certainly been in enough doctors' offices because of her epilepsy. There was no pretense here, no trying to mask the purpose of this place. The slogan on all of the paperwork she filled out—CONQUERING CANCER TOGETHER—announced it. Giselle pretended anyway. She signed in, filled out the necessary forms, and sat down to disappear for a few minutes, drifting away until her name was called.

"Ms. Burgess," a medical assistant in muted gray scrubs and black sneakers shouted into the waiting room.

She followed the woman, who wore scrubs similar to ones Giselle herself had worn in her previous job, down a speckled hallway and into a small treatment room. She undressed, slipping out of her Girl Scouts button-down shirt and slacks, stripped down to her underwear, then shrugged into a hospital gown that opened to the front.

At a preliminary visit to review the treatment plan, the radiation oncologist had explained what would happen during her external beam radiation treatment, so she had a reasonable idea of what to expect. She lay down on a cold table and a doctor's assistant marked her lower torso as if readying her for a tattoo. The marks they put on her pelvis, in fact, looked like tattoos, and Giselle thought the machine used to make them looked like a rotary telephone. Lead protectors, meant to shield the rest of her body from radiation, pressed down on her chest and legs.

The table was beneath a machine that looked like a giant faucet. Her pelvis was lined up beneath the "faucet," which emitted the X-rays that were supposed to destroy the cancer. It didn't hurt; in fact, she couldn't feel the beams that were bombarding her abdomen at all. For thirty minutes, she lay still, thinking about what she would cook for dinner, what tasks she needed to complete the next day at work, and how she didn't want to die.

When the treatment was over, she dressed and headed to the subway, hoping she'd find a seat on the crowded train. She felt drained and sluggish, as if she had been out in the sun all day. Her head throbbed, and her body itched and ached.

"We made dinner," Karina told her when she walked into the house about an hour later. Since they'd been living in the Tudor house, Giselle had cooked dinner, a chore she normally relished. On this night, she was so exhausted that her daughters' thoughtfulness almost brought her to tears.

Karina and Hailey caught her up on what Christina, Judas, and Gillesy had done at school and then told their mother that she needed to rest.

"Go lie down," Hailey told her mother. "You're going to be fine."

||||||||||||||||||||||

About four weeks and four treatments later, Giselle stood in a huge community room at St. Francis College in Brooklyn fighting her radiation-induced nausea and watching Meridith prepare to speak. Her friend and boss stood at a podium beneath a sign that said WELCOME in a multitude of languages ranging from Slovak and Norwegian to Spanish and French. Flags from countries around the world hung from the ceiling, along with beach ball–size papier-mâché globes. The flags, the globes, and the poster board displays created by each group of girls had transformed the normally sterile room into a festive gathering spot. Hundreds of Scouts—294 to be exact—sat on the floor and fixed their attention on Meridith as she opened Troop 6000's first World Thinking Day celebration.

Every year, the Girl Scouts and Girl Guides chose a theme for the celebration, and in 2018 the theme was *impact*. "I can't think of a better group of girls to celebrate impact with than Troop 6000. You have made an impact on the city of New York. You have made an impact across the globe to everyone. It's resonated and your story and your courage and your confidence and your participation as a Girl Scout have really changed the world in just one year," Meridith told the group.

It had been a year to the day since Giselle had gathered her three oldest daughters and five other girls inside the breakfast room at the Sleep Inn, worried that the idea of a Girl Scout troop in a homeless shelter would never take root. Now dozens and dozens of girls in thirteen shelters throughout New York City were part of Troop 6000. To celebrate World Thinking Day, each shelter had picked a country to learn about; they would then present their findings knowledgeably to other Scouts. Row after row of folding tables were home to their displays, giving the room a feeling similar to that of a science fair, but without the miniature volcanoes spewing out baking soda lava.

The Jackson Avenue Family Residence, where Ebony lived, chose South Africa. They'd researched famous South African women on the Internet, then downloaded their photographs, enlarged the images, and placed them inside picture frames. Their photo gallery included the actress Charlize Theron, who was placed in a row next to Nomaindia Mfeketo, the minister of human settlements and former mayor of Cape Town, and Zukiswa Wanner, a journalist and an author. The Scouts added stuffed rhinoceroses and miniature toy animals, like a lion and an elephant. An artificial king protea—the national flower of the country—with its spiked petals around a large head, was prominently featured.

Visitors could crisscross the city and the globe by wandering through the maze of colorful poster boards. You could tour Mongolia if you visited the display of the Albemarle Family Residence in Brooklyn; explore Bangladesh with the Westway Motel in Queens; check out the exhibit of the East River Family Center in Manhattan if Portugal was your destination of choice. If Mexico was calling to you, it might be fun to take a look at the presentation set up by the girls from the Ruth Fernandez Family Residence in the Bronx.

For the OGs of Troop 6000, it was also a reunion. Since Hailey, Karina, and Christina no longer lived at the Sleep Inn, they only saw their sister Scouts at the weekly meetings now held at Evangel Christian Church. Sanaa, her two brothers, and her mother, Mickyle, had just moved into an apartment on Staten Island; getting to the meetings on Fridays was so challenging that she didn't know if she was going to be able to stay in the Girl Scouts. But she made it to World Thinking Day.

The OGs were amazed at the number of new Scouts who filled the room. "Remember how I said this was going to be a chain reaction," Hailey bragged. "Look." She nodded her head in an I-told-you-so fashion, as the pride she felt spread across her face in a huge smile.

David was working at an upscale convenience store in Midtown but still volunteered at Ruth Fernandez in the Bronx. He had helped the Scouts there make an elaborate display about Mexico. The girls had been inspired by the movie *Coco,* in which a young Mexican boy paints his face like that of a skeleton for a celebration of the Day of the Dead. Some of the girls painted their faces the same way and were having fun surprising visitors with their slightly ghoulish appearance.

Had World Thinking Day been a competition among the shelters, the Sleep Inn likely would have come in last place. Giselle usually poured herself into such projects, but not this time. Radiation treatments were slowing her down.

But she kept pushing herself. She didn't want anyone to think she wasn't doing her job.

What the Sleep Inn display lacked in visual presentation, Karina and Sanaa made up for with their nonstop enthusiastic recitation of facts. Even though Sanaa lived far away in Staten Island now, she quickly made up for lost time by glancing over the poster board and other materials and memorizing nuggets with lightning speed to tell passersby. "The national flower is the white nun orchid," she said, instantly retaining that curious fact, even though she'd never seen a white nun orchid before or heard of the flower.

"A woman hasn't been elected president there yet. But we hope so," Karina chimed in.

And then there was the food: The room filled with the aromas of curries and peppers and tomato sauce, smelling much like Roosevelt Avenue in Queens, where many immigrants made a living selling dishes from their native countries from trucks or carts on the street. Cori was in charge of the food, and she had ordered every different kind of cuisine she could think of that she could get for a decent price—Indian, Bangladeshi, Mongolian, Chinese, Greek, and Jamaican. Thinking she might need to satisfy the taste buds of Scouts still afraid to try new things, she added in American-style pizza that could maybe pass for Italian in the mix. David helped her assemble the trays.

After all of the girls ate lunch, they gathered in the auditorium next to the community room and sat on the floor. Meridith stood at the podium again and told the assembled Scouts that she wanted to introduce a special guest, gesturing to a slim woman next to her with light brown hair. Some of the older Scouts recognized the smiling woman in the suit right away; others thought she looked vaguely familiar. She had been winding her way through the poster board displays just like a Girl Scout.

"Every day we meet people, and I want you to keep in mind, whenever you meet a girl or a woman in your life, ask her, 'Were you a Girl Scout?' or 'Are you a Girl Scout?' " Meridith was saying.

"Most of the time you will find that that woman will say, 'Yes, I was a Girl Scout.' And immediately, you have something incredible in common with her. Whether she's ninety and was one of the original Girl Scouts or whether she's a brand-new Daisy. You have something in common. You belong to the same organization. You believe in the same things, and you respect the values and the mission of what we are committed to do to make this world a better place.

"We have the opportunity to welcome an incredible alum of the organization and actually she is a lifetime member of Girl Scouting." Meridith said the woman lived in New York City with her husband and a daughter named Charlotte, who would hopefully be a Girl Scout, too.

"Her name is Chelsea Clinton."

The girls clapped and cheered. Clinton, Meridith told the Scouts, was one of the many people around the world moved by the story of Troop 6000. The former first daughter got up to talk, opening her speech with shout-outs to Giselle and Heidi, and then, quick on her feet, added, "I've learned a lot about Syria and South Africa, about Senegal, about countries that don't begin with the letter *S*."

The crowd laughed as Clinton went on. "But most of all, I've learned why I'm so proud to be a lifetime member of the Girl Scouts, because you all are the best of what we hope for all of our children."

She told the girls they had to persist in every aspect of their lives. "You've inspired me, invigorated me, and you've encouraged me to be more optimistic about this world."

*Sanaa, Phoenix. Jessica, Christina, Hailey, Karina, and Genesis had met Chelsea Clinton months earlier at an event hosted by Seneca Women, a group that promotes the advancement of girls and women.*

World Thinking Day closed with all of the girls from all of the shelters singing "Lean on Me." They swayed and danced on the stage and in the crowd. Some of the girls belted the song out in such a way that they were more screaming than singing, but all of it sounded like pure happiness. Off to the side of the stage, Giselle, Cori, Meridith, David, and Heidi huddled like a football team ready to make a big play.

Giselle was feeling gratitude for this group of people who had held her up through everything—being evicted, living

in shelter, establishing the troop and building it up in a way she could never have imagined, moving into her new home, and now fighting cancer. As the song ended, they unlocked arms, emerging with faces glossy from tears. It wasn't just Giselle who was grateful for them. They were all grateful for one another. Cori, bumping into Sanaa, told her, "This was amazing."

*Months earlier, Sanaa studied the map at Jimmy Van Bramer's meeting on how to spend capital dollars in his district.*

Sanaa, growing wiser than her years every day, smiled. "It's not just us."

Eight weeks after her first radiation session, Giselle arrived at the treatment center prepared to learn whether or not she would have to consider a hysterectomy. Her primary doctor there, whom she called Dr. G, met with her in his office and spoke in a friendly yet authoritative tone. She didn't like that tone because it made it hard for a patient to immediately tell whether what was being said was good or bad.

But in this case it was good. Dr. G had positive news. "It worked."

That's all Giselle could remember him saying as she walked out into the March wind that whipped up and down Thirtieth Drive in Astoria. The trains on elevated tracks chugged by and Giselle stood outside on the sidewalk to absorb the news that she did not need major surgery, that her life was not over, that she was going to be fine, just like Hailey had been insisting all these weeks. The tumor had disappeared, shrunk into nothingness just as it was supposed to do, and Giselle was healthy again. She felt suddenly like she was walking on air. The wintry day, no matter the litter blowing on the streets, regardless of the dirty stanchions of the elevated tracks, seemed oddly beautiful.

"Thank you, Jesus," she said aloud. She could barely feel the cold or the gusting wind. No amount of subway hassles could bother her now.

When she got home, she sat everyone down in the living room. She came right out with it—why make them wait?

"I have good news. The treatment worked. Mommy is going to be okay," she said. "I promise till the day God comes for me I will keep fighting to be here for you." The children enveloped their mother with hugs and tears and kisses.

Except Hailey. She played it cool.

She was about to turn fifteen years old and had the maturity of a grown woman. Living in the hotel room had aged her, though her face could still look younger than her years, still as cherubic as ever when she allowed herself to smile.

Throughout the treatments, Hailey had refused to get emotional, asserting over and over again that Giselle would be healthy once more. Now, as her sisters and brother wept out of happiness, Hailey finally allowed herself some joy and she smiled one of her angelic smiles.

"I told you that you were going to be fine," she said jokingly yet authoritatively. Something in her tone suggested that maybe she actually *had* known.

And then Hailey moved on to the next task at hand: How was Troop 6000 going to sell Girl Scout cookies?

# 24

# MUSKOGEE TO UNION SQUARE

SANAA AND HER family had lived at the Sleep Inn for nearly eighteen months—a little more than the average fourteen-month stay for a family in a New York City shelter—before her mother, Mickyle, spotted their future home online. The Staten Island apartment was decent enough, with its exposed brick, a kitchen where Mickyle could bake strawberry cakes, and, better yet, a bed for everyone. But Micklye knew her children would really flip over something that was not in the apartment at all but across the street: the Stapleton Library.

A bookstore or a library was as enchanting to Sanaa as a candy shop or an ice cream parlor was to most kids. The Stapleton Library had opened in 1907 with the financial assistance of Andrew Carnegie, who had been a business partner of the father-in-law of Harriet Dyer Price Phipps, the philanthropist who had poured her heart and her friends' money into the Girl Scouts of Greater New York from the 1920s until her death in 1981. For thirty-one years, she served as president of the organization, succeeding Eleanor Butler Alexander Roosevelt, the daughter-in-law of President Theodore Roosevelt. Mickyle and Sanaa did not know the history of either the local Girl Scouts or the library. All they knew was that the Stapleton Library was both stately, because of its original limestone and brick construction, and state-of-the-art, with a modern extension enclosed in a wall of glass. Closed for about three years for renovations, it had reopened in 2013 and five years later still looked amazingly new.

Sanaa was a kid in her kind of candy store, and her currency was a library card. During spring break in April 2018, she was reading a book she'd picked up on Martin Luther King, Jr. That was her priority on her vacation—that and selling cookies. Troop 6000 was finally selling cookies, and she and her fellow Scouts were more than ready.

The lore of the Girl Scout cookie was 101 years old. In 1917, just five years after Juliette Gordon Low founded the Scouts in Savannah, the Mistletoe Troop hawked homemade cookies in a high school cafeteria in Muskogee, Oklahoma, as part of a service project. Cookie sales spread from troop to troop across the country. In 1922, a single sugar cookie recipe, with a base of one cup of butter and one cup of sugar, was shared in the Girl Scouts magazine; clearly in mind was a low budget and a high profit margin. For a total of 26 to 36 cents, six to seven dozen cookies could be made and then sold for between 25 and 30 cents per dozen. That was a serious profit at a time when the average salary was less than $3,500 a year.

Scouts throughout the states wrapped cookies inside wax paper and began selling them door-to-door. By the 1930s, the Girl Scouts of Greater Philadelphia boxed up the cookies and became the first council to use commercial bakers.

Clearly, by tapping into America's sweet tooth, the Girl Scouts were onto something, because in 1936 cookie sales were strong enough that the national organization licensed commercial bakers to produce the treats that would soon become part of its identity. Those boxes were then dispersed nationwide for Scouts to sell. During World War II, the price of flour, butter, and sugar made production prohibitively expensive, so the Girl Scouts sold calendars instead of sweets.

But America's cookie craving grew as returning veterans helped to drive the suburbanization of the country. As rural paths were replaced with concrete sidewalks and girls could more easily go from house to house, door-to-door sales became the Scouts' modus operandi. Supermarkets went hand in hand with suburbs, and Scouts could set up their booths outside them. Shopping malls popped up; troops caught customers there, too. The country's palate was crystallizing. Lovers of Girl Scout cookies grew most partial to a buttery shortbread (Trefoils), a chocolaty, minty cookie (Thin Mints), and a peanut butter cookie (Peanut Butter Patties or Tagalongs, depending on the maker). Those three types became the trifecta for the organization that continued to evolve its cookie-selling strategy; digital sales even allowed Scouts to sell online. By 2018, it all added up to two hundred million boxes of cookies sold annually, estimated to represent $700 million to $800 million in revenue.

If the Girl Scouts of the USA had decided to sell cookies all year long, the organization would no doubt have given favorite commercial brands like Oreos and Milanos a run for their money at the grocery store. But the Girl Scouts elevated cookie season to an unofficial holiday by limiting the period of time when cookies were available for purchase. Waiting for the delivery of cookies was like anticipating Christmas Day—except you knew what you were getting because you were the one who had placed the order. You got to pick which boxes of cookies you wanted and how many; say, five boxes of Thin Mints, three to be eaten right away and two to be hoarded in the freezer. In a 1976 public service spot, Girl Scout cookie lovers of different races, ethnicities, and incomes announce the arrival of their favorite season with successive proclamations of "The cookies are here!" Both advertisements and the annual sales helped solidify Girl Scout cookies as a tradition to be shared by everyone regardless of their roots or where they lived.

For all of the hoopla, tradition, and revenue, the Girl Scouts organization treated cookie sales as only one part of being a Scout, a pin equal in weight on a vest or a sash to a badge for coding or camping. But to Troop 6000, the cookie pin had always hovered out of reach, unattainable. They were not allowed to go door-to-door inside the Sleep Inn, nor were they allowed to set up a table out front on the sidewalk. And asking financially strapped parents to buy a box of Trefoils for $4 or Samoas for $5 would have been tone-deaf when that sum could pay for enough milk to stretch through the week.

The Girl Scouts had adjusted to the suburbanization of the country post World War II, an era that had helped the organization to grow and be baked into the country's psyche. In 2018, wealth was flowing back into cities, especially New York, and it was time for yet another adjustment to meet the needs of Scouts who lived in shelter. So how could Troop 6000 sell cookies? The first thought was for troop members to participate in the Corporate Cookie Connection, days when urban Scouts sell cookies in company lobbies. But that gave the Troop 6000 girls only one opportunity; they would have no chance to sell over the whole two-month-long season, door-to-door and through their parents' jobs, as Scouts in traditional troops do. The easiest sales were always to neighbors and parents' co-workers, but no solicitation was allowed in shelters, and the Girl Scouts in good conscience could not ask the parents of homeless children to make a two-month commitment to take orders at their workplaces, pick up cases of cookies, and deliver them—as Giselle had initially resented doing.

Kellogg's, a company known for its cereal, also made Girl Scout cookies through a subsidiary called Little Brownie Bakers. When Troop 6000 was founded, Little Brownie had reached out to Meridith about having the Scouts sell cookies, but Meridith explained that the troop was just getting off the ground and couldn't take on that commitment. And then, of course, there were all the complicated issues raised by the fact that the girls lived in shelters. By 2018, the timing was perfect, and Kellogg's offered its new café at Union Square in Manhattan as a pop-up for Troop 6000's cookie sales. All proceeds would go to the troop.

Sanaa had wanted to sell cookies almost as much as she had wanted to go camping. It was a coveted pin missing from her vest, but as the Union Square sale approached, she was worried. Because this was the first time Troop 6000 was selling cookies, she figured they would be lucky to sell a few hundred boxes. The OGs were all split up now. Scouts Genesis, Brithani, Juwanda, and Jasmine were still at the Sleep Inn. Kiara was still in Philadelphia. Sanaa was in Staten Island, and Giselle and her family were in Ozone Park, along with Jessica and her mother, Sue, and a few other Scouts. The fact that they were scattered all over the city didn't make them any less of a team, Sanaa knew, but she was still worried about how many cookies they'd be able to sell.

The Girl Scouts timed Troop 6000's special cookie sale with spring break for the New York City public schools so that the Scouts would not miss classes. From four to six P.M. of that week, Monday through Friday, the troop's Scouts would work the pop-up in Union Square. Different shelters were assigned to cover each day, as if they were in a relay race. The average Girl Scout in Seattle or Des Moines or Richmond sold 150 to 200 boxes of cookies over the course of cookie season, meaning she likely found thirty to fifty customers to buy cookies, since boxes of cookies were like potato chips and nobody could buy just one. But the Girl Scouts of Greater New York knew Troop 6000 was different. Though there were a few hundred Scouts spread throughout fourteen New York City shelters in April 2018, not every girl was available during spring break and logistically the event needed to stay fairly small.

So Troop 6000 set a reasonable sales target: six thousand boxes of cookies.

Through word of mouth, Girl Scout press releases, media coverage, and the sharing of a link to online sales, Troop 6000 had crushed that goal by the end of the business day on Tuesday, so Giselle decided to think big: She raised the bar to twelve thousand boxes of cookies. It would be up to the OGs, who were in charge of anchoring the contest on Wednesday, to continue the sales momentum and get Troop 6000 within sight of the ambitious new finish line.

Union Square was a rare open space in lower Manhattan. Surrounded by ornate office buildings built in the early twentieth century, including a Barnes & Noble bookstore, which was next to the Kellogg's NYC café, the square was always crowded. It was especially jammed because farmers from the Hudson River Valley and other places hawked their wares from booths in the well-known Union Square Greenmarket.

It was still cool enough for a coat in April on the Wednesday of the sale. Sanaa, her mother, and her brothers had to wade through throngs of people crowding the market to get to the Kellogg's café. "What's going on at Barnes & Noble?" Sanaa asked. A bottleneck had formed on the sidewalk in front of the bookstore, and she wondered if there was a famous children's author signing books inside; maybe she could convince her mother to take her and her brothers there after the cookie sale.

Mickyle did not have an answer for Sanaa right away because she was coming to a realization. "Is this the line?" she asked no one in particular. Then, "This is the line!" she shouted. "This is the line!"

Word of mouth had turned the Troop 6000 cookie sale into a sensation. That Wednesday a stream of people flowed out of Kellogg's and curved onto the sidewalk, snaking past Barnes & Noble and winding all the way down the block.

Once she and her family made it inside the store, Sanaa bent down and slid a lanyard with a credit card reader around her neck as if she were getting a medal at the Olympics. Heidi helped straighten Sanaa's vest, then she noticed a badge was peeling off and she pressed hard to restick it. Hailey was behind the counter surrounded by cookie boxes stacked upright as if they were books on a shelf. Someone had drawn a Samoa, a Trefoil, and a Tagalong on poster board and had written WE ACCEPT CREDIT + SIGNATURE DEBIT CARDS. ALSO, CONTACTLESS PAYMENTS LIKE APPLE PAY, SAMSUNG PAY + GOOGLE PAY.

The operation was moving briskly, even chaotically in spurts. Although Hailey questioned whether they were setting themselves up for failure with the twelve-thousand-box goal, she marveled at how Christina, her nine-year-old sister, had thrown back her shoulders and assumed a no-nonsense demeanor for this sales endeavor. This was not the same girl who had whispered into the microphone in the Blue Room to announce the expansion of Troop 6000 nearly nine months earlier.

"Look at the cookie boss," Hailey said, laughing proudly.

But Hailey had taken the lead before the cookie sale had even started. Kellogg's NYC sold bowls of the company's cereals enhanced with all sorts of fun add-ons. For the week of the cookie sale, Hailey had helped to create special $6 cereal bowls that customers could buy if they could fight their way through the crowd clamoring for cookies: Mint-a-li-cious Goodness (Cocoa Krispies, Thin Mints, white chocolate chips, yellow cake mix, and fresh mint) and Special Troop 6K (Special K, toasted coconut, coconut whipped cream, strawberries, Samoas, and salted caramel sauce). All proceeds from the cereal sales would also go to Troop 6000.

Hailey was the oldest, most experienced Scout there, and girls and even adults were turning to her with questions about how much each box cost and how to use the electronic credit card reader. She took it all in stride.

"Wait. Wait," one Scout said to customers firmly but politely as she put her finger up, and several customers were tickled at the professionalism of a third grader. Her slick ponytail bounced up and down as she shook her head and counted $5 times two boxes and $4 times three boxes on her fingers. She had an electronic tablet that was supposed to calculate for her, but she wanted to make sure the number on the tablet and the number in her head matched. Sanaa stood over her shoulder and gently corrected her when necessary, helping the Scout with the card reader when people did not have cash.

While Sanaa was helping some of the younger Scouts,

Mickyle monitored text messages as friends on Staten Island sent her orders, which she plugged into the tablets before setting aside boxes of cookies.

"I should have never put this on Facebook and Instagram," Mickyle said aloud, chuckling to herself.

Jessica and her mother, Sue, listened to orders, retrieved boxes of cookies, and placed them in bags.

Cori, who had never been a Scout and was selling cookies for the first time just like most of the girls, passed by, shaking her head at the number of customers and saying under her breath, "I'm gonna find me a glass of wine when I leave here."

Giselle was keeping track of the inventory—the cases of cookies stacked against the walls and behind the counter. Some people were carrying out entire cases. "We're going to need more S'mores," she yelled out to volunteers within earshot.

Customers of all ages, races, and ethnicities kept flowing into the store. Many of them had rushed over from their jobs: men in suits, women in suits, people wrapped in puffy coats. A man wearing a Members Only jacket wanted twelve boxes of Thin Mints.

"What's in a Tagalong?" a woman with salt-and-pepper hair asked rhetorically. "I sold them when they were fifty cents a box."

At that moment, Jasmine and Juwanda, the sisters who were six and eight, hurried into the store with their mother, Ruby. The three had donned cookie costumes in an attempt to bring in more business. Juwanda and Ruby were Samoas and Jasmine was a Thin Mint. They'd wandered around Union Square making sure strangers knew why there was a line at the Kellogg's café and encouraging them to visit.

"We got customers! We brought in customers. I was jumping up and down," Ruby said, more enthusiastic than her daughters.

"Mommy, it's hot," Jasmine said, pulling at her cookie costume.

When the OGs took breaks, they were allowed to pile bowls high with crunchy cereals for free. It was an unexpected form of empowerment, and the girls crowded a counter to select their base cereal and toppings.

Inside the makeshift social services office at the Sleep Inn, there were hundreds of single-serve disposable plastic bowls of cereal, the kind with paper on top that peeled back like a sardine can. There were a few varieties to choose from, but the cereal was packaged for convenience and economy, and for parents and their children at the Sleep Inn, it was another reminder that being poor meant having fewer options. Someone somewhere had decided that a single small serving of cereal per day was good enough, and to many, each plastic container felt like a single serving of poverty. To experience homelessness was to live a life where everything, it seemed, was decided by the shelter staff, by the hotel staff, by the government. Every aspect of their lives was apportioned right down to the cereal.

So inside the Kellogg's café, the girls' bowls were heaped to the brim, and they kept stuffing their mouths with cereal covered in milk and mountains of whipped cream and fruit toppings—not because they were hungry, but because they could.

"Are we allowed to get two bowls?" Jessica asked.

Yes, they were.

By the end of the day, their bellies were full and so were the coffers of Troop 6000. Because the Girl Scouts wanted to make sure every customer in line was able to leave with the boxes of cookies they wanted, the allotted two hours had stretched into the early evening, and the Sleep Inn Scouts had sold more than twelve thousand boxes. Giddy with their success—and plenty of sugar—they headed back to Queens and Staten Island. On Saturday, after more Scouts from other shelters sold cookies on Thursday and Friday, the whole troop gathered at the Kellogg's café to get their cookie pins and patches, and they were cheered, applauded, and celebrated by Giselle, Cori, Heidi, Meridith, David, and special guests like Kathy Hochul, New York's lieutenant governor.

After the troop closed up shop at Kellogg's NYC, Giselle

found a way for some girls to get a more traditional experience, setting up an old-fashioned booth in front of John Brown Smokehouse, a barbecue restaurant about a twenty-minute walk from the Sleep Inn. For one Saturday in early May, Scouts from the original Troop 6000, including Hailey, Karina, Christina, Jasmine, Juwanda, and Jessica—plus Gillesy, who was the resident tagalong, and Maliyah and Melanie, the youngest daughters of Ebony—hawked their wares to passersby.

The first cookie sale that day was to the restaurant owner who had agreed to allow Troop 6000 to sell its cookies out front. "I'm going to buy some for the staff," he said, pulling out his wallet.

The wind blew hard that day and boxes of cookies kept tumbling off the table. The card reader swinging from Hailey's neck worked only sporadically, and some customers grew annoyed. "I have cash," a man said impatiently, handing her a wad of bills and going on with his Saturday.

Another man in sweatpants and flip-flops was more polite. "What do you recommend?" he asked.

"These are my favorite," Hailey said, pointing to a stack of Savannah Smiles.

"My favorites are Tagalongs," Christina said.

"Savannah Smiles," Karina chimed in.

Three young women rode up on their bicycles, amazed to stumble upon a random cookie sale on Forty-fourth Drive in Queens. The street offered a scenic view of the glittering Chrysler Building in Manhattan.

"This is so rare. It's like a unicorn," one of the young women marveled.

She opened a box of Tagalongs right there, sharing with her friends. "Shit. I'm so shook," she blurted out, as if tasting a gourmet meal for the first time.

The women did not ask the girls any questions other than the price of the cookies. They did not know that the girls of Troop 6000 lived in shelters. As far as the bike riders knew, these were just plain old Girl Scouts, sort of like Trefoils—nothing flashy and solidly good.

The cookie sale that day was nothing to write home about. There were no cameras, no long lines. Just a table and some cookies.

And that's exactly what Giselle wanted.

One day in June, Heidi arrived at her desk at the Girl Scouts office on Wall Street. Sitting by itself in the middle of her desk was an envelope addressed to Troop 6000. She picked it up and turned it over and beamed when she saw the Boston return address and the time stamp of Washington, D.C.

Inside the envelope was a handwritten note on the formal stationery of the United States Senate.

"Girl Scout Troop 6000—Congratulations on your historic cookie sale! I am sure there are more than 32,500 people across America cheering you on—I'm one of them! Elizabeth Warren."

To be precise, Troop 6000 had sold 32,569 boxes.

# 25

# CROSSING OVER

**BUSES ARRIVING IN** front of the Sleep Inn could mean one of two very different things: a field trip that might be the greatest day of a young Scout's life, or the dreaded return to PATH, which meant you were getting bounced out of one shelter and moved to another. One prompted joy; the other served as a reminder that being poor meant having little or no control over where you would rest your head from one week to the next.

The PATH bus was usually a yellow school bus, a cheap mode of transportation employed by the city because every day so many people needed to be ushered from the intake center to a place of lodging, or transferred from one shelter to another. More than 100 families applied for shelter at PATH each day.

Even if the decision to move families from one shelter to another wasn't arbitrary, at the very least it seemed that the transfers were carried out with indifference. Someone somewhere—a caseworker or management at a hotel or in the Department of Homeless Services—had decided that it was time for people to pack up and move. Genesis, Brithani, and their mother and little sister were moved from the Sleep Inn to a more traditional shelter that had a regular-size refrigerator and a stove in each room so that families could make home-cooked meals. In their new space, Genesis was grateful to see her mother stirring pots, not only because that meant far better food than they'd been able to eat in a long time but also because the packaged lunches and dinners handed out each day at the Sleep Inn had been meals that could stretch to satisfy an empty stomach—filled with starches that could also exacerbate diabetes, which Genesis's mother had developed. So having a stove and a refrigerator was good, because it meant healthier food. But the move came with consequences, too. Their new shelter was deep in East Flatbush, Brooklyn, about forty-five minutes away from the Sleep Inn. Genesis and Brithani had to start at new schools—again.

In the shuffle of the move, Genesis lost her Girl Scout vest. Material losses were common for people experiencing homelessness. Displacement was inevitably tied to misplacement. Stuffed animals, favorite toys or books, or mementos were jammed into bags that sometimes ripped or even disappeared. Often losses

*Genesis, Hailey, and Karina volunteered to feed
less fortunate people in November 2017.*

were not accidental. Enough missed payments on a storage unit could lead to a family's belongings being auctioned off. To help indigent families hold on to their belongings, the city's welfare agency spent nearly $19 million annually to pay for storage. Genesis's family had already lost furniture and clothes in the fire in Miami, so they had nothing to store. What Genesis accumulated at the Sleep Inn had become precious, especially the khaki Girl Scout vest that she had given back to Giselle and then retrieved. Now it was gone.

The missing vest was one more worry for Genesis, who wondered how she would make it through the next few years. She had to adjust to a new school in Brooklyn and find a way to get tutoring for the SAT, which she now understood was the test she needed to take to apply to college. Attending college was crucial. Genesis remembered the gangs in her homeland and being forced to stay inside because of how dangerous a simple walk to the store could be. "I can't go back to Honduras," she repeated over and over again. "I can't go back to Honduras."

Her younger sister Brithani was more hopeful, less in tune with reality, than Genesis. All she knew was that she did not like her new school, which was across the street from the shelter, and that she missed the Girl Scouts. A photo of Troop 6000 at Camp Kaufmann hung on the refrigerator. Unlike Genesis, Brithani still had her vest, which she was quickly outgrowing. But that Brownie vest stuffed in a drawer couldn't by itself give her back the feeling that she and Genesis now missed so deeply—the feeling of belonging to something fun and important.

⁕

By August 2018, there were Troop 6000s in sixteen different shelters across the city, but Genesis and Brithani had been placed in one of the hundreds without one. They had moved just as Genesis was finally embracing her role as an older Scout in the Sleep Inn troop.

Genesis had always been self-conscious about her Honduran

accent. She and her sister had been the only fluent Spanish speakers among the Sleep Inn Scouts. The ability to speak two languages was an asset, but Genesis carried her bilingualism around like it was an abnormality, an affliction that made her an outcast.

Months earlier, when the Scouts were still meeting at the Sleep Inn, Giselle had an idea: Phoenix, the ten-year-old who'd jumped up so enthusiastically at the Cipriani auction every time someone bid on something, was supposed to move up from Junior to Cadette. She needed to make it official by completing a task that would help her reach the next level. Learning how to recite the organization's pledge in Spanish would fit the bill. Giselle sought out Genesis and told her that Phoenix needed her help.

For twenty minutes, Genesis sat quietly and translated the Girl Scout Promise and Law into her native language and then spent another forty-five minutes huddled in a corner with Phoenix to teach her how to pronounce the words.

At the end of the meeting, both of them raised their hands, showing three fingers. Genesis told Phoenix to repeat after her.

"Palabra de honor . . ." Genesis began. The other girls watched in astonishment as Phoenix recited the pledge in Spanish following Genesis's lead. Genesis was not one to draw attention to herself, and now here she was in front of the room acting as a mentor to Phoenix and proudly speaking in her native language. All of the girls understood that it had been an important moment.

Months later, Genesis, Brithani, their younger sister, and their mother were transferred to another shelter. Now no longer residents of the Sleep Inn and unable to coordinate permission slips and transportation from so far away, Genesis and Brithani were going to have to miss Troop 6000's most ambitious undertaking since being formed a year and a half earlier: a mass one-day return to Camp Kaufmann for Scouts from homeless troops around the city and their entire families.

In front of the Sleep Inn on a Saturday morning, a driver gripped the wheel of the charter bus and looked through the large window up at the sky, a mass of gray with no sunshine in sight, as girls and their parents piled into the seats, their clothes dampened by a misty rain and chilled by the air-conditioning.

The event had taken tremendous coordination, from transportation and permission slips to head counts. David worked hard to help pull things together at the Ruth Fernandez shelter in the Bronx; Sanaa and Mickyle had begun holding meetings at a shelter for domestic violence victims and their daughters in Staten Island, and Mickyle had taken the organizational lead there. Giselle and Cori had arrived at Camp Kaufmann ahead of the big trip to take care of business on that end. Giselle, Cori, and Heidi had spent nearly every weekend that summer at Camp Kaufmann, chaperoning small groups of girls from each shelter so they could experience a weekend of camping. The third weekend in August, the weekend of the big trip, would mark the end of the summer and a chance for the girls to show their parents and siblings what they had been up to: swimming, archery, rock climbing, marshmallow roasting, fishing, and singing songs.

But as usual, there were too few parent helpers, so Evelyn and Manny volunteered to be the main chaperones on the bus that picked up families from the Sleep Inn and the nearby Westway Motel.

Evelyn had continued to watch her daughter with a mixture of amazement and pride as Giselle had grown into a leader respected by all around her. She still couldn't believe Giselle's focus and dedication as she built Troop 6000 girl by girl, shelter by shelter. And she'd marveled at how her daughter had stoically battled her cancer. After all those youthful and not-so-youthful missteps, she'd turned into a woman who could command a room.

On the morning of the trip, Evelyn carried a clipboard with a list of everyone who was supposed to be on the bus. Manny loaded breakfast bars and juices to pass out to the children and their parents for the hour-and-a-half trip. That day he was wearing a Mets jersey with pitcher Jacob deGrom's name emblazoned on the back; Manny never needed a special occasion to wear a Mets jersey, but still, this was a special occasion.

They made the bus ride a family affair: Mateo, Giselle's brother, and Hailey passed out the breakfast bars, and Hailey also monitored the route with her phone's GPS, just in case the bus driver got lost. Miranda, Karina, Christina, and Gillesy were also on the bus, excited about spending the day at the camp with so many friends. Judas was spending time with his father, Wally, who had been released from jail after serving a sentence for eluding police in New Jersey. Wally had moved from jail straight into a halfway house. He had reestablished contact with his children, and longed to be back in a relationship with Giselle.

Evelyn had been jumpy all morning. It wasn't as if she had never been camping before; she was something of an expert. But Giselle had asked her to be in charge of a bus carrying dozens of girls and their parents, and she wanted to live up to the moment. She'd spent years evolving from irresponsible teenage mother to good, more mature mother to exceptional grandmother. She'd never been in charge of so many little girls, so many parents. She was on edge, worried that something would go wrong, and the threat of a rainstorm wasn't helping.

"I'm sitting down. I'm excited. I'm sorry. I feel important today," she said aloud, though she was really talking to herself.

The bus driver, an older man, sensed Manny and Evelyn's nervousness. He wore a crisp blue shirt and a newsboy cap, a sartorial choice that showed he took his job seriously and that he had been around the block, traveling the highways and byways of strangers' lives with them.

"You guys going to be outside today?" the driver asked Evelyn. "I hope the sky opens up."

Then he paused, realizing that he had only made Evelyn more anxious. "We need the rain. Otherwise, God wouldn't make it," he said, grinning.

He peeled off Thirteenth Street and headed to the Westway

Motel, a no-frills budget inn that looked like a giant concrete block, holding little charm yet serving as a useful marker to alert frequent fliers that they were nearing LaGuardia Airport. Its name in giant red letters could be seen from the Grand Central Parkway.

Its initial use for the housing of homeless people was in 1990, when a few dozen families were moved in, but by 1993, the city had transferred them elsewhere. Challenged by protesters—and in court by none other than Steven Banks, when he was an attorney for the Legal Aid Society—the city emptied Westway's rooms because they lacked kitchens, at that time a requirement for family shelters. For nearly twenty-one years, until 2014, Westway became a true last resort, the place the city turned to for housing in emergencies: for families burned out of their homes on Jamaica Avenue in Queens; for a group of undocumented Mexican immigrants, many of them deaf and mute, who had been smuggled into the United States and forced to sell knickknacks in the subway; or for families from New Orleans and its environs who fled homes soaked beyond recognition during Hurricane Katrina.

Westway rarely operated solely as a motel during those twenty-one years, and in 2014, the city quietly gave Win, its largest provider of services and shelter to families, a contract to operate the motel as a shelter for four years. All 121 rooms would be used for shelter services, prompting NIMBY protests, even though the hotel had been used as a shelter for as long as most people could remember.

"Hello, my loves," Toni Ostini greeted everyone as she got on the bus outside Westway. Toni—Meridith's friend who had served as a chaperone at Troop 6000's very first trip to Camp Kaufmann the preceding summer, and who had made the troop's T-shirts for their appearance at the Yankees game—had taken over as the head Girl Scouts volunteer there. As Troop 6000 grew and bumped along, Heidi, Giselle, and Cori realized that each site needed a person who was not experiencing homelessness to be a co-leader, because the parents in shelter who

volunteered were juggling work, parenting, and problems related to homelessness; or they were transient, occasionally having to move to a different shelter or, in the best of cases, finally
leaving the system altogether.

Toni was the volunteer who made sure girls at Westway
could meet every Wednesday, and because of her involvement in
Troop 6000 since shortly after its inception, she was a constant,
familiar face for girls in every troop location. Toni, like Giselle,
had battled cancer and was still healing when she got on the bus
that day, but she had decided she couldn't miss this momentous
excursion.

The driver loaded more strollers into the luggage compart-
ment and then they were on their way, rolling up the highway
and onto back roads in Dutchess County. The bus driver got lost,
as predicted, and Hailey, GPS in hand, shouted out directions:
"We're seven minutes away. . . . We're here!" she announced, as
she watched the virtual bus on the map on her phone inch closer
and closer to a virtual Camp Kaufmann. The sun peeked
through the low-lying clouds, dripping light onto the leaves.
The parking lot at the bottom of the slope called Purgatory Hill
was filled with a half dozen buses just like the one they were on.

Giselle, dressed in Wonder Woman knee-high socks and
Wonder Woman sneakers, jumped on the bus, and the girls
screeched at seeing the woman they knew was in charge.

"Gigi!"

"Miss Gigi!"

"Giselle!"

She calmly held up the three fingers on her right hand and
waited for the bus to grow silent. Four-year-old Gillesy was still
wiggling in her seat, eager to give her mother a hug. "Gillesy,
have a seat, babe," she said, and then addressed the crowd on the
bus.

"We're gonna go over some rules and expectations that Miss
Toni probably has not covered yet," she said. "Before we get you
started, I just wanted to express a couple of things to you. One,
super excited to see you all here today, very proud.

"Two, we're going to have a great time."

After reviewing the ground rules, she led the girls and their parents off the bus, and some of the group who were at Camp Kaufmann for the first time looked around and realized that the parking lot was enveloped by trees, which had the mysterious effect of making the world beyond them disappear. It was as if they had stepped out of their normal day-to-day lives and into a magical new land. Moments later, they realized that to actually get to that new land, they would have to climb Purgatory Hill.

A thunderous voice that slid into a high pitch could be heard in the distance, as much a part of the air as the chirping of crickets and the rustling of leaves in the breeze. "Signs up! Signs up!"

"David!" one of the girls cried.

David was between jobs, having left his upscale convenience store position in hopes of getting a better-paying gig as a home health aide. He'd taken time off from his job search that day to chaperone the Scouts from the Ruth Fernandez shelter in the Bronx. He had finally been able to move out of the New York City shelter system and into an apartment in Jersey City, where he could test out his recipes for pasta with shrimp and mussels, Cobb salad, flapjacks, and fried chicken. He spent hours perfecting his Philly cheesesteak, slicing the beef just so and smothering it with melted cheese. Even though he had to take three trains to get to Ruth Fernandez, Troop 6000 gave him a meaningful activity to focus on, a different kind of purpose, a necessary diversion from being so far away from Kiara, who remained in Philadelphia.

Now his voice pierced through the windows of Cookie Hall, where he was standing, and out into the open air and all the way down Purgatory Hill, where Westway and Sleep Inn families gathered in the bus parking lot before hiking up the knoll. When they finally reached Cookie Hall, where the families would split up to go on different adventures, Giselle's middle daughter was raring to get started. "Who wants to go first? Me," Christina said, asking and answering her own question.

She held Gillesy's hand all the way to the pond. Christina,

who was entering the fourth grade, was about to move up and become a Junior. She had four years of Girl Scouting under her vest and probably a dozen visits to Camp Kaufmann, so she walked Gillesy, who was about to enter kindergarten, through the woods, showing her how to take a shortcut, a well-worn path that required navigating rocks and a bit of mud. "That's poison ivy," Christina told Gillesy, pointing to the plant with three green leaves that had already been marked. "See? A red flag."

They wound their way up and down along twisting paths until they came upon a grassy hill, practically tumbling down it to get to the pond, where Sanaa and Mickyle were putting on their life jackets and helping new Scouts buckle theirs on, too. Mickyle took photos with her phone, proud that she was now serving as an outside volunteer and leading her own shelter of Troop 6000 Scouts on Staten Island.

Tall reeds surrounded the dock that led to the pond and the canoes. Sanaa jumped on a boat with ease and swiftly rowed her group of girls into the middle of the pond, the muscles in her arms bulging with each circular motion.

"I see you, baby!" Cori yelled out to Sanaa as if she were her daughter.

The ground was marshy from the morning rain and sneakers sank into the mud, but no one seemed to care. The *thump-thump* of oars hitting the canoes, and the sounds of girls laughing, and crickets chirping, and fishing lines splashing on the water filled the air with the music of summer. Everyone was learning new skills and logging firsts—the first time touching a worm, the first time rowing, the first time seeing tadpoles, the first time catching a fish, the first time throwing it back. For their part, the fish—pumpkinseed sunfish, largemouth bass, bluegill sunfish, and green sunfish—danced in the water, often outsmarting the girls and their hooks, able to nibble at worms without getting caught.

After fishing and canoeing for two hours, it was time for lunch inside Cookie Hall, where White Lightning appeared to announce that dessert would include ice pops. This time there was no fighting, and Giselle, who hadn't realized she was nervous about it, was relieved. But the rain, in the form of a severe thunderstorm, came at around three o'clock, and all around camp the girls and their families rushed for cover—leaping out of the pool, descending from the rock-climbing wall, stopping the roasting of marshmallows—to gather under a pavilion and cover themselves in ponchos.

After lunch, while everyone was out swimming and boating and exploring the camp, and outrunning the storm, the middle of Cookie Hall had been transformed. The staff set up a footbridge that had been built years earlier by one of Meridith's brothers for the Sunnyside & Woodside troops to use in their bridging ceremonies; it was stored most of the year at St. Sebastian, the church where the Sunnyside & Woodside troops held their meetings.

Bridging ceremonies marked the Scouts' move from one level to the next—from Daisy to Brownie, for example—and took many forms: from simply walking across a room to making the increasingly popular one-mile trek on the pedestrian walkway of the Brooklyn Bridge. This was Troop 6000's first big ceremony, and it seemed fitting to use the footbridge crafted by Meridith's brother. After all, the roots of Troop 6000 were in the Sunnyside & Woodside troops where Meridith and Giselle first met and bonded, with no idea that they would both end up working full-time for the Girl Scouts of Greater New York and founding a troop for girls living in the city's shelter system.

The bridge had six posts, and balloons in a rainbow of colors—orange, yellow, green, blue, purple, and fuchsia—were tied to each of them. Outside, the rain came down harder. Many of the girls and their parents were still wearing the ponchos they'd put on when they'd got caught in the rain, and the protective gear stuck to their sweaty skin like plastic wrap. Girls wore barrettes of every imaginable color, and cornrows of every thinness and thickness, and braids that were either short or long, and Afro puffs that ranged from as small as plums to as big as grapefruits.

Cori wore a black wig with bangs and she had plaited a braid on one side; Giselle's hair had shrunk tightly from the drench of perspiration and rain.

Now she stood in front of the bridge and led the room in the Girl Scout Promise.

> On my honor, I will try:
> To serve God* and my country,
> To help people at all times,
> And to live by the Girl Scout Law.

"How many of us had a great time today?" Giselle asked when they'd completed the promise, waving her hands like a cheerleader encouraging a crowd to scream for the home team. She usually asked the girls to be quiet, but in this moment she wanted them to hoot until they grew hoarse.

She told them how Troop 6000's first camping trip a year ago had seventeen girls and three troop leaders. "Now," she said, beaming, "we're here today with three hundred and thirteen of you!"

The rain continued to pummel Cookie Hall, but the thunder and lightning outside couldn't compete with the sounds of excitement inside as the bridging ceremony was about to start. One by one, girls who were moving up a level walked across the bridge to be greeted by an older girl on the other side. Sanaa stood on one side of the bridge and Christina on the other, and the room erupted into cheers as Christina walked over it and shook Sanaa's hand. Christina was now officially a Junior. Then, Sanaa went around to the other side of the bridge, walked over, and was greeted by Karina. Sanaa was finally a Cadette. And Gillesy was finally an official Daisy.

Cori and Heidi high-fived girls after they crossed. For a few minutes, David grew quiet, standing next to the stone fireplace, his arms folded as he thought about Kiara and how she would

---

* According to the *Girl Scouts Handbook*, members may substitute for the word *God* in accordance with their own spiritual beliefs.

have been a Cadette. But he roused himself from his sad thoughts and joined Giselle and Cori because they had a tradition and they were going to follow it.

The three gave one another knowing looks; they had an understanding of what it had taken to get to that moment. Their lives were not perfect. Cori was stumbling at work, trying to master organizational skills that she'd never learned and to remember to always hit spell-check and look closely at her grammar before sending memorandums and emails. David was grappling with abandoning, temporarily, at least, his dream of being a chef or a caterer, and he continued to miss his daughter tremendously. Giselle was struggling for balance in romance; Wally was in and out of her life again, as he returned to being involved in the lives of his children. He helped out with their care, and he'd helped Giselle when she'd been weakened by the radiation treatments. But Giselle had new ground rules, the most important of which involved Wally's temper. There would be no blowups, no hitting, no yelling, or he could leave their lives. Wally took one look at Giselle and knew beyond the shadow of a doubt that she meant it.

Cori told Giselle, "If you love him, I'll love him. If he hurts you, I'll kill him."

Those were the bumps in their personal and professional lives, but they had something more now. They had communal lives that they shared with every new member of Troop 6000.

David blew a whistle to get everyone's attention and made the Girl Scouts sign with his fingers. "Signs up!"

After the room had hushed, Giselle yelled out as loud as she could, cupping her mouth with her hands, "There's one more thing before we leave!"

Some girls wondered if they were in trouble, but then Giselle, David, and Cori yelled out in unison, "This is a repeat-after-me song!"

And everyone laughed and sang about the moose who drank a lot of juice. The Scouts from different shelters hugged one another, and some parents were teary-eyed at the awesomeness of this sisterhood as they trekked back to the buses to return to New York City.

Juniors, Cadettes, Seniors, and Ambassadors stayed behind that night. They encircled a firepit, where Meridith used her expertise to get some flames going on waterlogged wood. Some Scouts helped her, adding tampons to the mix, the little trick they had learned earlier in the summer during those more intimate weekend trips to Camp Kaufmann. Gooey marshmallow stretched over graham crackers and melted chocolate.

Because of a mix-up by the charter bus company, five girls from Staten Island, including Sanaa, rode home the next day in a luxurious Mercedes-Benz Sprinter, so clean, black, and shiny that they could see their reflections in the polished surface as if it were a mirror. Sanaa and her new friends sank into the seats and quickly fell asleep, exhausted. Before too long, though, they were all awake again, eager to talk about the trip they had taken.

The last girl to get dropped off, a fourth grader, told the driver, "That's my house!"

The driver looked to his right and saw the brick building. He knew it was a shelter.

"That's your house?" he asked.

"Yeah," she said, nodding. She grabbed her backpack and her new sleeping bag and jumped out of the SUV. She couldn't wait to tell her mother, who was standing out front, all about the trip.

"Look, Mom! It's a limo!" the new Junior Scout cried.

Her mother caressed her head. "Did you have fun?"

The girl looked up, all smiles. "Yeah," she said. "I got to make s'mores with my friends." With her mother's arm draped around her shoulder, the girl walked back into the shelter, and the driver slowly eased away from the curb.

# 26

# ONE PERSON, ONE DAY

AUTUMN BROUGHT COLOR to Ozone Park, with its carpet of flame-colored leaves, and yards decorated with pumpkins, scarecrows, witches, ghouls, and goblins. Halloween had always been something for Giselle's children to look forward to, and she had never forgiven herself for missing it seven years earlier when she'd left Hailey, Karina, and Christina in Queens to pursue what she thought would be a better life in Florida.

Hailey dressed as Mrs. Incredible and Karina went as Veronica from *Riverdale*, the *Archie* comic spin-off. Christina and Judas teamed up as Gwen Stacy and Spider-Man, while Gillesy was Wonder Woman, adopting her mother's obsession with the comic book hero. They were all anticipating collecting candy from parties at school and at the huge bash Meridith threw, as she did every year, where Jimmy Van Bramer, now with his eye on becoming Queens borough president, showed up wearing a suit, as usual.

Giselle and her family were finally on their way to being stable—not all the way, but closer to it. She had settled into her fancier new title at the Girl Scouts of Greater New York: program manager. She was earning more money—although, with five children, she still qualified for food stamps—and had a house where she and her brood could spread out. They could plop down on the couch in the living room, where Judas kept a pet turtle in an aquarium, or they could squeeze into the booth in the kitchen beneath the faux Tiffany lamp, or they could retreat to the relative privacy of their bedrooms. The children could play on the concrete in the backyard. Giselle had enough money to spend a few dollars at Dollar Tree for decorations this Halloween. She hung a creepy sign just underneath the half-moon window over the wooden door. KEEP OUT, it read, with a skeleton and a rat peeking out from behind it.

On some nights, as she lay in bed watching the shadows of tree branches play on the bedroom ceiling, she marveled at all she'd experienced and seen, and how the chance invitation to volunteer at a Girl Scout troop on Saturdays had led her on this grand adventure and to so many people who had, each in his or her own way, helped her as she'd helped them—from Luana and Meridith, to Heidi and Jimmy, to David and Cori and on and on. And she marveled at how she'd witnessed so many shy, lost little girls become more self-assured as they racked up badge after badge and sold more cookies than anyone else. Watching them splash in puddles in the woods, open their eyes to the vastness of the world around them, and learn to resolve their differences continued to bring her happiness. But it was their newfound courage and confidence and pride that thrilled her the most.

From Juliette Gordon Low to Giselle and her daughters, and all the girls of the Sleep Inn and the other shelters, and all the Scouts all over the city and the country, there was an unbroken line of shared values and sisterhood. To the members of Troop 6000 in particular, the Girl Scouts had given hope and a future. Giselle had not yet met her long-term goals for financial stability, and continued to be fearful that she could not pay the rent and give her children all the things they needed. She certainly couldn't give them all the things they *wanted*. Every day was a balancing act. She longed for a nuclear family and hoped that one day she would remarry. Remarriage or not, though, she appreciated that she had five healthy children, and she knew she wouldn't trade them for anything in the world. It was on nights like this beautiful autumn one, when she was reflecting on her gratitude, that Giselle drifted most happily off to sleep, rolling all these miracles over in her head.

〜〜〜〜〜〜〜〜〜

But outside, the fight went on.

Ozone Park may have bubbled with Halloween excitement on the surface, but it had become the latest battleground in the war over shelters. The de Blasio administration was not going to meet its promise to open forty new shelters by 2019, its efforts having been blocked and delayed by lawsuits, fickle politicians, and angry residents. As of October 2018, the city had opened only fourteen, with just four other sites announced. Everywhere the city tried to open a shelter the opposition appeared, as if playing a particularly nasty game of whack-a-mole.

The situation in Ozone Park was not as tense as it had been in Floral Park a few years earlier when David and Kiara were bused to a museum so that children staying at a Quality Inn would not be upset by angry protesters. No one was yelling "White lives matter!" but the sentiment was the same: Residents worried that homeless shelters would bring down their house values—their homes were their biggest financial investments—and their quality of life. And there was the unspoken racism. Homeless people were not only undesirable to some residents in Giselle's little corner of Tudor Village, but maybe something to fear, like the monsters and ghosts they had hung in trees and planted in their yards for fun. A dozen homeowners had banded together to file a lawsuit against a men's shelter, and others were knocking on doors to get support to stop what they viewed as a proliferation of shelters in general.

Because she now lived in Ozone Park, Giselle could no longer be on the community board in Long Island City, and Jimmy Van Bramer had told her she should join the community board that included the neighborhoods of Tudor Village, Ozone Park, and Howard Beach. But Giselle realized she was not going to be welcomed onto the Ozone Park board, which was less liberal than the one in Long Island City. Instead, she familiarized herself with the roster of politicians in the area and the issues they supported.

The young members of Troop 6000 had become attuned to politics, too, through their visits to City Hall and Gracie Mansion, the mayor's home, and their attendance at meetings that delved into the nitty-gritty of government policy. Some of the OGs attended a meeting held by Jimmy to gauge how his constituents would want to spend $1 million in capital funds in his district. When Jimmy asked who would want to run for office someday, Sanaa, Karina, and Christina had raised their hands.

The adults around the girls were getting more vocal, too. Heidi Schmidt was appointed to a community board in lower Manhattan, where she lived. In another part of Queens, Meridith attended town halls and spoke in favor of shelters even as her neighbors were trying to drown her out with their NIMBY screams.

Giselle was moving toward testing the political waters. When she was in high school, she'd barely known what was happening with her student government, and now she was becoming a political force. She had

*Jimmy Van Bramer points out an area of Long Island City on a map at a meeting where members of Troop 6000 offered ideas on how to spend at least $1 million in capital funding.*

wanted to raise her hand so badly when Jimmy asked the Scouts who would want to run for office someday. She was scared, but she had been nervous about starting Troop 6000, and look how that all turned out.

One fall evening, as it began getting dark earlier, Giselle heard a knock on her door.

A woman, her face lit only by the streetlights, was standing there, holding a clipboard. She wanted Giselle to sign a petition.

"What is this about?" Giselle asked politely yet suspiciously.

"We're trying to prevent more shelters from opening in our neighborhood. They're making it unsafe. This is a problem for us."

Giselle paused for a second.

"What's wrong with having shelters in the neighborhood? What's the issue?"

"Well, you know, a lot of people who are in shelter, they're coming from jail, some of them have drug problems," the woman replied.

Giselle couldn't stop herself: "I'm just coming out of shelter."

The woman's face froze.

"Yes, I was formerly homeless," Giselle continued. "I moved to this house coming out of shelter. Do I look dangerous to you?"

Giselle desperately wanted to rant, but despite her fury she felt pity for this ignorant woman.

"I don't see anything wrong with family shelters being opened to help those in need. What you should do is start a list of people in the community that can help these people who have issues, that need help, resources. Why aren't you walking around seeing how we can help these families that are living in shelter find resources that can help them stay out of shelters?"

The woman finally mustered up some words in the form of a question. "Really, you were homeless?"

"Yes, I was homeless, and I live here now. I am not signing that petition because I think that petition is very wrong."

The woman rolled out a rote list of talking points that protesters were using: Mayor de Blasio had failed to give Ozone

Park timely and adequate information; too many shelters were being sited in one area; shelters for single men were particularly troubling and would bring loitering to the neighborhood.

Giselle sighed. "I'm actually partnered with the mayor right now. The mayor gave the Girl Scouts of Greater New York $1.1 million so that we can start programming for girls who are living in the New York City shelter system, and that's what I do for a living now."

Giselle thought about how she herself had once been so ignorant about homelessness; her pre-shelter existence almost seemed like another lifetime. Living in a shelter had given her time to get on her feet. That was the whole purpose of shelter. It was the same for the others: Cori was now living in a second-floor walk-up. True, there was only one bedroom, but she'd turned the living room into a space for her son, Trey, and they lived comfortably. Many of the Troop 6000 girls and their families had left the shelter system, including sisters Tiana and Tanae, Jessica, and Sanaa. It was taking longer for Brithani and Genesis's family, but they were surviving, as were Phoenix and her family, who were living in a Bronx shelter, and Ebony and her daughters, who also still resided in a shelter in the Bronx. Juwanda, Jasmin, and Ruby were still in a shelter. They were scattered, but they had a sisterly bond that seemed as if it would last for the rest of their lives. They had started a troop that gave girls some hope and friendship at a time when they could easily feel alone. Like millions of other women, one day they would say, "I was a Girl Scout."

In 2018, about 133,000 individuals had, at some point, lived in the city's primary shelter system, the one that Giselle and her family had lived in for a year. That didn't count the thousands of people who were in the city's special shelters for families escaping domestic violence and youths aging out of foster care. It also did not take into consideration the tens of thousands of school-age children living doubled and tripled up, sleeping on floors and four to a bed, the way Hailey, Karina, and Christina had had to do intermittently in their young lives. About seventy-four thousand students in the city's public and charter schools were known to live in overcrowded housing that left them little room to stretch out to do their homework, let alone to fulfill big dreams.

About 14 percent of people experiencing homelessness in the United States in 2018 lived in New York City, which unlike so many cities across the country actually shelters the needy. That means about a million people in the city had at one point in their lives been homeless, whether living on the street, or in a shelter, or sleeping on a couch because they had nowhere else to go.

Hailey was a few months away from her sixteenth birthday, and everyone at her school knew that she had been homeless. And that was fine. She had been interviewed for a piece for *Scholastic Action* magazine called "Homeless, Not Hopeless." She recalled how her mother had sat them down in the living room in the decrepit apartment on Maple Avenue to tell them they were being evicted and going into shelter. She talked about how she had been embarrassed but was not anymore.

"I've realized that everyone faces some kind of challenge. We shouldn't push others to the side because they're different. We're all the same, no matter where we live," Hailey said in the *Scholastic* interview.

Hailey, who had been sitting on the couch when her mother answered their neighbor's knock that evening, stood up and walked behind Giselle, waving her siblings over to join her. Karina came out of the kitchen, and Christina, Judas, and Gillesy filed down the stairs.

They were now flanking their mother like soldiers as she kept talking to the woman in the doorway.

"Keep in mind it takes a village to raise a child. What you need to do is really take into consideration how you can help people. I was homeless and now I'm not. Tomorrow, you could be homeless if you lose your job. Then what are you going to do?"

The woman had nothing else to say. "Have a good day," the woman said meekly.

Giselle turned around to see her children, their mouths agape at her eloquence and boldness. Then they spoke in unison.

"Ooh, Mommy!"

Giselle smiled. She'd had so many encounters, large and small, in public and private, with people who had misconceptions about homelessness and those who were trapped in it. Somehow, dressing down the petition-wielding woman, her *neighbor*, was one of the most satisfying. Homelessness was not a plague to be feared; it was a crisis that engulfed tens of thousands of people in New York each year. And it was being felt in every major city in the United States. Had she changed the woman's mind? Probably not. But she'd made her think about what the face of homelessness looked like. There were so many people who still did not understand. Maybe the only solution was to educate one person at a time, one day at a time, for as long as it took.

She shut the door against the night.

# ACKNOWLEDGMENTS

I CAN'T REALLY remember wanting to be anything other than a journalist, and I had a whole lot of help along the way, from my family to teachers and a school counselor who had gotten wind of my interest to my first instructors at the Dow Jones/Western Kentucky University Minority Journalism Workshop. To all of my mentors, especially the black women and men and their allies who made a path for me, thank you.

I'd also like to thank Giselle Burgess, Hailey, Karina, Christina, Judas, and Gillesy, and all of the troop leaders, Scouts, and their parents for letting me into your worlds, for giving me a play-by-play of arguments with caseworkers and shelter staff, for sending me photos so that I lived with you inside those hotel rooms, even when I could not be there. I know I asked a lot of you during one of the lowest and most heartbreaking points of your lives. You had no obligation to me yet you were gracious. I am forever grateful that you trusted me to share your story with the world. This especially goes to David, Cori, and Mickyle. I found the story thanks to Jimmy and Matt, and thank you to Jim Dwyer for passing it along. I nailed the story with the help of Anat, Meridith, and Isaac. Also, thank you, Sam, for capturing beautiful photos from the very beginning.

To the Girl Scouts of Greater New York and the Girl Scouts of the USA, I regret that my family could not afford for me to participate when I was growing up in Killeen, Texas. What you do to empower girls is absolutely amazing. To see how you have embraced girls, now subsidizing dues to make sure that any girl, regardless of the income of her household, can participate, brings tears to my eyes. This world is a better place because of Girl Scouts.

Pamela Cannon, my editor, loved this book before I put it on the page. Thank you for your confidence in me. Your team was incredible, from Lexi to Ada, to Karen and Taylor. To Larry and Sascha, thank you for giving me time and space, for not rushing me, for connecting me to the people who helped make all of this possible. I would not have met you without Kim, who, along with Sheri, always encouraged me. Thank you to Jon Schuppe for advice and Wendell for the nudge and guidance. And thank you to Nan Gatewood Satter for the last-minute assist. You brought things out of me I did not know I had.

I also could not have done this without my support groups: the Crew; my MV Family; my Sands and Sorors of Alpha Kappa Alpha Sorority, Inc.; my *Star-Ledger* brothers Jeff and Barry; and members of the National Association of Black Journalists, with much love to Vanessa and Betty. I also am forever in awe of my newsroom ally and cheerleader, Nikole. Your friendship means so much to me. Taja-Nia, thank you for lifting me at one of my toughest points. Raquel, thank you for appreciating Tex-Mex, etiquette, and entertaining as much as I do.

But everything starts at home. I don't see you often enough. I love you, JoAnn, Bridgitte, Terry, Bonnay, Jovan, Ethan, and Cicely. Love to the Viloria family, as well.

Elbert Lano "Pops" Stewart, Jr., who told nurses on his deathbed, "She works at *The New York Times*!"—we did not have enough time. Same goes for Paul Ellis. To Josephine, who read her Bible, the newspaper, and *Reader's Digest* every day, I hope you can see me. To my ancestors, the McQueens, the Gohagans, the Masseys, and the Vontreeses, you endured so that I would flourish.

Finally, a special thanks to the man who stood up when I bumped into his chair.

To Ella, my little drummer girl: This is especially for you.

# ABOUT THE AUTHOR

**NIKITA STEWART** is a reporter covering social services for *The New York Times*. The Newswomen's Club of New York recognized Stewart in 2018 for her coverage of homelessness, mental health, and poverty. She has been a finalist for the Livingston Award and an Investigative Reporters and Editors Award. She joined *The New York Times* in 2014 after working at *The Washington Post*.

Twitter: @kitastew

# ABOUT THE TYPE

This book was set in Walbaum, a typeface designed in 1810 by the German punch cutter J. E. (Justus Erich) Walbaum (1768–1839). Walbaum's type is more French than German in appearance. Like Bodoni, it is a classical typeface, yet its openness and slight irregularities give it a human, romantic quality.

To learn more about how you can support
the expansion of Troop 6000 in New York City,
please visit www.girlscoutsnyc.org/troop6000.